A Few Planes for China

EUGENIE BUCHAN

A FEW PLANES

FOR CHINA

The Birth of the Flying Tigers

ForeEdge

ForeEdge

An imprint of University Press of New England

www.upne.com

© 2017 Eugenie Buchan

All rights reserved

Manufactured in the United States of America

Designed by Mindy Basinger Hill

Typeset in Adobe Caslon Pro

For permission to reproduce any of the material in this book,
contact Permissions, University Press of New England, One Court Street,
Suite 250, Lebanon NH 03766; or visit www.upne.com

Library of Congress Cataloging-in-Publication Data

Names: Buchan, Eugenie, author.
Title: A few planes for China : the birth of the Flying Tigers /
    Eugenie Buchan.
Description: Lebanon NH : ForeEdge, an imprint of University Press
    of New England, 2017. | Includes bibliographical references.
Identifiers: LCCN 2017018922 (print) | LCCN 2017019594 (ebook) |
    ISBN 9781512601299 (epub, mobi, & pdf) | ISBN 9781611688665 (cloth)
Subjects: LCSH: Flying Tigers (AVG), Inc. | Sino-Japanese War, 1937–1945—
    Participation, American. | Sino-Japanese War, 1937–1945—
    Aerial operations. | China. Kong jun. American Volunteer Group.
Classification: LCC DS777.533.A35 (ebook) | LCC DS777.533.A35 B83 2017
    (print) | DDC 951.04/2—dc23
LC record available at https://lccn.loc.gov/2017018922

5 4 3 2 1

For Janet, my mother

Contents

Illustrations follow page 118

The Flying Tigers were a small, privately organized air force that fought the Japanese over Burma and western China at the start of World War II. Before Pearl Harbor and the American entry into the war, the Flying Tigers were known as the American Volunteer Group (AVG), but soon after war broke out with Japan, the Chinese dubbed the pilots "flying tigers," and the name stuck.[1] From December 1941 to June 1942 the Tigers rarely had more than forty airworthy planes, but they managed to destroy close to three hundred Japanese aircraft.[2] Their emblems were well known worldwide: the Curtiss-Wright P-40 fighter plane with shark's teeth painted on the cone; the figure of a tiger cub leaping out of the V for Victory, designed by Walt Disney; the tough features of "the old man," their commander, Claire Lee Chennault. The Tigers became so famous that in 1942 Republic Films cast John Wayne as a Chennault proxy, Jim Gordon, in the movie *Flying Tigers*.

Since World War II, there have been countless books, articles, and documentaries about the Flying Tigers, so why write another now? In history, as in crime, new evidence overturns old verdicts. I became intrigued by the Flying Tigers in 2006, when I came across a paper bag full of old files in a closet at my parents' home in Washington, DC. They belonged to my grandfather, Captain Bruce Gardner Leighton of the US Navy. The files revealed that he played a part in organizing the Flying Tigers in 1939–1942 while he was vice president of a long-forgotten aviation firm called the Intercontinent Corporation. Its president was William Douglas Pawley, whom I remember as a close friend of my grandparents.

In the 1950s, Daddy Bruce, as all the grandchildren called him, had a farm near Stuart, Florida. He was tall, bald, and wore khaki fatigues most of the time. I don't remember ever having a conversation with him, but fifty years after his death, I finally got to know him as I went through layers of onionskin duplicates.

Bruce was an early naval aviator, who earned his wings at Pensacola in 1915. He flew in World War I and then worked for the navy's Bureau of Aeronautics until 1928, when he resigned with the rank of lieutenant commander. That year, he joined Wright Aeronautical as its first vice president for marketing, just before the merger with the Curtiss Aeroplane and Motor Company. In the early thirties Bruce sold Curtiss-Wright military aircraft in Turkey and the Balkans. In May 1937, he left the relative security of the Curtiss-Wright Export Corporation and became vice president of the Intercontinent Corporation. Intercontinent's president was William Douglas Pawley. The new job took Bruce, his wife Ethel, and daughter Janet (my mother) to Shanghai.

Although my mother had vivid memories of Hong Kong, she knew little about her father's business in China, apart from the fact that Bill Pawley had built an aircraft factory for the Chinese government at Hangchow, south of Shanghai. A month after the Sino-Japanese War broke out on July 7, 1937, my mother and grandmother were evacuated to the Philippines. They soon resettled in Hong Kong, while my grandfather stayed in the interior of China; whenever it was cloudy, he might catch a passenger plane to Hong Kong to see them. As the Japanese army swept into the Yangtze River valley, Daddy Bruce and the factory moved west, one step ahead of the enemy. At the end of 1938, Intercontinent relocated the factory to its final resting place at Loiwing in Yunnan Province, near the border of Burma, then a British colony.

In December 1939 Bruce and his family came back to the United States. He commuted between New York, Washington, and Miami, where he managed an airplane assembly plant owned by Intercontinent. In 1942, he rejoined the navy and became its representative on the West Coast, to serve as liaison with manufacturers producing aircraft for the navy. That was all I knew about him before he moved to the farm in Florida.

In the paper bag was a folder labeled "CAMCO, AVG" that caught my eye: on the front my mother had written, "BGL's account of the establishment of the AVG." At the time I had no idea what these abbreviations stood for, but the bag of files contained a booklet about the AVG, *Americans Valiant and Glorious*, which triggered a childhood memory.[3] When we used to stay with my grandparents, I liked looking at it because of the tiger cub on the cover and the brightly colored tassel binding.

In the first few pages, Bill Pawley offered his version of how the Flying Tigers came about. In May 1939, he, his brother Ed, and Bruce met with Dr. H. H. Kung, the finance minister of China at that time.[4] Bill asked Dr. Kung what Americans could do for China and the Chinese Air Force. Dr. Kung replied that China needed a group of volunteer pilots like the Lafayette Escadrille, who flew on the side of the French before the United States entered World War I. Pawley said that he would do everything possible to put this idea before "men of influence" in the United States, and "thus the AVG was born."[5]

When I asked my mother about Bruce's involvement in the Flying Tigers, she was pretty vague, and when I asked her what CAMCO was, she drew a total blank. As far as she was concerned, her father had worked for Intercontinent. A quick Internet search revealed that CAMCO stood for Central Aircraft Manufacturing Company, the aircraft factory that Bill Pawley had built. It dated back to 1933 when Pawley set the plant up as a joint venture with the Nationalist government of Generalissimo Chiang Kai-shek.[6] It turned out that all the Flying Tigers had employment contracts with CAMCO.

As I searched through the web, I found little to suggest that Pawley and Leighton had been instrumental in forming the Flying Tigers: virtually all accounts focused on the pivotal role of Claire Chennault. In February 1942 *Time* magazine set the tone for subsequent works: "To no one man belongs credit for organizing and recruiting the A.V.G. But A.V.G.'s spark plug from the start, its commander in Burma now, is a famous U.S. flyer: lean dark Brigadier General Claire L. Chennault of Water Proof, La."[7] In 1942, Russell Whelan wrote *The Flying Tigers*, the first book about the group. Whelan was the radio director of United China Relief, an information and fund-raising organization for Nationalist China. According to Whelan, Chennault created the Flying Tigers expressly to fight the Japanese regardless of whether Japan and the United States were officially at war or not.[8] The following year, Robert Hotz of the *Milwaukee Journal* wrote *With General Chennault: The Story of the Flying Tigers*.[9] He made the story of Chennault synonymous with that of the Flying Tigers.

After the war, Hotz edited Chennault's memoir *Way of a Fighter* (1949) and incorporated passages from his earlier text into the autobiography.[10] Hotz may well have written this memoir drawing on conversations with Chennault and his own research and imagination. In a book review, Annalee Jacoby, coauthor with Theodore White of *Thunder out of China*, commented on the aptness of the memoir's title, because Chennault had fought with everyone: "These memoirs are so interestingly schizoid that they seem to be the product of three different men."[11] Nevertheless, over the years popular historians accepted *Way of a Fighter* as an article of faith. No one has ever challenged its main assertion, that Claire Chennault was the founding father of the Flying Tigers. The current authority Dan Ford opened his book, *Flying Tigers: Claire Chennault and his American Volunteers, 1941–1942*, by presenting Chennault as "the man behind the Flying Tigers."[12]

Nearly every book on the Tigers contains a potted biography of Chennault with his basic curriculum vitae. From 1919 to 1937, Claire Chennault served in the US Army Air Corps (AAC) as a flight instructor, squadron leader, and renowned stunt pilot. In 1937 Generalissimo Chiang Kai-shek, head of the Nationalist government of China, put his wife Soong Mei-ling in charge of the Commission of Aeronautical Affairs;[13] the CoAA was the Chinese equivalent of an air ministry, and it ran the Chinese Air Force (CAF). Although a military officer was always nominally in charge of the CAF, Madame Chiang, as chair of the CoAA, nonetheless held sway over the country's military aviation.

American flight instructors already based in China knew Chennault and encouraged Madame Chiang to invite him to inspect the CAF. In the spring of 1937, Chennault retired from the AAC and arrived in China just before war broke out with Japan. As it happened, he turned up about a week after my grandfather in Shanghai. They soon got to know each other: in 1937 and 1938 they played cards and watched Japanese air raids together; from 1939 to 1941 they conferred about the AVG project.

In 1937 and 1938, Chennault served as an air adviser to the Chiangs, and according to AVG chroniclers, Chennault continued to advise them in 1939 and 1940, although in this period he was based almost entirely in Kunming, the capital of Yunnan Province, where he was the chief American instructor at the CAF flight school.

According to all accounts, in November 1940 the generalissimo asked Chennault to go to Washington, DC, and help his personal representative, T. V. Soong (Madame's Chiang's brother) to lobby the US government for air assistance.[14] Over the next four months or so, as the accounts go, Chennault rapidly influenced key policy makers in the Roosevelt administration to support his concept of a small volunteer air combat unit to be based in China. Its purpose, according to *Way of a Fighter*, was to raid enemy targets in the occupied part of China and quite possibly to bomb Tokyo itself.[15] Several historians assert that in April 1941, Roosevelt discreetly "blessed" Chennault's proposal, and soon thereafter Soong engaged Bill Pawley and CAMCO to handle recruitment, personnel contracts, and some procurement tasks for the project.

My grandfather's AVG/CAMCO file contradicted this standard version of events in terms of chronology as well as protagonists. One batch of documents from January to May 1940 revealed Bruce's meetings with the navy to discuss his idea of a tactical air force based at CAMCO in Loiwing. During that time, his old friend Robert Molten had a top job in the Navy Department. Molten arranged appointments for Bruce with several senior officers, including the chief of naval operations (CNO), Admiral Harold Stark. In these discussions, Bruce outlined how his company could create *on strictly commercial lines* air combat units manned by Western pilots (not necessarily American); the factory at Loiwing would serve as the base from which these squadrons could carry out raids on Japanese targets in China. This mobile air unit could also be transferred to neighboring territory, such as the Dutch East Indies, if it faced the threat of enemy attack. Navy colleagues appreciated Bruce's views about how to help China in aviation but pointed out that US foreign policy prevented any such plan from being realized.

Another group of letters was dated mid-January 1941. Bruce referred to tense negotiations over the sale of a hundred Curtiss-Wright P-40 pursuit (fighter) planes between Intercontinent, the US Treasury Department, and T. V. Soong. It turned out that since Intercontinent had the exclusive right to sell Curtiss-Wright planes in China, it was due a sales commission on the

P-40s, which the US and Chinese governments did not want to pay. Bruce's letters revealed that Secretary of the Navy Frank Knox had asked his assistant, Captain Morton Lyndholm Deyo, to contact Bruce about organizing the air mission to China entirely on his own. Mort Deyo was an old friend of my grandfather; they had met most recently in Shanghai during 1937 while Deyo was assigned to the USS *Augusta*, the flagship of the US Asiatic Fleet. In a letter to Deyo, Bruce pointed out that no single man could handle such complex logistics on his own: only an organization such as Intercontinent could do it. A few weeks later, toward the end of January 1941, Treasury officials and Bill Pawley worked out a compromise about Intercontinent's sales commission. Then all parties agreed that Intercontinent should manage the China air program. Intercontinent subsequently stayed involved with the Tigers until July 1942, when the group was finally disbanded.

It seemed to me, based on Leighton's papers, that in January 1941 the president's closest advisers decided to outsource a covert air mission in China to Intercontinent, an early "private military contractor"—even if that term did not yet exist. As Bruce did not commit to paper the precise nature of this mission, another question arose: What bearing did this project in January 1941 have on the scheme that Chennault and T. V. Soong allegedly hatched in April 1941? I found no answers in the Flying Tigers canon.

As I read around the subject, I was struck by other anomalies. Why would Roosevelt have endorsed air action against Japan, which could have detonated an all-out war in the Pacific, when, in the view of most historians, he did his utmost to avoid conflict with Japan in the years before Pearl Harbor? If the Flying Tigers were destined to fight the Japanese in China, why, from July 1941 until Pearl Harbor, were they based in Burma, a British colony? These inconsistencies begged the questions: Who set up the Flying Tigers, when did they do so, and why? The answers form the substance of this book.

To the greatest extent possible, I have used primary sources to reconstruct the decision-making process that led to the formation of the Flying Tigers. The central thesis is that the Flying Tigers were not a strictly Sino-American venture, as most historians have insisted. The historical and strategic significance of the AVG stems primarily from Sino-British military cooperation in the year before Pearl Harbor. The man behind the Flying Tigers ultimately was Winston Churchill.

As this book shows, the British government consistently took the AVG seriously as a combat unit that could help reinforce its slender air assets in the Far East once Japan declared war on the British Empire. The British side of the story has been almost entirely ignored for several reasons, but one significant factor has to do with nomenclature: the British rarely referred to the group as the AVG; instead they called it the International Air Force (IAF). The National Archive in Kew, outside London, is full of files labeled IAF or Aid for China, which became "open" to public view in 1972, but I have never come across any reference to these documents in popular histories about the Flying Tigers.

Before war broke out in Europe, the British were at pains to avoid armed conflict with Japan. Once they were at war with Hitler, they could not afford a war on two fronts, and so they continued to concentrate resources in Europe rather than Asia. It was not long before they saw the strategic importance of the AVG for the defense of their colonies in the Far East: then they did everything possible within limited means to help the AVG's "supervisor" Claire Chennault transform it into a combat unit.

In 1944, Bruce Leighton wrote a long letter to a Chinese colleague, General C. T. Chien. Leighton referred to the spectacular accomplishments of the Flying Tigers and "the much less spectacular" account of the difficulties that dogged the group's formation: he and others (including Chennault) worked in "extreme secrecy; the arrangements with government agencies had to be handled entirely by word of mouth, with knowledge of the true nature of the project confined to a very restricted group."[16] This "back" story of how the Flying Tigers were formed may be less spectacular than one about "Americans Valiant and Glorious," but it goes further to explain the rationale for the Flying Tigers, the group's significance in prewar diplomacy, and its connection to the airpower strategy that the United States eventually used to defeat Japan in 1945.

A Few Planes for China

Chiang's Rotten Air Force 1

In early February 1939, Generalissimo Chiang Kai-shek and Madame Chiang invited to their residence in Chungking the new British air attaché in China, Group Captain Robert Stanley Aitken of the Royal Air Force. Over tea, he hoped to find out more about their requests to buy British aircraft and bring RAF advisers to China to reform the air force.[1] Madame interpreted for her husband in flawless English with a slight southern accent. She told Aitken that the administration of the air force was "absolutely rotten" and offered poor value for money. On Chiang's behalf she stated, "We have had to do without a Navy, we would be better off without a rotten Air Force." She claimed that the British would have "carte blanche" to reorganize China's air ministry, the Commission on Aeronautic Affairs (CoAA), and the air force.[2]

This was not the first time that the Chinese Air Force and its "ministry" had been labeled as rotten. In October 1936, Aitken's predecessor, Wing Commander Harold Kerby, reported that China's ruling couple were "thoroughly disgusted" by standards at the main flight school at Hangchow and described its white buildings as "a cloak for the rottenness within."[3] At the end of the month, the generalissimo appointed his wife as chairman of the CoAA. Chiang's chief air adviser at that time was General Silvio Scaroni of Italy's Regia Aeronautica. He warned Madame Chiang, "Your Air Force is rotten and as a weapon of war, it is entirely useless."[4]

Rarely if ever did foreign military attachés have anything good to say about China's air force or army. The founding father of such critiques was Major John Magruder, who served as the US military attaché in Peking from 1926 to 1930. He would later return to China in the autumn of 1941 as the head of the American Military Mission to China (AMMISCA). In an April 1931 article for *Foreign Affairs*, Magruder described the Chinese as "practical pacifists."[5] Whereas Japan had a deep reverence for the fighting man, according to Magruder, the Chinese had no martial spirit, and with the exception of an increased use of machine guns, the Chinese had hardly modernized their armed forces. Military aviation was in a "period of transition from military stage property to a moral auxiliary," and the Chinese army did not regard it as "a necessary arm"; owing to the inferior performance of army air bureaus, the air force was an "an overrated scarecrow."[6]

CAF pilots fought bravely in the first three months of the Sino-Japanese War but lacked leadership as well as reserves to prolong the war in the air. When the conflict began on July 7, 1937, Japan's air forces had outnumbered the CAF by four to one: Japan had 620 army planes with 25 percent reserves, and 600 navy aircraft, all produced by Japanese manufacturers. The Chinese had only 250 airworthy planes, all of which were imported: 230 came from the United States, the rest from Italy or Germany.[7] By the end of November 1937, the CAF had lost all its prewar stock and was down to about 27 planes.[8]

After the air force collapsed, the Chinese started to rely on Russian airplanes and pilots. In August 1937, Chiang had signed a nonaggression pact with the Soviet Union, which became the basis for military assistance. The terms of the pact featured low-interest loans with which the Chinese could buy hardware, especially aircraft. Planes began to arrive in November 1937. Over the next three years the Nationalists received a total of nine hundred Soviet planes, of which 80 percent were delivered by the end of 1939.

With equipment came advisers, and the mission known as Operation Zet began to expand. In the Soviet Union the pilots achieved heroic status comparable to that of the Flying Tigers in the United States.[9] In January to February 1938, Russian crews carried out 150 bombing missions against the enemy.[10] By the end of the year, three hundred Russians were involved in Chinese military aviation.[11] Nor was their service risk-free: from 1937 to 1940 some two hundred Russian volunteers died in China.[12]

Operation Zet was so well established by 1938 that the Chinese Air Force seemed to have transferred its loyalty from the Chiangs to the Russians. Such was the conclusion of the assistant US naval attaché, Marine Corps captain

James McHugh, who during a long tour in China for the Office of Naval Intelligence (ONI) reported in detail not only about military aviation but also about the intrigues of the generalissimo's family circle involving his various Soong in-laws.[13] McHugh was of enormous influence in shaping how the US Navy perceived the shifts of power in the Nationalist regime, as well as at the State Department through his special reports to the US ambassador, Nelson Johnson.[14]

At the end of February 1938, Madame Chiang gave up her chairmanship of the CoAA. Exhausted and in ill health, she retired from aviation affairs and persuaded her brother T. V. Soong to take over as chairman of the CoAA. As McHugh reported, Soong was content to let the Russians assume responsibility for the country's air defense because they provided much-needed credit and better airplanes than the "superseded models" available from the United States.[15] In a letter to Bill Pawley, Bruce Leighton also observed that Dr. Kung was "relinquishing all initiative in the purchase of aircraft . . . and passing it all over into the hands . . . of T. V."[16] From 1933 to 1938, Dr. Kung in his role as finance minister had handled nearly all negotiations with Bill Pawley of Intercontinent to buy Curtiss-Wright "Hawk" fighter planes. In 1933, Pawley and Kung set up a joint venture between three American partners — Intercontinent, Curtiss-Wright, and Douglas Aviation — and the Nationalist government: the Central Aircraft Manufacturing Company (CAMCO) was designed to save the Chinese government money on the cost of importing planes in their large principal parts — fuselage, wing, and motor. The arrangement was to take advantage of lower labor costs and local raw material to make certain parts in China and assemble the planes there.

This business model worked well until the outbreak of war, which had the effect of greatly increasing the cost of plane parts from the United States and inducing the Chinese to rely on less-costly Russian equipment. In April 1938, Leighton noted that the USSR provided planes at costs that were much lower than anything Intercontinent could offer. Therefore, the prospects for selling American planes were "far from brilliant."[17] By October 1938, the Nationalists had 207 airworthy combat planes, of which 95 were Russian and 80 were American. There also were 14 French Dewoitines, 10 British Gloster Gladiators, and 8 German Henschel bombers.[18]

T. V. Soong willingly accepted dependence on Soviet aid, but others in the family circle were uneasy about it, especially Dr. Kung and Madame Chiang and her closest confidant, W. H. Donald.[19] Donald gave special briefings to British diplomats, particularly the air attachés. At the end of 1937, Harold Kerby reported Donald's suspicions that the Russians and Japanese would settle their differences and carve up China between themselves.[20] Two years later, Aitken, the air attaché, discovered that "mention of the Russians was not welcome": Madame Chiang flatly commented that "they [the Russians] look after themselves," while others confirmed that "they will not talk."[21] Aitken surmised that absolute secrecy was one of the conditions of Soviet aid, and if that condition were broken, Stalin might withdraw his helping hand. There were reports that Russian pilots were just using China as a "sort of training ground." Even so, the Russians inspired universal respect for their courage and efficiency when they chose to fight; they appeared to be in China for the long term, as some eighty Sino-Russian interpreters were teaching Chinese personnel to speak Russian.[22]

Donald had invited Aitken to come to Chungking and arranged his appointments. He too told the new British air attaché that the air force was in a hopeless state, mainly because of its incompetent officers: Donald singled out for special sanction General Mao Pang-chu (also known as Peter or P. T. Mow), the head of air operations.[23] Because General Mao was "irresponsible and corrupt," Chiang had appointed General T. C. Chien (Chien Ta-chun), a loyal and honest army officer, to replace him as head of the air force.[24] General Chien, however, knew so little about aviation that he had to rely on Mao for guidance. Madame Chiang asked Aitken to keep the real nature of his visit a secret from T. C. Chien, who proved to be equally cagey toward Aitken. When the latter asked for hard numbers about air force capability, the former said that he could not possibly release these to a British air attaché.[25]

To his surprise, Aitken found that General Mao spoke more common sense about aviation than anyone else, even if he was a "corrupt scoundrel."[26] His was a pragmatic approach to combat: pilots engaged the enemy only if they had a reasonable chance of success, and they were not allowed to "indulge in heroic deeds against impossible odds."[27] He showed Aitken a new air force chart that featured at the top the generalissimo, Madame Chiang, and her brother T. V. Soong, as well as a few military men. In Aitken's view the organization was nothing more than "a heterogeneous collection of terminologies bunched indiscriminately in groups."[28]

At Kunming, the capital of Yunnan Province, Aitken met the senior CAF officer in charge of flight instruction, General Chow (Chou Chih-jou), as well as the chief instructor, an American called Colonel Chennault.[29] The conversation was hampered by language difficulties, the evasiveness of Chow, and the deafness of Colonel Chennault.[30] When Aitken asked Chennault what he thought of Mao's new organization chart, the latter dismissed it as "hopeless" but had no views on improving it: Aitken surmised that "organization was not his forte."[31]

Aitken understood that there were a dozen or so American Army Air Corps reserve officers training CAF cadets.[32] By all accounts, however, the Americans had poor relations with their students as well as with Chinese officers, who resented the Americans telling them how to teach. There had been a "mutiny" at one school when Chinese instructors told cadets that once they had flown solo, they did not have to mind their American superiors.[33]

One of the American instructors was William MacDonald, an old flying companion of Chennault. In the mid-1930s, Mac had been a wingman in the latter's AAC aerobatic trio, Three Men on a Flying Trapeze. Although Mac refused to admit that he had flown combat missions, he nonetheless alluded to one: he had tried to instill a true sense of loyalty and duty in Chinese crews, but the first time that he led them against an equal number of Japanese (nine), they deserted him immediately.[34] Aitken understood that MacDonald received a handsome reward for each enemy aircraft that he brought down. When the Chinese reduced his bonus to "a thousand dollars gold," by which he meant a thousand US dollars, MacDonald objected that on those terms the Chinese could "shoot the blankety things down themselves."[35]

Aitken got hold of a questionnaire in which Chennault listed for the generalissimo the CAF's countless defects: weak organization, poor training, bad discipline, and lack of initiative on the part of Chinese personnel, as well as the shortage of reserve aircraft and spare parts. In his view, pilot error due to unsound and inadequate training had caused the air force to lose half its planes in the first six months of the Sino-Japanese War. Nonetheless Chennault believed that Chinese pilots, if properly drilled and equipped, could carry out "guerrilla air action" against Japanese supply lines. The CAF already had a few Curtiss Hawk 75 planes suitable for such air strikes, and he recommended the procurement of more long-range single-seater fighter planes armed with heavy guns or cannon.[36] Aitken disagreed with Chennault's tactics on the grounds that fighter planes flying over long distances would be vulnerable to enemy attack. Given their air superiority, the Japanese could easily destroy whatever equipment the Chinese might deploy.[37]

Although the CAF seemed to be a lost cause, the Chiangs gave every indication of wanting to reform and revive it. On December 13, 1938, US diplomats in Chungking had reported that the generalissimo was intent on "revamping and expanding the Chinese Air Force." The government also was about to sign a large contract for planes to be built at a new CAMCO factory located in Yunnan Province.[38] Aitken, however, made no mention of these significant developments. It would appear that the Chinese managed to keep secret their renewed commercial relations with the Intercontinent Corporation, its partner in CAMCO. In December 1938, after a yearlong break, Dr. H. H. Kung resumed his responsibility for American aircraft procurement. He entertained tenders from Bill Pawley as well as another aircraft broker, A. L. "Pat" Patterson. Kung was in the market to buy as many as three hundred new American combat planes from one or the other.

At about this time, Kung also approached the British ambassador to China, Archibald Clark Kerr, about securing export credits worth £10 million to purchase aircraft.[39] Kung raised the possibility of building an aircraft assembly plant at the port of Rangoon (Yangon) in Burma, from which finished planes could be flown to Yunnan Province. This might be necessary because, as Kung pointed out, the transport of oversize aircraft parts on the Burma Road would prove "extremely difficult."[40]

In February 1939, Aitken was aware of the proposal for a Chinese-owned aircraft factory in Burma. In his secret report, he took issue with the idea of allowing any foreign interests to build and operate aircraft factories "in our possessions."[41] He concluded, however, that a few RAF officers should come to China to promote British aircraft because they might have a better chance than any other foreign agents to gain a foothold in that market.[42]

Such was the conundrum that enveloped Chinese military aviation during 1938 and 1939. On the one hand, Chiang wanted airpower but had no faith in

Chinese subordinates to deliver it. On the other hand, he could not dispense with the *Chinese* element of air defense: no matter how incompetent senior air force officers might be, the generalissimo needed an air force manned by his own people for the sake of prestige, if nothing else.

Since the Chinese were entirely dependent on foreign planes, foreign personnel were always required to teach the Chinese how to man and maintain their imported equipment. The Chiangs presided over an air organization that resembled the spokes of a wheel: foreign experts had little interaction with each other and formed separate relationships with the CAF clique that flew American, Italian, or Russian aircraft. At the hub was the generalissimo, who demanded the loyalty of foreign as well as Chinese air personnel. The Chinese saw nothing contradictory about the Soviet Union providing nearly all aircraft and personnel for air operations while they themselves explored the possibility of engaging RAF officers to reform the air ministry, the CoAA.

The Chiangs had learned no lessons from past experience about the drawbacks that such cohabitation inflicted on the air force. For example, from 1933 to 1937, thanks to misguided procurement policies, the Chinese ended up with an official Italian air mission, as well as a privately organized group of American flight instructors. The commander of the American group was Colonel John Jouett, a retired officer of the US Army Air Corps. In 1934, he stated categorically that "oil and water cannot mix and it cannot be expected that Italians and Americans with totally different racial characteristics, ideas, methods of training, etc. could work harmoniously together."[43]

Last but not least was the problem of logistics, which more than any other factor was bound to restrict procurement of Western aircraft. In December 1938, Dr. Kung pointed out to the British ambassador the difficulty of transporting large aircraft parts over the Burma Road. So even if the Chinese ordered planes from Britain or the United States, there was no reliable way of delivering components to Yunnan. The Soviet air mission, by contrast, faced no such obstacles in sending planes to western China: since 1937, they had assembled aircraft near the railhead of the Turkestan-Siberia Railway at Alma Alta (Almaty) in Kazakhstan and flown them to their main base at Lanchow in central China (Gansu Province). From there, planes went on to the large CAF base at Chengdu in the western province of Szechuan, of which Chungking was the capital.

The Russian ferrying operation probably inspired Dr. Kung to believe that a comparable system could be established whereby planes assembled at Rangoon could be flown up to Yunnan. That, however, would require the consent of the British, who were caught between their desire to help China and the need to avoid conflict with Japan. "Nonprovocation" of Japan prevailed and ruled out the possibility of ferrying planes from Far East ports over British territory into China. Therefore in Washington and in London, officials faced the awkward reality that in order to help China in the field of military aviation, they had to rely on the unreliable Burma Road. So, unfortunately, did Intercontinent.

Toward the end of 1937, the Chinese began to widen and extend an old mule track that wound through the mountains of Yunnan into Burma.[1] The result was the 720-mile-long, hard-packed Burma Road that ran by twists and turns from Kunming down to Lashio, the terminus of the Burma Railroad. It was opened in December 1938 to considerable fanfare.

That month, the us ambassador to China, Nelson Johnson, drove the full length of the road. The *New York Times* reported, "The fact that his party was able to make the journey smoothly and easily, he said, spoke for itself. . . . And if a light car could make the trip . . . it is obvious according to experts here, that trucks bearing munitions and other supplies could make the same trip."[2] It was "a miracle of modern construction accomplished by methods older than ancient Rome."[3] The miracle was the product of forced labor. Across Yunnan, village headmen had "volunteered" work teams who used their bare hands and the most basic implements for construction: they were not allowed to return home until their section of the road was finished.[4]

But the new highway was not all it was cracked up to be. The road was dangerous and, as Dr. Kung had realized, could not bear the weight of heavy cargo such as large aircraft parts. Kung's misgivings found an echo in confidential comments by foreign observers. In December 1938, James McHugh of oni accompanied Ambassador Johnson on his car ride over the Burma Road. McHugh privately reported on the hazards for two-way traffic caused by the road's narrow hairpin turns as well as landslides during the monsoon. He concluded that in most sections of the road, "the geology is such that constant patrolling and repair will be required."[5]

In October 1938, the Japanese seized Canton and Hankow, but China-bound cargo from Hong Kong continued to move into the southern part of free, unoccupied China.[6] Soon thereafter, in February 1939, the Japanese invaded Hainan Island, where they established naval as well as air bases: it became a jumping-off point for the Gulf of Tonkin and north Indochina. The Japanese put pressure on the French in Indochina to block the shipment of munitions and most other cargo from Haiphong and Hanoi by rail to Yunnan. By November 1938, the Burma Road had become the last truly secure route for bringing matériel into China from the West. If the Japanese ever imposed the same demands on the British in Burma, they would be able to cut off all delivery of fuel and weapons to China.

The Nationalists had a lot riding on the Burma Road. In September 1938, Dr. Kung sent a special envoy, the venerable financier K. P. Chen (Chen Kuangpu) to the United States to negotiate a large new loan; its execution would depend entirely on the transport of commodities over the new road to Lashio in northeast Burma and from there down to Rangoon for shipment west. Chen was already thinking about the military hardware, including aircraft parts, that would go back up from Rangoon by water, rail, and road to the border. Therefore, in November 1938 it was music to Chen's ears when Henry Morgenthau Jr., the US treasury secretary, suddenly mentioned that the president had asked him if the Chinese had bought any planes recently.

Chen immediately replied that his government had already drawn up a list of American aircraft and munitions worth US$100 million for delivery over the Burma Road. He downplayed the drawbacks of the new route and played up its potential for improvement. He added that the Chinese were talking with the British authorities in Rangoon about allowing the passage of arms and planes over the Burma Road to Yunnan; Chen assured Morgenthau that all the Chinese needed was the money to start procurement.[7] Morgenthau became excited and told Chen that he would bring his wish list to Roosevelt's attention: "I don't make any promises, but I am doing everything I can, Mr. Chen."[8]

Nonetheless, Morgenthau anticipated problems with transport. He pointed out that the Burma Road could not carry more than 140 tons a day; people were bound to question the use of granting loans to the Chinese if they could not deliver tung oil, or other items.[9] Morgenthau was not the only one perplexed by geography and logistics. He mentioned to Chen that the president kept asking questions about the different routes in and out of China, which no one had been able to answer. He hoped that Chen would explain everything to the president. The eminent banker could not have been more delighted to produce memorandums about China's transport system.[10] Chen assured the president that the Burma Road was "destined to be one of the most important highways linking China to a safe foreign seaport and will play a vital role in her struggle for national independence."[11]

In December 1938, the administration announced the so-called wood oil loan, whereby the Chinese received a credit of US$25 million: this constituted advance payment for deliveries of oil extracted from the seeds of tung trees, which is used for varnish. The Chinese regarded this loan as the first real show of American support since the war began in July 1937. K. C. Li (Li Kuo Ching), a wealthy Chinese American businessman known as the "tungsten king," wrote to Dr. Kung that "the $25 million is only the beginning . . . further large sums can be expected. . . . This is a political loan. . . . We will have two years [of a] sympathetic Washington administration, possible six. Our political outlook is now brighter."[12]

The Chinese elite—Chiang and his Soong in-laws, diplomats, educators, and other opinion formers in China as well as the United States—put on a good show in leading the world to believe that Western gestures of goodwill boosted the determination of the Chinese people to fight Japan. The Chinese made propaganda out of their high spirits as well as their black moods to exert pressure on the Western powers for political or material support. In this case Chinese elation about the loan was probably genuine. It certainly fueled the perception of the Roosevelt administration that not only the loan itself but the *timing* of publicity about it had a significant psychological impact on China's people and leaders. The wood oil loan of $25 million was a drop in the bucket compared to Soviet credits. Nonetheless, the administration saw it as a small stone thrown into a big pond that generated ever-widening ripples of good feeling across China.

In response to the new loan and anxiety about future Russian assistance, the Chinese revived their interest in buying American aircraft. K. P. Chen probably assured Dr. Kung that the White House would help in some way to facilitate sales of aircraft. It seems more than likely that Kung, like W. H.

Donald and Madame Chiang, objected to China's dependence on Soviet air aid. Now Dr. Kung had a chance to do something about it: he solicited bids for three hundred planes from Bill Pawley of Intercontinent and another aircraft broker, A. L. Patterson of Consolidated Aviation.

Bruce Leighton and Bill Pawley were just as aware as Dr. Kung that the Burma Road posed an obstacle to their business: even if they managed to sell planes to Chiang's regime, they might not be able to build and deliver them. At the start of the Sino-Japanese War, they had been forced to move the CAMCO aircraft factory from Hangchow to Hankow, a major treaty port farther up the Yangtze. After the Japanese took Hankow in October 1938, Leighton and Pawley had to find a home for the factory at a safe remove from the enemy. In November 1938, their surveyor Ed Gourlie found a new spot for the plant in the south of Yunnan Province. It was a valley called Loiwing, just across the Shweli River from Muse in the Shan territory of northeastern Burma. The viability of this new location depended as much on Burma roads as it did on new orders from the Nationalists.

In December 1938, Leighton wrote to a colleague in New York that it would be some time before the Burma Road would be up to the standards required for a flatbed truck to haul engines and other heavy aircraft parts from depots in Burma into Yunnan.[13] Gourlie had come up with an alternative: the company could have cargo shipped from Rangoon up the Irrawaddy River to the terminus at Bhamo, and from there trucks would go over the seventy-five-mile road to Muse, just on the other side of the Shweli. Gourlie was confident that this Bhamo Road would accommodate the fifteen to twenty trucks required to transport some three thousand tons of material to CAMCO at Loiwing.[14] Leighton, however, surmised that the track from Bhamo to Muse would be impassable much of the time, especially in the rainy season from May to October. He conjectured that if aircraft could be assembled at Bhamo, then delivery of completed planes could "readily be made by air."[15]

Technically Leighton was correct, but he did not take into consideration the need for British consent. After war broke out in China, the British continued to let passenger airlines operate between Hong Kong, Rangoon, and the mainland, but they were reluctant to allow military planes to be assembled in their territory and then flown into China. From 1937 to 1939, various members of the Nationalist regime, as well as Bill Pawley, submitted proposals to build planes in Hong Kong and fly them to China. British authorities carefully weighed the pros and cons from the standpoint of neutrality, the security of British territory, and the need to somehow support China's war effort. But the basis of all policy in the Far East was to avoid provocation of Japan, which might lead to armed conflict. Therefore, on each occasion the cabinet rejected requests to assemble planes and fly them from Hong Kong to China, because the Japanese might attempt to shoot a plane down and then treat the "incident" as a casus belli, an excuse for aggression and incursion into British territory or interference in trade with China.[16]

The British government debated whether the risks to Hong Kong, on the threshold of the war zone in southeast China, applied to territories farther afield such as Burma or India. In February 1938, the Far East Department of the Foreign Office suggested that the Chinese government or a private entrepreneur such as Pawley could use Rangoon instead of Hong Kong as the site of an aircraft assembly plant because it was still a safe distance from Japanese air forces based in China.[17] Not only would an aircraft factory be of commercial value to an underdeveloped port, but it could offer strategic advantages from the standpoint of imperial defense.[18] Nigel Ronald of the Far East Department hoped that Bill Pawley and his associate in Hong Kong Stanley Dodwell could be encouraged to invest in an aircraft factory at Rangoon. Pawley was unenthusiastic. He regarded Rangoon as a backwater that lacked the financial institutions and skilled work force available in Hong Kong.[19]

Dr. Kung met with the British ambassador, Archibald Clark Kerr, in mid-December 1938 to discuss the possibility of the Chinese owning and operating an aircraft plant in Rangoon. Clark Kerr immediately referred the matter to the Foreign Office. Some of the policy mandarins, like Nigel Ronald, were in favor of an aircraft factory at the port of Rangoon, while others argued that it would provoke Japan.[20] The British ambassador to Tokyo, Robert Craigie, had the final word: the Japanese would regard this sort of cooperation as a hostile act. Furthermore, the planes might "be destroyed at once either through Chinese inefficiency or Japanese attack."[21] In mid-January 1939, Foreign Secretary Lord Halifax and Prime Minister Neville Chamberlain decided against "any plan for the establishment in Burma of a plant to assemble aeroplanes for China."[22]

Curiously enough, British officials failed to communicate this decision to the Chinese. On hearing that Pawley was building a new CAMCO assembly plant on the Chinese side of the border, they simply assumed that Chiang's regime had lost interest in a facility at Rangoon.[23] Nonetheless, in January 1939 Milo Talbot of the Far East Department wondered how a new factory at Loiwing would ever produce any planes: "The difficulty referred to by Dr. Kung . . . remains — that of transporting the aeroplane parts by road and rail even so far as Pawley's intended factory just over the frontier." As the prime minister had ruled only against a plant owned by the Chinese government in Rangoon, Talbot reasoned that Pawley or another "enterprising person" should still be encouraged to build a factory there from which incomplete aircraft could be flown to the factory at Loiwing, where they could be fitted with armament: "This might enable us to help the Chinese without doing anything a neutral would not be allowed to do."[24] Talbot hoped to discuss the matter with Bill Pawley, who, he understood, might visit London in February or March.

In the first quarter of 1939, Pawley never made it to the Foreign Office because he was tied up in negotiations with Dr. Kung in Chungking: his bid to sell three hundred planes was vital to the future of CAMCO at Loiwing. To impress his Chinese clients, he imported two new Curtiss-Wright demonstrators, the CW-21 interceptor and the CW Hawk 75-Q. The Irrawaddy Flotilla Company delivered all the parts to Bhamo, where CAMCO staff loaded the oversize parts (fuselage and wings) onto trucks to be driven to Loiwing. During the summer of 1939 British observers commented that CAMCO was "coping" with the transport problem along the difficult road from Bhamo to Loiwing.[25] Perhaps that had been the case before the monsoon season, but once summer brought heavy rains, cargo destined for Loiwing began to pile up in Bhamo. Intercontinent soon discovered how much damage to its finances the weather as well as Burma roads could inflict.

Bill Pawley had already invested US$250,000 of his own money in the state-of-the-art complex at Loiwing, which boasted not only a factory and runway but a golf course, clubhouse, hospital, and modern housing.[26] It seemed increasingly possible that "Pawleyville," as it was sometimes called, would become a white elephant if CAMCO had to rely solely on roads through Burma to receive aircraft parts.

Pawley felt there was no choice but to persuade the British to let him fly material to Loiwing. After a brief visit to the United States in July 1939, he went to England, where he met up with his Hong Kong associate Stanley Dodwell. Toward the end of July, the two of them sought permission to use large transport planes to bring aircraft parts from Hong Kong to Loiwing. At the Foreign Office, John Henniker-Major minuted that air transport of this nature would be extremely "provocative" to the Japanese and "might lead to all sorts of incidents."[27] Nonetheless, officials in other departments still believed that Rangoon could become an aviation hub. Just before Pawley's arrival, B. E. Embry of the Air Ministry minuted that "it might be in the interests of the British Empire to encourage the establishment of an aircraft industry in Burma"[28]

On August 22, 1939, Bill Pawley went to the Colonial Office and Air Ministry to discuss his proposal for air transport from Hong Kong to Loiwing. He still had no interest in Rangoon.[29] The outbreak of war in Europe on September 4, however, brought discussions to a halt. On September 7, 1939, the Foreign Office decided that it would be too dangerous to allow Intercontinent to fly transport planes out of Hong Kong to Loiwing: the Japanese might try to intercept the plane and create an incident that the government was "at present more than ever anxious to avoid."[30] With the onset of war, British officials abandoned for the time being the idea of allowing planes to be built in Rangoon and flown into Yunnan.

Beginning in 1937, Bill Pawley and British authorities discovered that their interests were complementary if not exactly mutual: some British officials wanted Pawley to build an aircraft plant in Burma, while he only wanted one in Hong Kong. Even though he did not achieve his goal, Pawley planted in the mind of British officials the idea that he was an energetic entrepreneur who might be useful to them. At the same time, Pawley began to realize that British cooperation was the key to his business in the Far East. Given the hopeless state of Burma roads, the only way to deliver large pieces of equipment to China was by air transport.

The outbreak of war in Europe dealt a fatal blow to Intercontinent and its principal client, the Nationalist regime. As the Russians were already curtailing the flow of planes to China, Chiang hoped to procure planes from American manufacturers. But the window of opportunity in the United

States had already come down. After the Munich crisis in September 1938, President Roosevelt decided to commit nearly half of all US aircraft production to France and Britain. He became convinced that if the French and the British could supplement their own production with American imports, they would have fleets large enough to deter Germany from attacking its neighbors. For the time being, Roosevelt's "plane aid" was exclusively for Britain and France, and there would be few planes left over for China.

Plane Aid 3

F ranklin Roosevelt had been intrigued by aviation for some time, but in the autumn of 1938 for the first time he explored how airplanes could be used as instruments of deterrence. His emphasis was entirely on the quantity of aircraft rather than the quality of air forces. He was no different from many of his contemporaries in mistaking air strength for airpower and believing that the sheer presence of modern aircraft stationed in strategic locations could act like a scarecrow and keep the enemy away.

The US ambassador to Germany, Hugh Wilson, wrote confidentially to Roosevelt in July that Germany was producing six thousand to seven thousand planes a year and had the capacity to build at least seventeen thousand a year. In fact, German aircraft output in 1938 was 5,235.[1] Wilson was neither the first nor last to exaggerate German air strength, and Germany's allegedly colossal capacity to put planes in the air made a deep impression on Roosevelt.[2] The president went so far as to say that if he were conducting Germany's war he would make the war "principally of the air."[3] He expressed concern about how far behind American air strength lagged compared to that of Germany: at that time the US Army Air Corps had only 1,800 aircraft, of which 350 were deemed obsolescent.[4]

On September 28, 1938, as the crisis over Czechoslovakia reached its peak, the US ambassador to France, William Bullitt, secretly reported to Roosevelt how anxious French officials had become about the superiority of the German air force. If war broke out in Europe, the French would have only six hundred military aircraft to field against the enemy's fleet of sixty-five hundred, of which two-thirds were bombers. Bullitt repeated what the French air minister Guy de la Chambre had told him: "The destruction in Paris would pass all imagination." Chambre pointed out that his country did not have the industrial capacity to expand the fleet in the short term; the only way to increase air strength was to import American combat planes.[5]

On September 29, 1938, Chamberlain and Hitler sealed the fate of Czechoslovakia at Munich. The French were convinced that superior air strength had allowed Hitler to lord it over his European neighbors. They believed that if France and Britain had already possessed air forces comparable to the Luftwaffe, they could have credibly threatened Hitler with retaliation and thus kept him from occupying Czechoslovakia.[6] Roosevelt also embraced this conditional logic, for psychological rather than strictly military reasons. As the historian William Emerson put it, "From the Munich crisis onwards, Roosevelt pursued diplomacy of deterrence in which military appearances, including aid to allies, were no less important, in many respects were more important, than military realities."[7]

The Munich crisis convinced Roosevelt that the most effective way for England and France to project power and keep Hitler at bay was to rapidly add American planes to their fleets. Furthermore, aircraft sales to allies would have economic as well as strategic benefits for the United States, because they could subsidize the expansion of the US manufacturing base without increasing appropriations by Congress for US military orders. Air strength supplemented by American imports would enable the Allies to intimidate Hitler: if and when war broke out, their superior air strength would deal the fatal blow to Germany without requiring US military intervention.[8] As the head of the Army Air Corps, General Hap Arnold, later stated, Roosevelt was only interested in aircraft: barracks in Wyoming would not scare Hitler — the president wanted "airplanes now and lots of them."[9]

In mid-October 1938, Roosevelt rang Treasury Secretary Morgenthau and announced, out of the blue, that the country should build fifteen thousand aircraft a year. For Morgenthau the president's wish was always his command. Even so, Morgenthau was taken aback: the target could not possibly be realized in the current economic and fiscal climate.[10] In November, Roosevelt scaled his goal back to ten thousand planes, only to see it further reduced by the US Congress: in 1939 Congress authorized a ceiling of 5,500 planes for the Army Air Corps, although procurement to that level was unlikely, given that in 1938 manufacturers built only 1,823 airplanes.[11] Nonetheless, by the end of 1938, Morgenthau shared his boss's zeal for having plenty of planes to sell to European allies. After the cabinet debated the matter, Interior Secretary Harold Ickes agreed that "from a strictly defense point of view, it would be better for us to let France have planes than to insist on having them ourselves."[12] In December 1938, Roosevelt put Morgenthau in charge of all aircraft business with the French and British governments; Morgenthau became, in effect, the administration's aviation czar.

In September 1939, the outbreak of war in Europe demonstrated the flaw in Roosevelt's concept of air deterrence: to him, the prospect of his foes having lots of planes did not stop Hitler in his tracks. Nevertheless, FDR continued to treat aircraft sales to the Allies as the cornerstone of "all aid short of war." "Aid" was a misleading word: planes were neither free nor bought on credit. Britain and France paid hard cash for aircraft. It was aid only in the sense that the Allies took precedence over the US armed forces in procuring planes and munitions. Over the course of 1940, Morgenthau channeled well over half of all available military aircraft to the Allies. In the second half of 1940, the British took delivery of 1,160 combat planes, the US Army 256, and the US Navy 208.[13]

The army protested against the president's new policy of allowing British and French purchasing agents to see and test the latest military aircraft.[14] Under pressure from Roosevelt, Secretary of War Henry Woodring authorized a French pilot to secretly fly the prototype of a new Douglas attack bomber, the DB-7. When the plane crashed on January 23, 1939, killing the French and American test pilots, isolationists on the Hill and in the army used the episode to criticize the president's policy. When called before a Senate committee, General Arnold admitted that, at the request of Morgenthau, he had given permission for a French air force officer to test a new Douglas fighter plane. A senator pointedly asked him, "Who is running your Air Force: the Secretary of the Treasury or the Secretary of War?"[15] The honest answer would have been Henry Morgenthau, not Harry Woodring.

This was just the start of plane aid. At the end of 1938, Morgenthau decided that France and Britain should have "the best airplane in the world," which in his view was the Curtiss-Wright P-40 fighter.[16] At that point Curtiss-Wright had not even begun production of its new fighter. In 1938 and 1939, Curtiss-Wright designed and built the prototype of the Hawk 81, the eighty-first in the series of Hawk fighter planes designed since the first in 1922.[17] When the Hawk 81 won the AAC competition to replace the obsolescent P-36 (Hawk 75), the AAC gave it the designation P-40. In April 1939, the War Department ordered 524 P-40s.

In October 1939, just after the outbreak of war in Europe, French purchasing agents drew up a contract for one hundred Hawk 81As (the export version of the Hawk 81) and 265 Hawk 75s, all to be built to their own specifications.[18] The French contract for 265 Hawk 75s had the effect of pushing Chinese orders down the scale of priorities. If Intercontinent could not procure parts to assemble Hawk 75s and other aircraft at Loiwing, its transport problems would become irrelevant. The future of CAMCO was also compromised by the failure of the Nationalists to shoulder their share of the investment in the Loiwing factory: Bill Pawley had paid for the construction of the CAMCO complex at Loiwing out of his own pocket, even if the Nationalist government still owned half the shares. He was beginning to panic about his losses and wondering how much longer he could keep Intercontinent afloat in China.[19]

Without some intervention by the US and British governments, there could be no planes for China. The Roosevelt administration needed to relax its policy of plane aid for France and Britain to make some equipment available to China. From the British government, the Chinese and Pawley needed permission to fly transport planes or military aircraft assembled in Hong Kong over Burma directly to Loiwing and thus bypass Burma's abysmal roads. At the end of 1939, Pawley went to work on the British, while Leighton went home to convince his old friends at the Navy Department that it was a strategic necessity to let China have its fair share of American aircraft.

Bruce Leighton's Guerrilla Air Corps 4

For a brief period in September 1939, the outlook for Intercontinent had never been brighter. In the summer, Dr. Kung had signed a contract with Bill Pawley worth US$4.4 million to build 125 planes, including 49 Hawk 75s (P-36As), 29 C-21 Interceptors, 30 Hawk IIIs from a previous contract, and a few Curtiss-Wright trainers. Bruce Leighton did not anticipate much profit, just enough to maintain the office in Chungking, but at least the contract would create a production schedule for the new Loiwing plant.[1]

In March 1939, Dr. Kung had also awarded a contract to Pawley's rival A. L. Patterson for 209 planes worth US$8.8 million: 64 Seversky P-35 fighter planes, 25 Chance-Vought dive bombers, and 120 trainers.[2] Almost immediately, however, Kung's associates in the United States, K. P. Chen and K. C. Li, had found so many faults in the Patterson contract that in the summer of 1939 the Chinese government effectively let it lapse.[3]

At the same time, the Chinese were becoming anxious about the decline in Russian aircraft deliveries, a development that worked to the advantage of Intercontinent. In October 1939, James McHugh (now promoted to major) discovered an astonishing twist in the tale of Sino-Soviet relations. During the spring and summer of 1939, Yang Jie, the Chinese ambassador in Moscow, had assured Chiang that some seven hundred Russian airplanes were on their way to China.[4] This allegedly was the real reason for dropping the Patterson contract. But then, according to McHugh's source, Chiang found out that Yang had never even started the negotiations for the seven hundred Russian planes.[5] Suddenly the Chinese had nothing like the deliveries that they had expected. This shortfall may explain why, in October 1939, Dr. Kung awarded a further aircraft order to Intercontinent worth US$7.5 million, which included seventy-five Vultee V-11 single-engine fighter planes.[6]

In October 1939, Dr. Kung invited Leighton and Pawley to his home in order to put the finishing touches on the new Vultee contract. This was the same meeting Pawley had described in *Americans Valiant and Glorious*; in 1944, Bruce Leighton confirmed much of the detail in a letter to Bill Pawley. After talking about business, they turned to international affairs. Then Pawley asked how "he and his organization might be of service," to which Dr. Kung replied: "The greatest service which you can do to China—and to your own country if you but knew it, for your country cannot avoid war with Japan, if Japan's present designs in China are permitted to succeed—is to convince your government that a free China is essential to the interest of the United States, that China must be permitted to obtain modern aircraft, and a nucleus of pilots and mechanics familiar with their operations, as the basis for developing a Chinese air force capable of coping with the Japanese."[7] Leighton and Pawley both traced the origins of the Flying Tigers to this seminal meeting with Dr. Kung.

Hindsight, however, exaggerated the significance of Kung's remarks in October 1939. The finance minister did not call for a mercenary air force manned by Western aviators. What he wanted was the restoration of a level playing field in aircraft trade. Plane aid had pushed China and every other country to the back of the line. Neither Intercontinent nor the Chinese Air Force could survive unless the Roosevelt administration accepted the premise that China's war with Japan was just as threatening to US interests as the war with Germany. Therefore, the Chinese deserved the same commercial access to aircraft as America's allies in Europe. Furthermore, in the interwar period, the Nationalists had always required foreign aircraft suppliers to provide foreign technicians and pilots to help the CAF with training, maintenance, and operations. Such had been the case with the Italian mission, the American "Jouett" mission, and the Russian mission. Dr. Kung wanted the US government to restore the status quo ante in aircraft procurement; then China could once again buy American planes and hire American experts to instruct the Chinese how to fly and maintain their equipment. In the short run, Americans would be in charge of the planes, but the object was to transfer technology and operations to the Chinese. That was in line with the prescription of the Chinese Republic's founding father, Sun Yat-sen, who believed that the Chinese initially had to harness foreign capital and expertise to realize national economic reform but eventually should manage all new technologies themselves.[8]

In December 1939, Leighton and his family returned to the United States. In China, he had tended to play second fiddle to Pawley, but in Washington he took the lead. As Leighton recalled in 1942, he and Pawley decided that "at that stage of the matter it would be better that . . . [Pawley] not enter the discussion at the Navy Department."[9] In January 1940, Leighton started to contact old friends across the Navy Department in order to explain the situation in China. In developing his "pitch" to the US government, however, Leighton went beyond the strictly commercial demands that Dr. Kung had put forward in October 1939. He advocated creation of an air guerrilla corps based at CAMCO in Loiwing.

During the previous three years, the US Navy had developed a reputation for being more supportive of China and tougher on Japan than was the army. This was largely thanks to Rear Admiral Harry Yarnell, who commanded the US Asiatic Fleet from 1936 to 1939. The Asiatic Fleet had its base in the Philippines, to which it returned after patrolling the waters of the South China Sea and stopping at treaty ports around the east and south coast of China. In August 1937, Yarnell commanded the flagship USS *Augusta* at Shanghai as the Sino-Japanese conflict escalated into all-out war in and around the city. Yarnell ordered marines and other officers to help Chinese refugees flee the invaders as well as protect US citizens and property. His immediate response to the crisis contrasted sharply with the reaction of the State Department: its officials called right away for the withdrawal of all Americans, including military personnel, from China in order to avoid any incident with Japanese troops.

Yarnell indirectly criticized the State Department when he briefed the press on September 22, 1937. He defended the rights of American citizens to pursue their business or profession in China. He felt that even after Americans had been warned to leave China, it was the duty of the US Navy to help the American community continue their life and livelihoods in China; he implied that by staying on in China, Americans would be standing up to the Japanese invaders.[10] His pronouncements deeply irritated Roosevelt, who complained to the chief of naval operations, Admiral William Leahy, that Yarnell had not consulted the State Department before holding forth.[11] Leahy apologized and promised that it would not happen again.

After retiring from the navy in November 1939, Yarnell continued to criticize the US government for its weak response to Japan.[12] In January 1940, he became an honorary vice-chairman of the American Committee for Nonparticipation in Japanese Aggression, which urged the US government to stop exporting American munitions to Japan. Yarnell lectured across the country, calling for greater US defiance to the dictators and deployment of the US fleet to protect American rights and interests.[13] In contrast to Admiral Yarnell, senior army officers rarely made public pronouncements. The World War I hero Sergeant Alvin York was perhaps the only army figure who exhorted Americans to wage war against Japan.[14]

Bruce Leighton had known and admired Harry Yarnell for years; from 1937 to 1939 they saw each other off and on when the *Augusta* anchored at Hong Kong. Leighton shared Yarnell's forthright views about China. He hoped to find a pro-China audience in the Navy Department, where his contacts were well placed to help him meet the top brass. One was an "old and close personal friend," Captain Robert P. Molten.[15] Molten had graduated in 1911 from the Naval Academy, two years ahead of Leighton. In January 1940 he was aide to the CNO, Admiral Harold Stark, and the assistant CNO, Admiral Robert L. Ghormley.[16] On Friday, January 5, 1940, Leighton received a short handwritten note from Molten: "Dear Bruce, Have discussed several matters which you mentioned with Ghormley and he took it up with Adm[iral] Stark. Adm. S. wants to see you and arrange for you to see the President. Better get down — See me first. I will be away 9th and 10th [January 1940] Always Bob." As the tone of his letter suggests, Molten was ready to open doors to the navy's highest-ranking officers and maybe their commander in chief.

On January 16, 1940, Leighton called on Admiral Walter Stratton Anderson, director of the Office of Naval Intelligence. Two officers joined the meeting: navy commander John M. Creighton and Marine Corps major Rodney A. "Danny" Boone from the Far East section.[17] Both had closely followed the Sino-Japanese War during the previous two years: Boone had been his regiment's intelligence officer on the *Augusta* during the battle of Shanghai in August to October 1937.[18]

After this meeting, Leighton prepared a one-page memorandum, which Admiral Anderson forwarded to Admiral Stark.[19] Leighton stated that Japan's military position would become vulnerable if mobile air forces attacked Japan's essentially waterborne supply lines in China. Chiang's regime backed such tactics but recognized that the CAF lacked the pilots, equipment, training, and organization required for such operations. If American banks (with support from the US government) loaned US$25 million to the Nationalist government, the Chinese could acquire a hundred bombers, a hundred fighters, and fifty transport planes. Leighton suggested that his firm could employ American and Western military reserve pilots for the new air corps. Once the program was up and running, it would cost $5 million a year to maintain it. Leighton emphasized that his company could manage the new enterprise "under commercial contracts with the Chinese government, without any direct participation by the U.S. government." Not only would his firm take care of personnel, but it would handle all aspects of importing, assembling, and maintaining the planes at an advance training base and aircraft facility in China. Leighton was prepared to turn Intercontinent into a private military contractor, perhaps the first of its kind, even if he never employed that term in his proposals.

In a separate conversation with Danny Boone, Leighton offered more details about the Intercontinent Corporation. Its factory at Loiwing was close to the border with Burma and the Chinese section of the Burma Road. The facility could produce two hundred planes per year and had modern Western-style housing for Chinese as well as American workers.[20] In January 1940, it was assembling thirty Curtiss Hawk III biplanes (the last to be produced under a 1937 contract) and had a contract for seventy-five single-engine Vultee bombers, as well as fifty P-36s (the Curtiss Hawk 75-L) and 30 CW-21 Interceptors, another Curtiss aircraft. Intercontinent also had ordered materials from the United States to build sixty Russian planes at a government factory in Chungking. Nevertheless, his company was having great difficulty in acquiring parts from American aircraft manufacturers (including Curtiss-Wright) because of their commitments to other customers. It would be at least fifteen months before Intercontinent could secure the resources to fulfill its China contracts.[21] In the meantime the Loiwing factory carried out maintenance and repairs: some 450 aircraft engines needed complete overhaul. He acknowledged transport problems in Burma. Cargo came by river steamer up the Irrawaddy to Bhamo and then was brought over a "rather poor" seventy-five-mile-long road to Loiwing.

As Leighton later recalled, the ONI officers expressed their *"personal* concurrence" with his ideas but saw little prospect of greater aid for China.[22] Soon thereafter, Leighton had lunch with Captain Oscar Badger, the secretary of the Navy General Board, an advisory group of brass hats who had no direct authority over operations.[23] Badger gave him much the same message: many officers stationed in the Pacific felt that the United States should help China to serve "as a friendly springboard for American activities in the event of trouble; none felt, however, that anything constructive could be done at that time because of national policies."[24] Thanks to Badger, Leighton met the General Board toward the end of January 1940. He repeated most of the points made to ONI and stated that, given Intercontinent's current operations, nothing prevented the company from "setting up some form of 'flying school' and hiring pilots for 'tactical exercises.'"[25]

In February 1940, Bob Molten arranged for Leighton to speak with Admiral Ghormley for an hour or so and then to see the CNO, Admiral Stark.[26] Leighton had expected to see him alone, but on arrival he found a gathering of some twenty officers, to whom he gave roughly the same presentation as he had to the General Board. Leighton suggested that a "comparatively few mobile naval dive bombing squadrons" assisted by radio communications could make the Yangtze River untenable as the line of communication for the Japanese; a hundred planes would be the minimum to start with.[27] At the end, Stark turned to Captain Dan Callahan, Roosevelt's naval aide, and suggested that he take the president a brief memorandum prepared by Leighton about his China air proposal.[28]

On May 6, 1940, Leighton wrote a final letter to Captain Badger that summarized the key elements of his proposal: Intercontinent had "American management with carefully hand-picked American supervisors" for assembling up to three hundred planes a year in China and maintaining or repairing engines and other equipment. Therefore, it would not be difficult to handle shipments of two or three times that number of dismantled planes in the same manner. The Chinese were eager to expand these existing facilities; all that was required were credits from private banks to allow "a continuous program underway apparently on a purely spontaneous commercial basis, without direct formalized plans on the part of our government."[29]

Then, as Leighton later recalled, the trail went cold. On a subsequent visit to Washington, he saw Dan Callahan, who explained that he had done nothing about the China proposal but would keep him posted.[30] Clerks filed away all the memorandums that Leighton had drafted for the navy during January to May 1940. He had pitched his program to all the right people in the language of "Plan Orange," the navy's plans in the event of war with Japan. His highly original contribution was to suggest that a private company, rather than the US military, was in the best position to enhance China's resistance to Japan by means of airpower. If the US government provided loans to China, Intercontinent and CAMCO would do the rest, by setting up a guerrilla air corps at Loiwing.

Fortunately for Leighton and Pawley, no one in the US Navy knew how desperate they were to keep CAMCO from the brink of collapse. In the spring of 1940, the prospects of acquiring parts from Curtiss-Wright took another turn for the worse. On April 17, the Anglo-French Purchasing Board (established on November 29, 1939) drew up a new contract for 600 Hawk 81As (equivalent to P-40s).[31] Suddenly Curtiss had six times as many Hawk 81As to build for the Allies. Many of the parts could also be used in the Hawk 75s that Intercontinent was trying to build for China. Soon thereafter the War Department agreed to stop taking delivery of P-40s so that Curtiss could forge ahead with the French and British contracts.[32]

If the US Army Air Corps could not get its orders filled, the prospects for the Chinese government and Intercontinent were even worse. They struggled to transfer to Loiwing materials already shipped to Rangoon: crates of components were piling up in Bhamo as the road from there to Loiwing proved to be unreliable, especially in the rainy season. The Chinese no longer felt obliged to pay for planes that CAMCO had little chance of building. As the company secretary, Mamie Porritt, recorded in a letter home, Pawley and the Chinese were in dispute during May 1940.[33] Foreign Office records reveal that Dr. Kung asked Pawley to resell fifty Vultee V-12 long-range bombers to the British. Kung portrayed this as a terrific sacrifice, which he and the generalissimo made for the sake of "international relations with the allies."[34] The British saw through the rhetoric. A few months later, an official in the

Burma office commented that the Chinese had decided to sell off the Vultees because they had "failed to meet their cash obligations towards Mr. Pawley," who was now trying to "find scope for his energies elsewhere."[35]

Being pressured to unload the Vultees onto the British may have been the last straw for Bill Pawley: he did not see how he could stem his losses at Loiwing, since the Chinese were too strapped for cash to pay for planes or their share of the investment in CAMCO. He was indeed looking for business elsewhere.

Pawley had formed a new partnership with an Indian entrepreneur, Walchand Hirachand, to build planes for the new Indian Air Force.[36] Over the next few months he cultivated British officials in the government of India who were "impressed by Mr. Pawley's enterprise . . . and by his achievements at Loiwing under conditions of far greater difficulty than exist in India."[37] On this new client depended the future of Intercontinent: Pawley hoped to transplant the bulk of his assembly operations from Yunnan to Bangalore in Hindustan.

The Chinese faced an impasse as far as their air force was concerned. On the one hand, Russian air assistance was drying up, and on the other hand, they could neither afford nor take delivery of American aircraft ordered through Intercontinent. The old arrangement between Kung and Pawley was breaking down; Chiang looked for other ways to procure airplanes, which did not involve sales commissions and negotiations with a "middleman" like Pawley. In March 1940, he sent two CAF officers to the United States to explore how best to bypass Pawley and get hold of American combat planes.

O n March 31, 1940, two Chinese Air Force officers, Colonel Hadson Wang and Colonel C. F. Wang (Wang Chengfu), arrived in California.[1] In 1935, Wang Chengfu had inspected aircraft facilities with Colonel Mao Pang-chu and other members of the CoAA. That tour took him to the Miami Air Races, where in January 1935 William D. Pawley hosted the Chinese visitors and introduced them to the Three Men on a Flying Trapeze, the Army Air Corps aerobatic team who were featured at the meet. This encounter marked the first step on the road to China for the flying trio's members, Claire Chennault, William D. MacDonald, and Luke Williams.[2]

The two Wangs were to locate planes that the Chinese government could buy immediately. On their way across the country they inspected aircraft factories and reached Washington in early May. Their instructions probably came from Dr. Kung; his associate K. C. Li, the "tungsten king," provided a letter of introduction to US government officials. On May 4, 1940, the Chinese military attaché Colonel Kuo Teh Chuan, armed with that letter, presented his fellow officers to Joseph Green, head of the Office of Arms and Munitions Control in the State Department.[3]

Joe Green had become the department's expert on US aircraft and arms trade because of his involvement in foreign munitions trade. Manufacturers and their foreign customers applied to his division for a license to export any military equipment abroad; through this procedure Green tracked the US contribution to the international arms trade in compliance with the Neutrality Act of 1935 and its revisions in 1937 and 1939.[4]

Green briefed them on the way foreign purchasing missions could buy aircraft: first they should submit requests to the president's liaison committee at the Treasury Department; it had been set up toward the end of 1939 to formalize the ad hoc power that Henry Morgenthau, the treasury secretary and "aviation czar," exercised over all foreign military aircraft orders. Green immediately made an appointment for the Chinese with the committee chairman, Captain Collins.[5] That morning the three Chinese officers met Collins but insisted that "their call was not a formal one." Instead of exploring China's aircraft needs, they discussed export licenses for propellers and machine tools. Collins explained yet again the procurement process for foreign purchasing agents: they had to submit their preferences to the liaison committee, which decided how many planes, if any, could be released for sale. The committee processed the order, and then the foreign client as well as his supplier applied for an export license from Joe Green's office.[6]

After their meetings with Green and Collins on May 4, neither the two Wangs nor any other member of the Chinese delegation appear to have contacted the liaison committee about aircraft orders again for months: the Chinese ambassador called on its directors only a few times before October 1940 without discussing specific requests.[7] Given the complete control of the White House over supplies, and stiff competition from the US and British military, the Chinese purchasing agents needed all the help they could get from official patrons if they were to secure any aircraft. Yet they ignored the protocol: they were determined to deal directly with manufacturers without resorting to any middlemen, including the president's liaison committee.

Just after the Wangs met Joe Green in early May 1940, Hitler invaded France. The US government introduced new measures to ensure that arms and aircraft did not end up in German hands. On July 2, 1940, President Roosevelt issued a proclamation that gave him sweeping powers to curtail or limit the export of any strategic commodities or equipment (including airplanes) deemed essential for national defense. Congress reinforced this executive power when it passed the so-called Requisition Act on October 10, 1940.[8] Whenever the president deemed it necessary, he could indirectly or directly block the shipment of military equipment or commodities to any country that was a real or potential enemy of the United States and its allies.[9] Roosevelt was not only commander in chief but became the chief controller of all strategic materials.

In the spring of 1940, Chiang had decided to send his brother-in-law T. V. Soong to the United States in search of financial assistance. Soong arrived in Washington on June 27, accompanied by associates from the Bank of China and Arthur Nichols Young, an American financial expert employed by the Ministry of Finance.[10] On July 7, Chiang told Soong to act as liaison with Colonel C. F. Wang about aircraft procurement and deliver the following message to President Roosevelt: the US government ought to reallocate to China all planes formerly destined for France, where the Vichy regime had just been established; Soong was to point out that if his country received "even one-tenth" of the military hardware already sent to France, it could win the war.[11] The Chinese, however, were unaware that on June 16, the day that Marshal Pétain became the French premier, Arthur Purvis, head of the Anglo-French Purchasing Board, had already arranged with his French colleagues to transfer all their contracts to the British Purchasing Commission (BPC).[12] The board was then dissolved, and the BPC took over all French contracts. With the blessing of Winston Churchill, the BPC also employed the top French purchasing agent, a banker named Jean Monnet, the future father of the European Union.[13]

In 1940, T. V. Soong was no more interested in military aviation than he had been in 1938 when he became head of the CoAA and delegated all the problems of the CAF to the Soviet air mission.[14] Instead, Chiang's brother-in-law poured his energy into high diplomacy and left Arthur Young to work with C. F. Wang on the search for airplanes.

As French orders for Curtiss-Wright P-40s were beyond their reach, Wang and Young looked for alternatives.[15] They sought help from their old friend Colonel John Jouett, former head of the American air mission to China from 1932 to 1935 and now president of the American Aeronautic Chamber of Commerce. Jouett brought to their attention Swedish aircraft contracts for nearly three hundred planes. The Swedes had ordered 144 Vultee Vanguards at US$57,000 each. From Republic Aviation (the successor to the firm of Alexander de Seversky) they also had ordered 112 combat aircraft, of which sixty EP-1 (single-seater) fighters cost $57,000 each and fifty-two 2-PA (two-seater) light bombers were priced at $67,000 each: the total bill, including armaments, came to $22.57 million.[16] Republic also had the parts for thirty-six combat planes that the Swedish government had initially ordered but decided not to buy. These, too, according to Jouett, might become available to China.

Although the Swedes insisted that the planes were for self-defense, the administration feared that the equipment would fall into German hands. As the Swedes recognized, they were bound to come under pressure to sell the planes back to the manufacturers, who in turn would resell them either to the US military or the British government.[17] In the meantime, however, the Swedish purchasing agent, Captain Jacobson, applied for an export license for the Vultee and Republic aircraft.

In early August 1940, Colonel Wang and Arthur Young approached Jacobson to see if China could purchase the entire lot directly from the Swedish government.[18] Once again, the British stole a march on them. In July 1940, Purvis expressed interest in taking over *all* the planes ordered by Sweden: Morgenthau set to work to block export licenses for the Swedish planes, starting with the Vultee Vanguards, which had not yet gone into production.[19] Eventually the US government blocked export of these Vultee planes on the grounds that they were needed for Western Hemisphere defense.[20] Toward the end of August, the State Department also turned down Sweden's application to export the Republic aircraft. The firm, however, had already started to build them and by the end of August had twenty two-seaters and twenty-two single-seater planes ready for shipment. Major Jacobson suggested that if the Chinese could obtain an export license, perhaps he could start to negotiate the sale of the Republic planes to China before the US government had time to seize them.[21]

There was a problem with the Republic order that irritated Arthur Young. The firm had given Bill Pawley of Intercontinent the exclusive right to sell its equipment to China, and he was due a commission on any contract for China until this agreement lapsed on October 17, 1940.[22] Young deeply disapproved of Pawley: in the summer and autumn of 1940 he complained to Joe Green about "the disgraceful behavior of Mr. Pawley," who in his view had sabotaged the Patterson contract the year before and was entirely to blame for China's lost opportunity to import US planes before the outbreak of war in Europe.[23]

Young hoped to get around Republic's commitment to Pawley. He suggested to Captain Jacobson that if the Swedes reinstated the contract for the thirty-six fighter planes for which Republic had parts, then the two governments could come to a deal. Republic's directors, however, felt that they would face some liability if the Swedes sold these thirty-six planes to the Chinese government before Pawley's agency expired. Young replied, "China naturally would have no obligation to pay anything to Pawley and . . . the Swedes could not be sued without their consent."[24]

The Republic deal was not the only project that occupied C. F. Wang and Arthur Young. They drew up a procurement plan designed to keep the CAF fleet at a constant level of 300 fighter planes and 100 bombers over the next few years. As the attrition rate might come to a quarter of all planes each month, Wang estimated that China would require, over a two-year period, 2,100 pursuits and 700 bombers delivered at the rate of 117 planes a month. Wang pointed out that, because of transport problems on the Burma Road, all the planes would have to be flown to China either from the Philippines or Burma, depending on their range. That was precisely the point Dr. Kung had raised back in December 1938: the only way for planes to reach China was by air, not by the network of river, rail, and road through Burma. Wang's two-year purchasing program would cost US$339 million: it also included an estimated $13 million to pay for the transportation and training of two thousand Chinese pilots in the United States.[25]

It was all pie in the sky. Given their lack of funds as well as influence in Washington, Young and Wang could not possibly realize this ambitious program. It fell to T. V. Soong to pry open doors at the highest level of the administration. In the summer of 1940, however, his mission seemed as doomed as that of his subordinates.

6 *T. V. Soong's Mission to Washington*

On June 19, 1940, Soong Tse-Vung had landed in the Pan Am Clipper at Treasure Island in San Francisco Bay, his first trip to the United States since 1933.[1] From 1928 to 1933, Soong had served as the first finance minister for the new Chinese Republic; in 1933 he succeeded in negotiating a US$50 million loan to buy cotton and wheat from the US government. At the end of that year, however, Soong quarreled with Chiang about the latter's excessively high military budget, which detracted from economic development. Chiang became suspicious of his brother-in-law's political ambitions and put pressure on him to resign. Soong did so on October 31, 1933, and was replaced by his more compliant brother in law, Dr. H. H. Kung, who remained finance minister until 1944.

Nevertheless, in the autumn of 1939, Chiang and Soong overcame their long-standing differences. Chiang had become disenchanted with Dr. Kung and considered reappointing Soong as finance minister. Martin Nicholson, the US Treasury's agent representative in Hong Kong, reported that before bringing Soong back to power, Chiang wanted him to hold high-level talks with President Roosevelt and Treasury Secretary Morgenthau. The focus of discussion was to be US Far East policy, the implications of the Ribbentrop-Molotov pact (August 23, 1939) for US-China relations, and China's economic problems.[2]

By the spring of 1940, the scope of Soong's mission had become more complex, owing to the decline in Soviet military aid to China. While Chinese diplomats in Moscow worked to restore the flow of arms and planes, Soong was to promote US-Soviet friendship in ways that would benefit China.[3] That was nearly impossible, because at the end of 1939, the Roosevelt administration had condemned Soviet aggression against its Baltic rim neighbors, a result of the secret protocol of the Ribbentrop-Molotov nonaggression pact. First came the Russian occupation of Poland in September 1939, then the invasion of Finland in December. Finally, in the spring of 1940 Stalin delivered ultimatums to Latvia, Lithuania, and Estonia: they either could accommodate various demands from the Soviet Union or face military occupation. By mid-June 1940 the Baltic states had caved in and established pro-Soviet regimes, which the US government refused to recognize as legitimate governments.[4]

Before meeting President Roosevelt, Soong intended to see the second-most powerful man in Washington, Henry Morgenthau Jr. Soong was not to know that he had managed to rub Morgenthau the wrong way well before arriving in the capital.

After suffering an assassination attempt in 1931, Soong became obsessed with personal security.[5] In 1940, his wife and two younger daughters, Katherine and Mary Jane, set off for the United States before he did. Soong asked Martin Nicholson to arrange special protection for them and to enlist Morgenthau's help to keep secret their arrival in the United States. In his daily meeting on May 27, 1940, Morgenthau read out a "very important . . . secret cable" from Nicholson, which was to be "treated with caution": the Soongs were coming to town, and it had to be kept secret. Morgenthau quipped, "Do two Soongs [Songs] make a White?"—he no doubt addressed this remark to his senior economist, Dr. Harry Dexter White.[6] Looking around the room, Morgenthau asked, "Seriously, who wants to be nurse to the two Soong children?" One passed the buck to the other: was it a shipping matter, a Foreign Department thing, or a currency stabilization problem?

Soong had planned to reach Washington on June 27 and go directly to Morgenthau's house. Instead he was granted an appointment at the Treasury the following morning.[7] On June 28, accompanied by the Chinese ambassador Hu Shih, he met Morgenthau, who straightaway asked if Soong had seen his old friend K. P. Chen: the latter had just returned to China after negotiating a second credit of us$20 million in the spring of 1940. This new loan was to be secured by tin exports. Morgenthau had enormous respect for Chen, whom he described as "a grand fellow. He's everything that a

story-book Chinese businessman should be and most of them ain't."[8] Soong
made his excuses: he had been on the Clipper from Hong Kong while Chen
was on the boat from Manila to Hong Kong—Soong probably avoided
Chen because he was an associate of Dr. Kung. Morgenthau let the matter
drop and asked, "Well, sir, what is on your mind?"

Soong explained that Chiang had wanted somebody to come and discuss
with the president and other members of the administration the internal
situation in China, its current military strength, and its relations with Russia—roughly the agenda foreseen by Nicolson.[9] Morgenthau immediately
tackled him about Soviet aid to China. Soong gave the impression that all
was well between China and Russia: the Nationalists still received regular
supplies from Russia, particularly of aircraft, which in quality matched those
of the Japanese. Nonetheless, the Chinese needed more planes than Russia
could provide. The Japanese were relentlessly bombing Chungking, with as
many as a 150 bombers at a time, whereas the CAF usually could field only
up to 25 planes to fend off the enemy. Morgenthau wondered what sort of
political demands the Russians had made in return for aid. Soong insisted
that there were none: the terms were strictly financial and commercial. After
asking about the state of transportation in and out of China, Morgenthau
somewhat abruptly brought the interview to an end.

Morgenthau was deeply wary of T. V. Soong and communicated his doubts
to the president just before Soong went to the White House on July 1. In
Morgenthau's view, Soong "could hardly be regarded with the same confidence as K. P. Chen": it was unclear whether he even favored continued
resistance to Japan.[10] Morgenthau was sure that Soong would ask for another
loan but advised the president against offering any further financial support at
that time: China's currency was not as weak as Chinese financiers pretended;
there was no point in giving Chiang's regime any more money, because even
if they spent hard currency on imports, enemy interference in the transport
network would prevent delivery. The Japanese had already pressured the
French to suspend shipments by rail from Indochina into Yunnan, and they
were on the verge of forcing Britain to do much the same in Burma.

Gone was the enthusiasm that Morgenthau displayed in the autumn of
1938 when he seemed happy to deal with K. P. Chen and write off every dollar
that he was about to lend to China. If the president's right-hand man was

unsure about Soong, it was virtually a guarantee that Roosevelt would offer tea and sympathy to him but no money.

Soong, however, was not looking for the usual handouts. Instead, he presented a grandiose proposal for cooperation between the United States, China, and the Soviet Union.[11] The president appeared to be intrigued by Soong's scheme and asked Morgenthau to explore ways to get aid to China by means of a trade arrangement with Russia.[12] Roosevelt apparently gave little thought to the policy conflict between such a deal and the State Department's recent condemnation of Stalin's aggression against his Baltic neighbors.

On July 12, 1940, Soong submitted to the US government a substantial wish list from Chiang Kai-shek: US$50 million to stabilize China's currency; three hundred fighter planes and one hundred bombers at an estimated cost of US$40 million; other military supplies worth US$30 million, to be procured either in the United States or in Russia. Chiang also requested funds and expertise to improve China's transportation, of which paving the Burma Road was a top priority.[13]

The administration could not reject Chiang's demands without the risk of demoralizing the Chinese. Roosevelt hoped that some sort of deal with Russia would offer a diplomatic way out of that dilemma. On July 15, Harry White came up with the concept of a three-way swap: the US government would pay $100–200 million up front to the Soviet Union for strategic minerals (manganese, chromite, iron ore, and the like) to be shipped over the course of the next four years. As security against failure to deliver, the Soviet Union would earmark a certain amount of gold for the United States. In exchange for this large advance, the Soviet Union would immediately offer China an equivalent credit with which to buy more Russian military supplies: this new credit would be in addition to the US$50 million that, according to Soong, was left over from the third and final credit (US$150 million) granted by the Russians in July 1939. White concluded that if the scheme was adopted, the US government would acquire much-needed strategic materials from the USSR and promote Soviet aid to China without incurring any political risk vis-à-vis Japan.

By mid-July, China's transport situation undermined any such deal. In June 1940, the Japanese had put pressure on the new British prime minister Winston Churchill to suspend the transit of all military goods, including aircraft parts from the Far East ports of Hong Kong and Rangoon, into China. Churchill could not afford a confrontation with Japan at a time when Hitler had just launched the massive air offensive that became known as the Battle of Britain. To avert the risk of war on two fronts, Churchill ordered the Burma Road to be closed for three months as of July 18, 1940: British customs agents refused to let cargoes of military items cross the border into China, while deliveries of nonmilitary items continued.

As Chiang pointed out to Soong, this fresh disaster made all the more urgent the need for us-Soviet cooperation: if the United States and Russia could exercise responsibility in the Far East, they could turn the situation around.[14] Hopes for a us-Soviet-China alliance against Japan were soon dashed. On July 23, 1940, the State Department expressed American solidarity with Latvia, Lithuania, and Estonia and condemned the "predatory activities" by "one of [their] powerful neighbors" in annihilating their sovereignty and territorial integrity.[15] For the time being, Morgenthau and Roosevelt abandoned the trilateral scheme and let the entire question of us economic aid for China slip back down the scale of priorities.

There can be little doubt that in the summer of 1940, Soong's mission to Washington was bound up entirely with the problem of Sino-Soviet relations. He cultivated the Soviet ambassador to the United States, Konstantin Oumansky, who later revealed that in all their conversations, Soong expressed his hopes that the poor state of relations between the United States and the Soviet Union could be improved.[16] Moreover, as Soong's talks with Morgenthau and Roosevelt revealed, the administration contemplated aid to China only within the framework of an agreement with the Soviet Union. Morgenthau, however, was not interested in any deal—bilateral or trilateral—to funnel a small amount of aid to China, because in his view it would have no impact on Japan. He wanted to play hardball and impose bold economic sanctions, which by depriving Japan of raw resources would cripple its war effort and undermine its capacity to invade China's neighbors, particularly the oil-rich Dutch East Indies.[17]

In August 1940, Morgenthau told Stanley Hornbeck, head of the Far East division at the State Department, that Treasury had nothing more to offer to the Chinese. He advised T. V. Soong to go elsewhere for a loan, perhaps to Jesse Jones, who had recently left the Reconstruction Finance Corporation

(RFC) to become head of the Federal Loan Agency: Morgenthau wondered if Jones could use his influence to extract help from the government's two major lending institutions, the RFC and the Export-Import Bank.[18]

Soong had been in Washington for three months. Discouraged by Morgenthau's attitude, he felt like giving up and going home.[19] Chiang Kai-shek agreed: since trilateral cooperation with the USSR was doomed, Chiang was ready to drop that idea, recall his brother-in-law, and work out some other strategy with the Russians. On August 15, Chiang wrote to Soong about a new position in his Kuomintang government, and a week later he asked Soong to come home to serve in a new Ministry of Economic Warfare: Chiang thought it would be a good idea if Soong returned via Russia and showed "some good will on our side."[20]

On September 5, T. V. Soong finally saw Jesse Jones and expressed his frustration with Morgenthau, who had "given him the run around." Jones expressed sympathy but had nothing to propose, apart from a small loan of $5 million "as evidence of our interest in the Chinese at this time."[21] Before proceeding, however, Jones needed to check with the State Department.

For years, the secretary of state, Cordell Hull, had exercised extreme caution in dealing with the Far East crisis. He consistently opted for a policy of "nonprovocation" of Japan and avoided any overt support for China. His appeasement of Japan irritated cabinet hawks such as Henry Morgenthau and Harold Ickes. In 1938, during negotiations over the wood oil loan, Morgenthau objected to the way that Hull thwarted efforts to help China through his "adamant policy of doing nothing which could possibly be objected to by an aggressor."[22] Two years on, however, Hull was finally flexing his thin muscles. He was outraged by Japan's threats to occupy part of French Indochina and enter a formal alliance with Germany and Italy. In cabinet on September 6, Hull warned that if the Japanese did not "pipe down," the United States should impose a ban on Japanese silk imports, an economic embargo, and give China a loan of $20–25 million. Morgenthau was astounded to hear Hull sound off with such passion.[23]

The president tempered Hull's zeal for stiff economic sanctions against Japan but supported his idea of a big new credit for China. Then Hull began to have second thoughts. In principle he favored an injection of funds for China, but, as in 1938, he worried about the impact of a "political" loan on

Japan. To "depoliticize" it, he and Roosevelt decided to keep the State Department in the background and let Jesse Jones handle the publicity. Jones would portray it as a purely commercial arrangement to acquire tungsten for the government's stockpile of strategic materials. At the same time, Jones was to privately assure Soong that once China had exhausted this credit, he could have another.[24] Since Morgenthau had passed the buck to Jones in the first place, Roosevelt left the treasury secretary out of further China loan discussions, at least for the time being.[25]

The administration was still looking for a big stick with which to beat Japan. As a last resort, Roosevelt asked Morgenthau to revive US-China-Russia trade discussions. On September 19, 1940, when Cordell Hull heard about this scheme for the first time in cabinet, he was aghast.[26] He immediately warned Morgenthau that "this Russian outfit" would never do more for China than it was already doing and that the United States should not perpetuate China's dependence on Soviet military aid by embarking on a three-way trade deal. He proposed an alternative to the "Russian method": let China use the US$25 million loan to buy whatever armaments it wanted in the United States, even if that meant turning a blind eye to statutory prohibitions on using US government loans for military procurement.[27] Hull had rarely been so impulsive: he was ready to scrap long-standing restrictions on the use of foreign loans for military procurement. His proposal was radical and technically illegal, but in his view anything was better than strengthening Russia's hand where China was concerned.

On September 20, Morgenthau met with Jesse Jones and the Soviet ambassador, Konstantin Oumansky. Jones tried to summarize T. V. Soong's idea about a three-way deal: if the United States bought more metals such as manganese or other items from the Soviet Union, then the Chinese could get more help from Russia. Oumansky replied that in his many conversations with Soong, he had never heard the latter talk about increasing US-Soviet trade in this fashion. He understood Soong's desire for trilateral cooperation but wanted to make clear at once "that such a triangle requires good relations between every two angles of that triangle. Our relations with China are very close, very friendly. Your relations with China are very close very friendly. Sorry that we cannot qualify in the same relations between my country and your country."[28]

Oumansky demolished the proposal: How did Morgenthau imagine that Russian manganese and other metals would be delivered to the United States, since most trade routes between the two countries passed through war zones and were currently blocked? He doubted that US-Soviet trade could develop satisfactorily as long as moral and real embargoes kept his country from receiving commodities already ordered from the United States.

Once Oumansky had pointed out all the pitfalls in the initiative, Roosevelt dropped the US-China-Russia scheme once and for all. The Soviet Union wanted to keep each of its bilateral relations separate from the other and not be locked into any agreement that would give more advantage to nations other than itself. In this period, Stalin rebuffed a similar overture from the British for closer trade and strategic ties: these he argued could not offer the benefits that he enjoyed through certain commercial arrangements covered by the nonaggression pact with Hitler.[29] Chiang was forced to accept the inevitable. In early October he warned Soong that Stalin wanted China all to himself and would "by no means give us aid" if China tried to form a relationship with the United States or indeed the UK.[30]

After the failure of the three-way deal, the Roosevelt administration went back to the drawing board to come up with new economic measures against Japan. In Hull's view it was a foregone conclusion that the Japanese would soon occupy French Indochina. Therefore, the matter at hand was how to keep them from carrying on to the Malay Peninsula, and thence to the island of Singapore, where Britain had its major Far East naval base; their next stop would be the Dutch East Indies. On September 20, he groped for words to arrive at a new formula that would allow the United States "to go as far as possible on a loan [to China] and on an iron scrap embargo [on Japan] as quickly as Japan settles in Indo-China, and it's a question of how far we can go without running too much risk of a military crash."[31] Interior Secretary Harold Ickes described Hull's approach as pointless: on September 15, he had written in his "secret diary" that even though Hull feared that Japan would march into Indochina and then into the Dutch East Indies, "it seems to be his policy to wait for Japan to make these forward moves before doing anything about it."[32] Morgenthau felt the same way: once the Japanese had occupied Indochina, "what the hell do they care if we put this or that or the other thing on? The horse is gone."[33]

On September 22, 1940, the pro-Vichy governor of Indochina finally succumbed to Japan, which was allowed to establish twenty-five thousand troops and four air bases in the French colony. On September 26, Jesse Jones announced a new US$25 million loan to China, to be secured by its sales of tungsten to the United States—no doubt K. C. Li, the "tungsten king," would have a large slice of the business. Jones did his best to portray it as something other than a response to the latest Japanese aggression: it was a purely commercial arrangement to acquire strategic commodities for national defense and thus primarily of benefit to the American people. The US government intended to purchase $30 million of tungsten from China while offering an immediate credit of $25 million to meet China's foreign exchange needs.[34]

Jones withheld one crucial piece of information about this loan: for the first time ever, the US government had placed no explicit terms and conditions on the credit, only that it would be repaid through tungsten exports from China. Therefore, Chiang's regime would be free to use the funds to buy anything it needed, including arms and aircraft. Hull had prevailed, and the US government would now turn a blind eye if the Chinese used its new loan for military procurement. Few people knew that this was the case, including Henry Morgenthau, who did not find out until early December.[35]

The following day President Roosevelt announced a prohibition on all steel and scrap iron exports, which though universal in its application was calculated to affect Japan the most. Morgenthau was as unimpressed with the new ban on steel and scrap iron exports as he was with the new loan to China. He told his colleague Harry White that the administration's efforts to help China and punish Japan were too little, too late: the time to put pressure on Japan had been months before.[36] Chiang Kai-shek had a similar reaction. In a telegram to Soong on September 26, he damned the new "tungsten" loan with faint praise because it wasn't big enough: Chiang and his advisers had sought a loan of at least US$100 million that would impress their own people and international lenders as much as the enemy. Oddly enough, Chiang was under the misapprehension that the credit on offer was for US$50 million rather than $25 million, but even so, he complained that $50 million was not enough to cover China's needs. He concluded, however, that since even this unsatisfactory loan would be of some help, it would be "impolite" to turn it down.[37]

In a second message to Soong on September 28, Chiang stressed that China needed American economic assistance to reinforce morale and sustain the war effort. If the US government was willing to cooperate on military aid, the only weapons needed were airplanes.[38] Having secured a new loan with no strings attached, Soong was now under pressure to spend it on military equipment. He had in hand C. F. Wang's purchasing plan, and on September 27, he cabled Chiang to suggest that "it would assist in convincing authorities here if program transmitted were supported by Colonel Chennault."[39] On October 8, Chiang sent Soong a long list of aviation requirements to present to the government. It was now critical to the future of China for him to "negotiate in earnest and get some results as soon as possible."[40]

A few days later, Chiang summoned Chennault to Chungking to discuss the possibility of going to the United States to help Soong with aircraft procurement.[41] At that time, Chennault was based in Kunming, where he was in charge of CAF advanced training. As his diary reveals, this appeared to be the first communication that he had received from the generalissimo for eight months.[42] Chennault had become thoroughly tired of life as an instructor in the CAF and given up all hope of the CAF approaching the standards of a Western air force. Just before leaving Kunming, he told the assistant US naval attaché, Marine Corps captain Francis J. McQuillan, that the only solution for China's present problem of "how to deal with the Japanese Airforce" was to turn the whole air force over "lock, stock and barrel" to the nationals of a foreign country. Chennault said that if he had four hundred foreign pilots and the latest aircraft — a hundred bombers, a hundred long-range pursuits (fighters), and a hundred interceptors (short-range fighters) — he could "very nicely organize a force that would protect Free China from Japanese raids and wreak havoc on the Japanese forces in China."[43] This in a nutshell was Chennault's blueprint for the future Flying Tigers. It was not very different from the concept that Bruce Leighton outlined to the navy earlier in the year.

Despite the uncertainty hanging over the Swedish contract, Republic kept to its schedule and by mid-October 1940 had at least sixty combat planes ready to ship.[44] It now seemed inevitable that the US government would intervene, especially after passage of the Requisition Act. On October 17, 1940, Swedish representatives put a "double-barreled case on record" to the effect that the planes should go only to the US government and no other customer.[45] On the same day, Arthur Young made a final appeal to Sumner Welles, the under secretary of state. Young suggested that once the US government had formally taken over the Swedish contract, the planes should be resold to China. He argued that the Chinese would deploy them against the Japanese, whereas the British or US military would only use them for training.[46]

Chiang, however, had given up on the Swedish planes. On October 18, he told Nelson Johnson that "time does not permit ordering them from manufacturers. US government has to allocate [to us] those that are already made or now in the service of the US Army Air Corps and ship them to China. This would encourage our troops and general public to continue resistance."[47] He gave Johnson the impression that Soong was already petitioning the US government about aircraft. In fact, Soong was still dragging his feet about planes and attending to high finance: after securing the $25 million tungsten loan, he had plans to seek at least another $50 million for currency stabilization.[48]

Given their sensibilities about national sovereignty, the Chinese did their utmost to control military procurement. This was understandable. Even the British ambassador to the United States, Lord Lothian, complained about the administration's interference in his government's contracts for arms and planes. He commented to Henry Morgenthau that the war in Europe was actually America's war because the Americans decided what the British could or could not have.[49] After months of wasted effort, however, the Chinese had learned that beggars could not be choosers. They had tried to do business the Chinese way; now they had to do business the American way.

A Few Planes for China 7

After the failure of the us-Sino-Soviet deal, the administration tried to work out other economic measures to contain Japanese aggression. Privately, the president, like his secretary of state, was outraged by recent pronouncements from Tokyo. A secret tape recorder in the Oval Office captured his reaction when, on October 4, 1940, the Japanese prime minister declared that his country would treat as an act of war any aid or comfort that the United States gave to Japan's enemies. Roosevelt pounded the desk and asserted that just because, under us neutrality laws, any belligerent could buy military hardware in the United States, that did not make the United States a belligerent. If Japan treated the United States as a belligerent and declared war on the United States because it was selling arms to England, then the United States would defend itself.[1]

On October 8, the tape recorder immortalized other comments: a Japanese press officer had proclaimed that his government would not declare war on the United States if it recognized the new order in Asia and demilitarized all us bases in the Pacific, including Hawaii. Roosevelt flew into a rage: "God, that is the first time that any damn Jap has told us to get out of Hawaii and that has me worried more than any other thing in the world."[2] He was anxious about what might happen when the British reopened the Burma Road, because that would be "a pretty definite challenge" to the Japanese. For the past five years, Germany, Japan, and Italy had played "a damn smart game," but if they finally did some "fool thing," the United States would get involved.[3]

That day, Cordell Hull ordered consuls in China and Japan to ask American women and children to leave. He also planned to withdraw all US troops, which otherwise might be exposed to insults from the Japanese. Hull had word from Chiang Kai-shek that the Japanese were planning to thrust southward through Indochina toward Singapore, which renewed anxiety. Hull wanted the Japanese to know that "the United States meant business," and that if Japan went too far, it would find itself at war with the United States.

At the same time, the British were organizing a defense conference in Singapore with military representatives of their dominions in the Pacific.[4] To the greatest extent possible, the British hoped to coordinate their Far East policies with those of the United States. Hull had tended to avoid international consultations that might arouse Japan's suspicions about the democracies ganging up against it. Now his sense of urgency was such that he pushed for staff talks among representatives of the United States, Britain, its dominions, and Dutch authorities in the East Indies to explore defense cooperation in the Pacific.[5]

Chiang seized the opportunity to send identical warnings to Britain and the United States about the collapse of Chinese resistance if aid was not forthcoming.[6] When the British ambassador Clark Kerr forwarded Chiang's message to London, the Air Ministry suggested the possibility of sending some "obsolete types of aircraft not required by the R.A.F."[7] That was hardly what Chiang had in mind: for weeks he had sent cables to Soong in Washington about aircraft procurement.[8] Soong was to tell Roosevelt that Russian planes were no match for the new Japanese fighters: unless China received the latest models from the United States to tackle the enemy, the morale of the Chinese military and people would not hold up much longer.

Furthermore, Chiang warned Soong that the USSR might start to back the Communists if the United States did not adopt a policy of active aid to Chiang's regime.[9] On October 18, the generalissimo raised similar specters in conversation with Ambassador Johnson: he had already instructed T. V. Soong to press for five hundred planes within three months and another five hundred within the year, not to mention "American volunteers . . . to aid us in carrying on hostilities."[10] What those volunteers were to do was left open-ended.

The president and his secretary of state were not immune to Chiang's pleas for aircraft. They had no intention, however, of supplying five hundred planes. Nevertheless Hull felt that the US government should sell at least a few to Chiang to boost Chinese morale.

After talking to Cordell Hull on October 23, Secretary of War Henry Stimson rang up Morgenthau. As Stimson put it, Hull "for once" seemed eager to help China, a development that was "right down your alley as well as mine."[11] Stimson wondered if there was any way to get hold of planes sold to Thailand, which were sitting on a dock in the Philippines, and send them to China: it would be better to sell China these new planes currently bound for Thailand instead of "some old junk . . . that wouldn't be much of a service to the Chinks and . . . probably kill off some of their pilots." In addition to the Thai planes, Stimson wondered if Morgenthau also could get hold of other equipment—Vultee and Republic—ordered by Sweden. Stimson surmised that aircraft parts could be shipped and then transported over the Burma Road, which had just been reopened by the British—although, in his view, it would be even better to have the planes flown from the Philippines to China. Morgenthau replied that "he would love to go to work on it."[12]

At Stimson's request, Philip Young, now chairman of the president's liaison committee, sought the president's approval to divert the Thai planes to China: ten North American dive bombers already in the Philippines and another six still at the manufacturer. Morgenthau portrayed this proposal as Hull's "brainchild," and therefore, once Hull gave it the okay, "it would go down the whole line."[13] In fact it probably was the president's brainchild.[14] The whole line, as Young pointed out, included at least four levels of bureaucracy: export control, consultation with the US military, compensation to Thailand for the requisitioned planes, and finally, payment by the Chinese government.[15] Nonetheless, Young saw no problem: it had all been done before and could be done again for the Thai planes.

On October 24, Cordell Hull instructed Nelson Johnson how to respond to Chiang's appeal for assistance: he should emphasize that it was the policy of the United States, except in time of war, "to avoid entering into alliances or entangling commitments." Nevertheless, officials would discuss Chiang's communication about aircraft with T. V. Soong and the Chinese ambassador: within the framework of existing laws and policies, the department would do what it could to help China.[16]

On the morning of October 31, Hull confirmed to Morgenthau that the day before, he had ordered the release of the Thai planes for resale to China.[17] In the afternoon of October 31, however, Joe Green, chief of export control at the State Department, called Philip Young about the Thai planes and explained that in the past day or so, Hull and Stimson had talked the whole thing over and decided that "the Air Corps needed them so badly that China wasn't going to get them." Stimson assured Morgenthau that "there wasn't a word of truth in it." Both men were taken aback; they had devoted considerable effort to this deal. "I'd like the Chinese to get these planes," said Morgenthau, and Stimson, with a laugh, replied, "So do I. I was the one who, I think, originally initiated it."[18]

On November 1, Young recounted his conversation with Green in a memorandum to Morgenthau. Not only had Green stated that Stimson and Hull had given up all thought of this diversion, but Green gave Young "a calling down for having this bright idea" in the first place. Young had told him, "Well, you might be interested to know whose idea this is. It isn't mine, it is Mr. Hull's," which, Young added, "left Green breathless." Morgenthau passed Young's memorandum with "the inside dope about Joe Green" to Stimson, who became so "agitated that he walked over to the State Department and put the document on Hull's desk." Hull went "through the ceiling" when he realized that Green had overruled his instructions about the Thai planes for China.[19]

The scramble for airplanes had begun. The most likely explanation is that the proposal to divert these dive-bombers to China conflicted with recent decisions by the War Department to upgrade air defenses in the Philippines. This Far East outpost of American interests had long been deprived of modern aircraft and other resources. The War Department was beginning to revise its attitude to the Philippines on the grounds that their reinforcement might help to deter Japan.[20] From this point onward, China's ambitions to secure air weaponry would be frustrated as the administration not only allocated air weapons to Britain but increasingly to the Philippines. Over the next seven months, the War Department gradually came to the view that the colony under its administration (about two thousand miles south of Japan) was a more secure and advantageous platform for bombing Tokyo than were any of the air bases in unoccupied China.

On October 18, General George Marshall, the army chief of staff, had intervened to ensure that the Republic planes coveted by China went to the Philippines instead. He asked the president to approve the dispatch of forty-eight of the sixty Republic EP-1s to the Philippines, and on October 23, President Roosevelt authorized the War Department to seize them: the firm immediately began to load the planes onto flatbed trucks for shipment to the Philippines.[21] The US Army Air Corps eventually designated these as P-35As.

It seems likely that as soon as Marshall got wind of the scheme to divert the Thai dive-bombers to China, he or General Arnold informed Joe Green that the army needed these, as well as the Republic fighters, for the Philippines. Stimson, by contrast, seemed absolutely certain that the Air Corps had no designs on the planes for Thailand, even if he knew about the AAC appropriation of the Republic aircraft. Therefore, it looks as though Marshall or Arnold maneuvered behind the secretary's back. Green may have discreetly gone along with an instruction from Marshall because he too felt that the dive-bombers would be wasted on the Chinese. That would explain the tone of his subsequent remarks during meetings with Chinese representatives from October 31 to November 7.

After failing to obtain any planes through their own devices, members of the Chinese delegation finally went cap in hand to US officials. On October 31, Joe Green received Hu Shih and reviewed recent efforts of the Chinese delegation to buy planes. Hu agreed with Green that his colleagues had a "mistaken policy" in trying to obtain small orders for immediate delivery, which had produced no "tangible results." Much as the ambassador had tried to dissuade them, his colleagues had persisted in doing business their own way. Hu had let the matter drop because he presumed that they knew more about buying planes than he did.

Green suggested that the Chinese immediately get in touch with the liaison committee, which would advise them on securing small orders of twenty-five to fifty planes "that could be added to the large orders of planes of similar types already placed by the British, Canadian, and American Governments." Green assured him that Philip Young was aware of the State Department's desire for the Chinese to be "enabled to obtain as many planes as possible, as soon as possible."[22]

On November 5, Arthur Young also made his excuses to Joseph Green:

he had warned his Chinese associates repeatedly that they must place orders with American manufacturers as soon as possible. Once again he voiced his regrets about the abandonment of the Patterson contract, but he assured Green that the Chinese government would soon instruct its representatives to confer with the liaison committee.[23] The following day, November 6, 1940, Stanley Hornbeck, the State Department's Far East expert, sent Green a note about Hull's wish to make available to China "as promptly as possible a few planes — within limits, the more the better," preferably from stocks already held by the government.[24] He referred specifically to the sixteen airplanes requisitioned from the Thai government that should be sold to the Chinese. Green stalled the transaction: on November 7, Young reported to Morgenthau that "the deal was still off according to Joe Green."[25]

That Green was acting to keep the Thai dive-bombers for the War Department became evident in his meeting with T. V. Soong, who finally appeared at his office on November 7. Soong explained that his government had authorized him to obtain at least a few planes immediately. Up to that point the Chinese had refrained from doing so because they had relied on the Soviet Union for aircraft, but recently they had been disappointed by the small number of planes coming from Russia. Soong then asked about the Thai planes. Green cautioned that these were very powerful dive-bombers, and for a variety of reasons it would be far better for the Chinese to buy something else.[26] Soong asked Green to make an appointment for him with Philip Young. Green assured him that Young was aware of the department's wish for him to "arrange the delivery of at least a few planes to the Chinese government in the immediate future."[27]

It was bad enough that Hull and Morgenthau had been frustrated by Green, but Stimson had been foiled by his own department: Generals Marshall and Arnold had somehow gotten the better of him, with the complicity of Joe Green. On November 7, when Morgenthau found out what had transpired, he quipped, "Joe Green had better be careful."[28] Morgenthau did not like to lose out to anyone, especially someone junior to him at the State Department.

After five months of work, the Chinese delegation had little to show for their efforts: no planes, and one new loan, which Chiang and Soong regarded as inadequate in terms of purchasing power as well as political impact. During the presidential campaign, the administration had been reluctant to change the approach to international relations. For most of 1940, Roosevelt and Hull adhered to the traditional China policy: they occasionally offered financial assistance, which in their view would bolster Chiang's morale and his people's powers of resistance. But as soon as Roosevelt secured a third term in office, he and his closest advisers seemed ready to change tack on the Far East. Chiang and Soong saw an opportunity to launch a new diplomatic strategy for obtaining loans as well as aircraft from the US government.

Chiang had already decided in October to send reinforcements to Washington. On November 11, Colonel Claire Chennault and General Mao Pang-chu set off in the Pan Am Clipper from Hong Kong for the United States. They reached California on November 14 and arrived in Washington by November 18.[29] Arthur Young, Chennault, and Mao set to work on a detailed proposal for the president's liaison committee. They wanted to acquire 350 fighter planes from five possible manufacturers: on the list was the Curtiss-Wright P-40, about which they had reservations because they considered it too slow and ill-suited to the high altitudes of Western China.[30]

On November 21, Arthur Young, General Mao, and Colonel Chennault met with members of the liaison committee. The following day, Philip Young's colleague James C. Buckley went over the proceedings with Joe Green. To Buckley's surprise, the Chinese had no interest in acquiring fifty P-40s, which the committee intended to allot to them; he presumed that there must have been some "misapprehension" about the specifications of the P-40. If the Chinese persisted in this attitude, they would make the work of the committee "considerably more difficult."[31] The Chinese ambassador and Soong moved quickly to control the damage. They insisted that Young, Mao, or Chennault were very interested in the P-40s. On November 22, Buckley reported to Green that the Chinese were placing an order for P-40s that could be delivered in July or August 1941.[32]

On November 26, Soong and Hu Shih called on the secretary of state. Soong stressed how discouraged the Chinese people had become because the air force had no combat planes to resist the "overwhelming air control" of the Japanese. Russia had sold some planes to China, but these were wholly inadequate. Since Britain was preoccupied with its own needs, the Chinese had no choice but to turn to the United States. In addition to planes, Soong transmitted Chiang's request for us$200 to 300 million to stabilize the Chinese currency and thus help the regime buy arms and aircraft. Finally, Soong expressed his conviction that the Japanese were withdrawing troops from China in order to launch a campaign against China's neighbors to the south.[33]

Two days later, on November 28, Soong submitted a memorandum from Chiang for Hull to pass to the president; Claire Chennault and Arthur Young had probably drafted the section on aircraft and Soong the rest.[34] To Morgenthau's irritation, State Department officials kept this important communication to themselves. Morgenthau requested that in future Hull should pass to him all diplomatic documents with a bearing on Treasury business.[35]

Chiang stressed the weakening of Chinese resistance and the mounting enemy threat to British and European colonies around the rim of China. The Japanese had recognized that since they could never dominate all of China, they might as well withdraw troops to mobilize for the invasion of Indochina, Malaya, and the Dutch East Indies. China did not have the resources, Chiang stated, to keep these troops trapped within its borders much longer. Russia had stopped sending aircraft, and since September, Japan's new fighter planes were superior to anything that the Chinese could put in the air. To force Japanese troops to stay in China, Chiang needed planes and lots of them. "Experience has shown," he stated, that a striking force of five hundred planes could contain an enemy air force four times its own size.[36] One might well ask what was the source of this ratio. It was probably Chennault; but on whose experience and in which theater of war did he base such conviction? In the interwar period, airpower enthusiasts had no hard evidence to back up their theories.

Chiang wanted the us and British governments to provide men and planes for a "special air unit" that would restrain the enemy from launching its spring offensive against Singapore.[37] The Chinese could base this special force near the coast in order to threaten Japan, Formosa (Taiwan), and Hainan, which the Japanese had occupied since 1939: thus positioned, squadrons could "act as a most effective deterrent to Japanese designs on Singapore and Dutch East Indies."[38] But how? By attacking Japanese air forces or by sitting there like scarecrows? It appeared that once he had resources in place, Chiang would figure out how to use them.

Whereas Chinese pilots and mechanics would be on standby across the country, personnel for this special air unit were to be drawn entirely from British and American armed forces. As for logistics, the planes could be assembled in Rangoon or India and flown to air bases in China. Chiang's memorandum made no mention of the need for British authorization to allow the flight of armed aircraft from their territory into China, although that was by no means a given. The alternative was to transport aircraft parts by boat from Rangoon to the Yunnan/Burma border and assemble them there. In a separate memorandum on this subject, Chennault had stated that fighter planes could be "readily shipped" by river to Bhamo and then by road to Loiwing.[39] Yet Chennault, like his Chinese counterparts, almost certainly knew that Intercontinent/CAMCO faced chronic logistical obstacles in bringing aircraft parts to Loiwing from Bhamo.

By highlighting the threat to the British Empire, Chiang hit upon a far more effective justification for his demands than he had previously thought up. He could not have anticipated that his ploy would strike a chord with Roosevelt, who felt increasingly anxious about his commitments to help the British in the Far East if and when intelligence indicated that Japan was poised to attack Singapore.

8 Roosevelt's Dilemma

Since the outbreak of the Sino-Japanese War, Roosevelt and Hull had refused to be provoked by Japanese acts of aggression, whether threatened or executed. When the Japanese sank the USS *Panay* in December 1937, Roosevelt and Hull refused to retaliate: they waited for the Japanese to apologize and offer compensation. In 1938, after Hankow and Canton fell to the enemy, rumors circulated that Chiang's regime was on the verge of collapse. If Chinese resistance broke down, then the Japanese would advance on neighboring European colonies. Nevertheless, the administration watched and waited for further events. In December 1938, when Jesse Jones announced the wood oil loan of US$25 million, the timing impressed journalists as a reaction to Japanese aggression. Chen and Morgenthau, however, had been negotiating since September: through that loan Roosevelt wanted to bolster Chiang's morale and keep him fighting, but it was not calculated as a broadside against Japan.

After the Netherlands and France fell to Germany in May 1940, the Japanese announced that they would take French Indochina, the Dutch East Indies, British Far East territories, or "all of them."[1] Roosevelt and Hull made haste slowly: they considered trade sanctions against Japan and how to induce Russia to restore military aid to China. In September 1940, Japan entered into the Axis alliance and then invaded the northern part of French Indochina. As Harold Ickes noted at the time, it seemed to be Cordell Hull's policy to wait for Japan to make a move before doing anything about it, while Morgenthau felt that Hull never reacted until it was too late.[2] The following day the administration publicized the $25 million tungsten loan to China.

Once again, in September 1940, the press suggested that the new credit to China indicated some sort of warning to Japan after its invasion of French Indochina. In fact, its terms and content had nothing directly to do with that crisis: Cordell Hull had been so eager to loosen Stalin's grip on China that he had allowed the tungsten loan to slip through without any "encumbrances." The Chinese were allowed to buy arms or aircraft while the US government looked the other way.[3]

During the presidential campaign, Hull and Roosevelt had been determined not to give any impression that they were worried about war with Japan, lest voters believe that Roosevelt would involve the country in a Far East war. After his reelection, however, the president started to pay close attention to signs of Japanese aggression. There were alerts from the US ambassador in Thailand, Hugh Grant, about Thai-Japanese cooperation, followed by other intelligence that pointed to a Japanese offensive against Singapore in the spring of 1941. Roosevelt and Hull became convinced that preemptive measures were required. For the first time ever, the president seriously considered military action against Japan, an unprecedented departure from previous threat perception.

On Friday morning, November 29, the president rang up Morgenthau and told him that he was worried about China and "something going on between Chiang and Wang," referring to Wang Ching-wei, the Chinese governor of the Japanese-occupied eastern zone of China. Roosevelt mentioned "in strictest confidence" that he would order part of the US fleet to the southern Philippines. Although that order was never carried out, the very thought of doing so indicated a sharp reversal of long-standing policy: for decades the War Department had considered the Philippines to be indefensible and rejected any proposal to put destroyers from the US fleet there, not to mention ground troops and modern combat planes.

Roosevelt insisted on announcing almost immediately the biggest credit ever offered to China—$100 million. He wanted Morgenthau to take $50 million from the US Currency Stabilization Loan (a measure Morgenthau had previously resisted), while Jesse Jones of the Federal Loan Agency was to provide the rest.[4] The president wanted to issue a statement about this big loan within twenty-four hours—that is, on Saturday, November 30, 1940, when Japan and the regime of Wang Ching-wei at Nanking were due to sign their "Treaty concerning Basic Relations."[5] The president stressed that it was a matter of "life and death" for him to announce the new credit that day, because further delay "might mean war in the Far East."[6]

Roosevelt and Sumner Welles (his principal confidant on foreign policy) believed in the propaganda value of presidential pronouncements: if, at the right time, the president of the United States were to show confidence in Chiang's regime, he could have a tremendous psychological and political impact on both China and Japan. Both men felt that by announcing the biggest loan ever to China, the president would boost the morale of the Chinese people and inspire the Chinese military to redouble its efforts against Japan. Bogged down by Chinese resistance, the enemy would no longer be able to mobilize troops for an offensive against Malaya and the Dutch East Indies.[7]

Morgenthau could not understand why the president's press release could not wait until Monday, December 2, and therefore rang Hull to find out what was going on. The latter confirmed that there was "an emergency situation in the Far East" and that was why the president was "in such a hurry."[8] He did not expand on the precise nature of the emergency. Morgenthau said that he would raise the whole issue in the weekly cabinet meeting, which both were about to attend at 2 p.m.

Chiang's memorandum was the first item on the agenda, although, apart from Roosevelt and Hull, no one had seen it.[9] As Harold Ickes wrote in his diary, the president wanted the $100 million loan to China "right away": he seemed ready to advance funds to China against deliveries of tungsten and other commodities, which probably would never be shipped.[10] Roosevelt stressed yet again that half of the big loan should come from the Federal Loan Agency and the rest from the Currency Stabilization Fund: he wanted Morgenthau to go ahead and arrange his part of the credit without waiting to consult congressional committees on banking and currency.

This demand put Morgenthau in a bind. He had promised to seek guidance if not actual permission from Congress should the president ever want to use the stabilization fund to support a country at war.[11] As Ickes wrote, Morgenthau tried to persuade Roosevelt to postpone the announcement so that he would have time to consult Congress. Morgenthau feared that it would "destroy him and make it impossible to approach Congress on any other matter" if he did not honor his pledge to consult the relevant committees before drawing on the stabilization fund for China.[12] Ickes noted that Morgenthau was in such a "sad mental state" about spoiling his relations with Congress that, after returning to the office, he sat at his desk "with his head between his hands" and then went home to bed. Ickes commented that Henry depended almost entirely on the president and always wanted to please him.[13]

Ickes also described the consensus about aircraft for China: as the Chinese had airfields within striking range of Japan, with the right number of planes they could "rain" incendiary bombs on the wooden houses of Japanese cities; then the Japanese would know in the most definite way possible what war meant. Furthermore, everyone "pretty well understood" that the Japanese were "naturally poor air men" . . . and "cannot cope with the fliers of other nations, and the opinion was that China could get all of the American fliers it could use. . . . It looks as if we were getting around to the point of really helping China and perhaps even supplying it with some bombers."[14] On such prejudices and assumptions the administration built its air strategy against Japan right up to Pearl Harbor.

Something had changed not only in the intelligence but in the president's interpretation of it. First of all, the reports did seem more alarming than in the past. On November 28, 1940, Hugh Grant again quoted a reliable source about the creation of a secret Thai-Japan military alliance in line with the "New Order" in East Asia. If the Japanese had their way in Thailand, then their troops could walk into Malaya. Grant suggested that the Thai government had come under Japanese influence when it received Japan's assistance in a border dispute with French Indochina. Grant's warning squared with that of T. V. Soong that the enemy was already withdrawing troops from China to launch a campaign against neighbors to the south.[15]

Germany also was said to be working behind the scenes. On November 30, Sumner Welles told Morgenthau what he had told the president: Germany was pressing Chiang to accommodate Japan: the Chinese were on the verge of a "real psychological moral lapse" as a result of Japan's formal recognition of Wang Ching-wei's regime. Therefore, the president's announcement of a substantial loan would serve as "an immediate counteractive": it was crucial to do so as quickly as possible, since the delay of a few days would weaken the impact of his message.[16]

In conversation with Morgenthau, T. V. Soong repeated the same points made by Welles. He insisted that the Wang-Tokyo accord had created a very grave situation, which would put Chiang's regime under greater pressure than ever. According to Soong, the German foreign minister Ribbentrop had told the Chinese ambassador in Berlin that the rapprochement between Germany and the Soviet Union would give the former a free hand to defeat Britain; then China would not be able to look to either the British or the United States for help. It would be better for Chiang to make peace with Japan now, before the other Axis powers were forced to recognize Wang Ching-wei's regime. If Chiang did so, Germany would make sure that Japan did not go back on its terms; thus Germany would guarantee the survival of China, as well as its leader the generalissimo.[17] For all these reasons, Soong agreed that Roosevelt should announce the $100 million loan on November 30, the day that Japan signed the new protocol with Wang's puppet government: "any assistance given now would have very good effect, both politically and psychologically."[18]

On Saturday morning, November 30, Morgenthau remarked to his staff on the president's exceptional sense of urgency. He pointed out that "things like this had happened before, but no one expected the United States to act so quickly." Harry Dexter White agreed that Chiang and the Chinese were "making the situation appear a little worse than it actually was."[19] Everyone in the room would have preferred the president to take the entire $100 million from Jesse Jones's agency. In principle, the Currency Stabilization Fund was for propping up the US dollar in times of uncertainty, not for propping up failing allies in times of war. Another colleague, Merle Cochran, noted that the Chinese currency was fairly stable and so there was no point in lending the Chinese funds to support it or to buy any more items from the United States. In fact, the Chinese could not even take delivery of military items already shipped, since the Japanese had blocked rail transport from ports in China and Indochina into western China.[20] Finally, Morgenthau pointed out that even though Soong regarded Japan's recognition of Wang's regime as a grave situation, he in no way insisted that Chiang was threatening to make peace with the Japanese because of it.[21] He clearly suspected something was up with the president but could not put his finger on it.

Morgenthau had yet to learn what Roosevelt had probably already revealed to Hull and Welles. The president faced a terrible dilemma over Singapore. Most of his advisers were aware that Prime Minister Winston Churchill wanted the United States to base a large portion of the US fleet at Singapore in order to deter Japan from invading Malaya and the Dutch East Indies. Churchill believed that if some US destroyers were stationed at Singapore as well as Hawaii, he would not have to divert the Royal Navy from its main mission of fighting the enemy in the Atlantic and Mediterranean.

The US Joint Chiefs of Staff, however, adamantly opposed the dispatch of any US warships to Singapore. In November 1940, Admiral Stark outlined his "Europe first" strategy in the "Plan Dog" memorandum: he argued that the United States and Britain should focus entirely on the defeat of Germany and the survival of the British Empire; even if Japan attacked US or Allied territory in the Far East—for example, the Philippines and Singapore— Stark insisted that the United States would have to wait for victory in Europe before fighting a war in the Pacific to recover any territory lost to Japan.[22]

The army agreed entirely with the admiral's assessment. On November 29, in commenting on Plan Dog, General Marshall went even further: the administration should focus on the survival of the British Empire, the defeat of Germany, and effective operations in the Atlantic; "So far as Malaysia is concerned, we should avoid dispersing our forces into that theater."[23]

Roosevelt, however, seemed prepared to overrule the strategy of his military advisers and dispatch destroyers to Singapore. What could possibly have spurred him, after years of restraint, to contemplate an action that risked war with Japan?

The American historian Frederick Marks has found evidence in the private papers of Commonwealth leaders and other politicians that during the Burma Road crisis Roosevelt secretly assured Churchill that if Singapore or other British colonies in the Far East came under serious threat of Japanese attack, he would deploy the navy to protect those territories, particularly Singapore.[24] In the first week of October, Roosevelt was exceptionally agitated about Japan: secret tape recordings in the White House captured him pounding the table and threatening retaliation if the Japanese did any "fool thing."[25] On October 10, Admiral James Richardson warned Secretary Knox that the president was ready to take the country to war, even though the navy was not yet in a fit state to fight one.[26] FDR's belligerent mood and other observations suggest that Churchill was ready to brave the wrath of Japan when he reopened the Burma Road on October 18, 1940, because he felt confident of US naval support to deter a possible enemy attack on Singapore.[27]

Further evidence that Churchill received such a pledge from Roosevelt can be found in a crucial letter that the British ambassador Lord Lothian drafted for Churchill to send to Roosevelt: as Churchill noted, the Far East was "already in your sector of defense against totalitarian aggression."[28] "Already" implied an agreement with Roosevelt as follows: it was up to US armed forces to resist Japanese attacks on British as well as US territory in the Far East. Yet the US Chiefs of Staff had been explicit: if the Philippines fell to the enemy, US armed forces would make no effort to recover it until victory in Europe was secured. Then and only then would the Allies concentrate on defeating Japan.

Nonetheless, if Japan were mobilizing troops to head south toward Malaya, then the political as well as strategic stakes would be dangerously high for the president. First of all, if he involved the navy in a confrontation with Japan, he would break his campaign promise to American voters that he would not send their boys to war. Second, if he sent the fleet to help Britain protect Singapore, he would contradict his declaration that the United States would go to war with Japan only out of self-defense. Third, he would go against the recommendations of his top military advisers, who felt that the United States should concentrate on helping Britain to defeat Germany and Italy before tackling Japan. Finally, his military advisers had no confidence that US forces were in a fit state to win a war against Japan.

What mattered most at this time was the president's perception. If he deemed that a genuine threat to Singapore existed, then for all practical purposes it did: that threat would force him to honor his pledge to Churchill. Therefore he had to find a deterrent to relieve him of that burden. At first he and his advisers hoped that the biggest ever loan to China might send a signal powerful enough to boost China's resistance and put a brake on Japan. Chiang, however, persuaded him that it would take a great deal more than a loan to disrupt the enemy's plans to invade Singapore.

On December 1, 1940, Roosevelt received a memorandum from Chiang that presented the following case: the Japanese had realized that they could never conquer China, and therefore they had decided to break out of China and start their expansion into the rest of Asia.[29] In Chiang's view, the only way to keep the Japanese from invading British and European colonies was to deploy a huge air force against them. Roosevelt and Hull also were coming around to the view that airplanes in some way could avert the Japanese advance, although not in quite the way that Chiang had in mind. On November 30, the president and his cabinet colleagues had discussed the possibility of firebombing Japan. Henry Morgenthau was always eager to please the president. He took it upon himself to solve Roosevelt's dilemma: he devised a plan to bomb Japan into submission, which would disrupt the enemy's designs on Singapore and eliminate any need to send the US Navy there.

9 Bombing Japan

On Monday, December 2, Roosevelt left Washington for a long-planned cruise on the USS *Tuscaloosa* to recover from the campaign and to inspect naval facilities in the Caribbean. With his mind on Western Hemisphere security, he left problems in the Far East to cabinet colleagues. Before leaving, he almost certainly put Henry Morgenthau in the picture about the risk of being forced to send US destroyers to deter the Japanese from Singapore.

That afternoon, the treasury secretary received a visit from the British ambassador. A week before, Lord Lothian had returned from London and informed a crowd of journalists that Britain needed ships, planes, and munitions as well as "perhaps a little financial help." The American press saw through British understatement. Headlines proclaimed that Britain was broke: the UK treasury had nearly exhausted all its cash reserves in order to pay for American armaments. Existing US laws barred the British government from buying arms on credit. If war was a matter of money as much as arms, Britain was about to lose the war.[1] Morgenthau listened to gloomy remarks by the British ambassador and then abruptly changed the subject: he revealed his plan to sell three or four long-range bombers to Chiang Kai-shek and have Chinese crews trained in the United States to fly them on the condition that the Chinese bombed Tokyo. Lothian seemed enthusiastic and said that he would talk it over with T. V. Soong; instead, he referred the matter to London.[2]

On December 7, Lothian let Morgenthau know that the Foreign Office regarded the concept of bombing Tokyo as impracticable and provocative because if attacked, the Japanese would retaliate harder than ever.[3] The following day, Morgenthau put his idea to T. V. Soong. He told Soong that "asking for 500 planes is like asking for 500 stars." Nonetheless, it might be possible to sell China three or four long-range bombers, which in his view would have just as great an impact as all the planes that Chiang had demanded. Morgenthau would have Chinese crews trained in the United States on the condition that China used the planes "to bomb Tokio and other big cities." Bearing in mind Lothian's comments, he asked Soong if he was worried about retaliation. Soong replied that the Japanese were bombing them anyway, and bombing Tokyo would give his country a chance to "hit back."[4]

That was the beauty of Morgenthau's plan for bombing Japan. The United States would provide the air weapon, but China would take the blame. It never occurred to Morgenthau or his cabinet colleagues that helping the Chinese bomb Tokyo might not cause the Japanese to collapse. It did not occur to them that the bombing mission might fail, or that if it succeeded, the enemy might hit back at the United States as well as China.

On December 8, Morgenthau had already recognized that it would take too long to train Chinese pilots. Therefore, he assured Soong that he could find American crews to do the job. He asked Soong in strict secrecy to let Chiang know that the United States was going to send him a few long-range bombers. If the Chinese bombed Tokyo, "it would change the whole picture in the Far East."[5]

Although Morgenthau claimed that he had not discussed the plan with Roosevelt, he "intimated" that it was the president's idea. As he wrote in a file note, Roosevelt had mentioned that it would be a "nice thing if the Chinese would bomb Japan."[6] On November 30, the cabinet had talked about firebombing Japan, as well as the big loan for China. It seems more than likely that the president floated the idea of getting China to bomb Japan and wanted to see a plan developed to that end while he was on vacation.

For a few days thereafter, Morgenthau thought he was the only one doing anything about it. On the morning of December 10, however, he called on Cordell Hull, who, to his delight, volunteered that airpower should be used to scare the Japanese: either a fleet of five hundred American planes should be launched from the Aleutian Islands to fly over Japan, or the Chinese should drop some bombs on Tokyo. Morgenthau confessed that he had already promised a few long-range bombers to Soong and Chiang.

The bomber in question was the Boeing B-17, also known as the Flying Fortress. Hull wondered how the planes could be delivered. Morgenthau surmised that they could be flown to Hawaii, thence to the Philippines, and onward to China.[7] Neither knew anything about the problems that the Army Air Corps faced in deploying the B-17. In principle it had a range of about three thousand miles unloaded, but two thousand miles when charged with six thousand pounds of bombs. In early January 1941, one flew across the United States at an average speed of 190 miles an hour. Because of high winds and icy conditions, however, it had to descend to about seven thousand feet instead of maintaining its expected altitude of fifteen thousand feet, hardly ideal performance if deployed over a war zone.[8] The AAC had not even tried to ferry a B-17 across the Pacific: it conducted this experiment only after the War Department decided to reinforce the Philippines in the spring of 1941.

While Morgenthau pushed his bombing plan, the Chinese delegation pressed for more fighter planes. Thus far, the liaison committee had come up with only twenty P-40s to sell to Chiang's regime. On December 5, Arthur Young discussed this matter with Joe Green and reminded him that the Chinese preferred to deal directly with the manufacturer and not with a middleman, for instance Bill Pawley of Intercontinent. In Young's presence, Green called Guy Vaughan, the president of Curtiss-Wright, to discuss Young's concerns about aircraft brokers. Vaughan stated categorically that Intercontinent had a long-standing agreement as the sole agent for his firm in China. It had been necessary to do business this way in China, "as his company would not dirty its hands by paying the tips and commissions without which no business could be done with the Chinese government." Although he would be happy to negotiate with Arthur Young, the Chinese government would have to sign the contract with Intercontinent.[9]

The Chinese soon learned that they could have fifty P-40s, only a tenth of the number demanded by the generalissimo.[10] On December 13, Chiang drafted a lengthy letter for Soong to transmit to Roosevelt. Chiang insisted that he needed a large air force for a massive counteroffensive against the enemy. In his view, five hundred new American combat planes could destroy fifteen hundred enemy ones—roughly half the entire Japanese air fleet: "This is the most fundamental solution to eliminate the danger of Japan's further aggression in Pacific region."[11]

What was the source of this ratio? Once again, it probably came from Chennault but had no basis in reality. For airpower advocates, the few could perform miracles against the many, like David versus Goliath, if they had the right weapon, skill, and courage.

On December 16, Roosevelt returned from the Caribbean, well rested and enthusiastic about a groundbreaking new initiative. While on board he had received an important letter from Winston Churchill—the text was virtually the same as that drafted by Lord Lothian in November 1940. Churchill made clear that Britain was running out of cash and the war effort would be doomed unless the impending financial crisis was averted. Roosevelt thought long and hard about it. At lunch with Morgenthau on December 17, he suggested that the US government should "get away from a dollar sign" and let the British have whatever they needed; after the war was won, they could pay it back in kind.[12] That afternoon he called a press conference to outline the principle of lend-lease or lease-lend—the program had yet to be named. New legislation would override all previous laws that prevented Britain from buying munitions on credit. Morgenthau was tasked to draft a bill and send it to Congress as soon as possible.

On December 16, in anticipation of Roosevelt's return to Washington, Secretary of War Henry Stimson and Secretary of the Navy Frank Knox, along with their chiefs of staff General George Marshall and Admiral Harold Stark, talked over policies "in the immediate future to insure the survival of the British Empire."[13] There was no doubt in their minds that Japan intended to advance on Singapore. To deter the enemy, they came up with somewhat contradictory recommendations. On the one hand, the British should get more planes and ships to Singapore, but on the other, they should release some aircraft to China in January and February 1941. In Marshall's opinion, a few bombers and some fighters in the hands of the Chinese "would have a very important effect towards checking the withdrawal of the Japanese Army for possible use in Maylasia [sic]."[14]

The Chinese also continued to stress the clear and present danger to the British Empire. On December 16, T. V. Soong delivered two more memorandums from Chiang to Henry Morgenthau: Chiang warned that the Axis powers would synchronize an offensive against Gibraltar, Suez, and Singapore. Therefore, "in order to cope with the threat on Singapore, it is necessary for us to carry the war to Japan. For that purpose, I am most anxious to acquire as many of your latest Flying Fortresses as you could spare which from our air bases could effectively bomb all the vital centers of Japan, and harass their fleet and transports. The effect of this upon the Japanese people who are already much divided and dispirited will certainly be far reaching."[15]

Chiang easily exploited the situation because everyone in the US government seemed convinced that this time the wolf was at the door. They agreed that, to stop the Japanese from attacking Singapore, Chiang should have combat planes, but only if they did not come from the US Army Air Corps. On December 16, George Marshall decided that planes for China would have to come from British allocations. It was now just a question of how many and which type.

On December 18, Morgenthau rang the White House to get an appointment with Roosevelt to talk about the "very secret message" he had received from Chiang Kai-shek. To his surprise the president came straight on the line. He told Roosevelt that Chiang wanted to bomb Japan, and the president replied, "Wonderful, that is what I have been talking about for four years."[16] The following day, Morgenthau went over "the whole Chinese thing" with the president, who was "just as thrilled" as he was. Morgenthau suggested that bombing Tokyo would have a far bigger impact on the international situation than the current campaign of Greek and British forces against the Germans in the Eastern Mediterranean. Roosevelt agreed: "Much more. Much more."[17]

After the weekly cabinet meeting on Friday, December 20, Roosevelt discussed the bombing plan with Stimson, Knox, Hull, and Morgenthau — the "Plus Four." He asked them "to work out a program" and not to wait for any further authorization.[18] That was a key point: they were not obliged to run the blueprint by the president, who simply wanted them to get the job done. Such an arrangement between the president and his cabinet colleagues was in line with Roosevelt's style of governing: he preferred to discuss the big picture rather than going over details; he disliked formal processes of consultation.[19] Stimson called his fondness for ad hoc measures and informal consultation "government on the jump."[20]

The president asked Knox if he had a big four-engine "flying boat" that could do the job instead of a Flying Fortress.[21] That query revealed how little appetite Roosevelt had for diverting bombers from the army. A month later,

Roosevelt was still of the view that the navy, not the army, should take the lead in developing any future plans for bombing Japan.[22]

Later that day, Morgenthau had good news for Soong: he had sent Roosevelt the letters from Chiang. The president was "simply delighted particularly with the one about the bombers. . . . the President said he had been dreaming about this for four years." Therefore, the president had approved Morgenthau's idea of using a base in China for the attack on Tokyo.

On Saturday evening, December 21, Morgenthau invited T. V. Soong, General Mao, and Colonel Claire Chennault to discuss the project. Morgenthau assured them that the president would find a way to get some four-engine bombers for China despite the army's opposition.[23] Soong insisted that bombers were more important than fighters, but Chennault and Mao pointed out the need for fighters to escort bombers. Both highlighted the need for at least a hundred and thirty fighters to protect potential bomber bases in China and another hundred for defending the Burma Road against possible Japanese air attacks launched from Indochina. Morgenthau agreed to a minimum of a hundred fighters, "as ten to twenty would not do any good."[24]

Bombers nonetheless were the priority for the Chinese as well as for Morgenthau, who suggested that the Army Air Corps would have to release crews for the mission: each person would be paid at a possible monthly rate of US$1,000. Chennault then brought up the problem of range. In principle, the bombers should be stationed at airfields in the free zone of China (close the southeast coast) in order to raid Tokyo and return safely to base. A bomber such as the Lockheed Hudson, however, had a range of only eleven hundred miles, whereas the distance to Tokyo, as Chennault noted, was twelve hundred miles. That eliminated Tokyo as a target. Nonetheless, a medium bomber might be able to reach Nagasaki, Kobe, or Osaka. Morgenthau suddenly asked if he was having "a pipe dream": Could these big bombers be concealed from the Japanese by shifting them between different airfields in free China? Chennault asserted that they could be moved around and that they could do a lot of damage before the enemy detected and destroyed them on the ground.

Chiang knew full well that attacking Japan from China was impossible at that stage. In a telegram to T. V. Soong dated December 23, 1940, the generalissimo pointed out, first of all, that unless the Flying Fortresses had fighter escorts, the enemy would easily shoot the bombers down. He also may have known that the p-40 had a range of 650 miles, not nearly enough for a flight to Tokyo. Second, as he pointed out to Soong, the CAF had not yet developed an airfield near the coast that could support the weight of a Flying Fortress: he estimated that one would be ready in March 1941 at the earliest.

The Chinese delegation had no desire to change the mind of Henry Morgenthau or any other US official about bombing Japan to prevent its invasion of Singapore. That scare story had worked wonders by giving the Chinese their first real chance of securing bombers from the US government to use for operations in China, against Japanese targets and quite possibly the Communists.

Henry Stimson finally roused Morgenthau and the others from their pipe dreams. On Sunday, December 22, he wrote in his diary that T. V. Soong and his fellow countrymen wanted to set up a diversion that would help China and "perhaps sew up the Japanese from making their attack on Singapore. Morgenthau and Hull are hot for it. The president mentioned it the other day—on Thursday after conference." Stimson's first and foremost consideration was the impact that the scheme would have on his own department—it would take precious bombers away from the Air Corps. When the cabinet discussed the bombing plan on December 19, Stimson had found it "half-baked. It hadn't been thought out. It was the product of Chinese strategists rather than well thought out American strategy." That was why he was calling a meeting "to get some mature brains into it, before we got committed to it."[25] Stimson had conveniently forgotten that this was an ill-thought-out American strategy cooked up by the president and his cabinet colleagues.

On Sunday evening, December 22, Morgenthau, General Marshall, and Frank Knox arrived at Woodley, Stimson's mansion in Northwest Washington. Stimson turned the floor over to George Marshall, who listed all the drawbacks of wasting bombers on the Chinese, bombers that the British could make better use of. Marshall recommended instead that the British give up some of their fighter planes to the Chinese. Morgenthau agreed to work with Marshall on a new plan for deterring Japan based on selling fighters instead of bombers to China.[26] As long as the planes came from British stocks rather than the Army Air Corps, Marshall was all too willing to devise a new scheme for disrupting the enemy's designs on Singapore.

Tomahawks for China 10

The combat plane George Marshall wanted to divert to China was the export model of the P-40, the H-81A, which in December 1940 Curtiss-Wright was building to strictly British specifications at its Buffalo plant. By that stage, Curtiss executives, as well as the British, had christened it the Tomahawk, or, to be precise, the Tomahawk II. The nomenclature reflected a distinction with a difference.

In the spring of 1940, Curtiss started to work on the big P-40 contract that the AAC had signed in April 1939. In the ordinary course of affairs, the firm would have followed the principle of first come, first served and built all 524 planes for the Air Corps. In April 1940, however, the War Department complied with the president's policy of plane aid. Consequently, the AAC agreed to take delivery of only two hundred P-40s in 1940, and at the same time Curtiss would set up an assembly line to build modified H-81AS for the Allies.[1]

On May 12, 1940, the fourth AAC P-40 rolled off the assembly line, and four days later it was shown off in a demonstration flight from Buffalo to the New York World's Fair. It flew about 270 mph, but its top speed in principle was 367 mph, at least as fast as the RAF Spitfire.[2] Production was slow. In May the Air Corps received twenty-five, in June forty-six, and in July forty P-40s.[3] By early October 1940 Curtiss-Wright had completed two hundred P-40s, and it built no more for the army that year.[4]

In May 1940, the Curtiss factory at Buffalo also began to produce the H-81A. As the French had been first to sign a contract, in October 1939, Curtiss started to build 315 H-81AS to French specifications. Curtiss described the Hawk 81A and the P-40 as virtually the same plane; both versions had the same airframe and power plant, an Allison liquid-cooled engine.[5] The French plane took the V-1710-33, the army plane a V-1710-C15 — known as the C engine, for short. Both versions were to be fitted with two .50 caliber machine guns in the nose of the fuselage. In other respects, however, they differed: the French H-81A had heavier armor on the pilot seat, an external rubber cover on the fuel tank to protect it against bullets, and two Browning .303 caliber guns in each wing — so four guns in all. The AAC P-40 had only two guns: one .30 caliber gun in each wing; the army plane also had no protection to stop leaks from the fuel tank. Consequently the army P-40, being somewhat lighter, was also somewhat faster than the French H-81A.[6]

After the fall of France in May 1940, the British moved quickly to prevent all the planes that the French had ordered in the United States from falling into the hands of the Vichy government. The Anglo-French Purchasing Board was dissolved; the British Purchasing Commission took over all French contracts and also employed Jean Monnet.[7] From then on, all the planes Curtiss built for France were to be shipped to England.

Through the summer of 1940 Curtiss continued to build the H-81A to French specifications. On August 6, the BPC sent the first French plane to England, and more followed. The Air Ministry soon discovered how time-consuming it was to modify the French plane for RAF use. One of the most significant differences concerned armament. The RAF required four Colt .30 caliber machine guns in the wings, not the Browning .303 caliber guns used by the Armée de l'Air. It was some weeks before the BPC communicated this drawback to Curtiss-Wright. In the meantime, the Buffalo factory had built 140 "French" H-81As before the BPC called a halt to the French assembly line.

From mid-October 1940 onward, Curtiss-Wright built to RAF specification the remaining 175 "French" Hawk 81As; these planes bore the serial numbers 141 to 315.[8] By the middle of November, the Buffalo factory had completed all 315 H-81As originally ordered by the French during 1939 to 1940. The 316th plane was the first built under strictly British contracts for a further 765 Hawks.[9]

By early November 1940, Curtiss-Wright and the BPC were calling the Hawk 81A the Tomahawk.[10] For its own bookkeeping reasons, however, the

BPC further refined the nomenclature. It decided to categorize all 315 planes constructed for the French orders as Tomahawk Mark I: it did so even though the H-81AS numbered 141 to 315 were in fact built to RAF specifications.[11] All the Tomahawks numbered 316 and upward were called Mark II because they had always belonged to a strictly British allocation. The BPC abbreviated these designations to Tomahawk I and Tomahawk II.[12] American engineers referred to the Tomahawk II as a Hawk 81A-2.[13]

In September 1940, Curtiss-Wright increased the capacity of the Tomahawk assembly line in order to use up all available Allison C liquid-cooled engines: the development of a more powerful Allison F engine was taking longer than expected. The daily rate of production increased from six in the summer of 1940 to eight or ten on average in November 1940 to January 1941. The president's liaison committee, with the agreement of the War Department, allowed the British to absorb all of this extra output. By December, however, Curtiss had assured the liaison committee and the BPC that it could build an extra three hundred Tomahawks for delivery between May and July 1941. The BPC immediately wanted to monopolize all future production in order to have in total 1,180 H-81AS for the RAF: 880 built by the end of March 1941 and 300 built in the summer.[14]

Curtiss faced countless obstacles in shipping fully functional Tomahawks to England. First of all, there were serious shortages of all sorts of materials. In the winter of 1940–1941, airframes (wing and fuselage) arrived without propellers or minus the correct number of tool sets and guns. In the long run, the most serious deficiency was the failure to deliver spare parts.[15] Second, the H-81A was not yet entirely standardized. To a certain extent, each plane had been individually crafted, and some parts were not interchangeable. For instance, "fillets" to be fitted at the joint of the wing and fuselage were not drilled in exactly the same pattern.[16]

Each plane underwent extensive tests that revealed a range of defects: some were easily corrected, but others were alarming. The RAF and AAC found that the Hawk 81A / P-40 was prone to ground-looping while landing, even when the pilot brought it down in near perfect weather conditions.[17] There were plenty of crack-ups, and by February 1941 the AAC estimated that of its 175 remaining P-40s, many were out of commission for lack of spare parts.[18]

Curtiss tried to find out what made the plane so difficult to land. According to company literature, pilots developed a new technique that overcame the problem. In the case of previous pursuit models, it had been the custom to stall the engine during descent and bring the plane down under force of gravity. They discovered that it was safer to bring the P-40 down under speed, land on the two front wheels, and then allow the tail to settle.[19] An AAC pilot described his method of avoiding a ground-loop: glide the plane in at 110 mph, maintain forward pressure on the stick, and land at speed on the front wheels with the tail high.[20]

In early March 1941, the Buffalo factory completed the British order for 880 Tomahawks. The P-40s that the Flying Tigers eventually flew were all Tomahawk IIs (H-81A-2s); the very last plane off the assembly line had the serial number MSN 15972. From January to early March 1941 a few Tomahawks were set aside each day for shipment to China.[21]

After building the last batch of Tomahawks for the British, Curtiss switched back to completing the original AAC P-40 contract.[22] Over the next two months or so, it built 324 P-40s in two batches. The first comprised 131 planes and had serial numbers that started where production of the Tomahawk II left off—MSN 15973 to 16103. The second lot, of 193 planes, had serial numbers MSN 16104 to 16296.[23] Curtiss engineers incorporated all the improvements made to the British Tomahawk II into the new P-40s for the AAC. These changes were significant enough for the army to assign new designations for the latest P-40s: P-40B for the first 131 planes and P-40C for the second group of 193 planes.[24]

In 1940 and 1941, Curtiss struggled to maintain the delivery schedule of Tomahawks to England. In early January 1941, the BPC understood that the Buffalo factory had arranged the shipment of about five hundred Tomahawks to England: all 315 Tomahawk Mark I planes and at least 185 Mark IIs.[25] As of January 10, however, the Air Ministry had received only 301 Mark I Tomahawks and none of the Mark IIs: 158 planes were apparently still en route, and thirty-four lost at sea.[26] It was not unusual if hundreds of planes ordered by the British ended up being stored at factory or at ports in the United States where they waited for a ship to transport them to England: such was the scarcity of freighters to transport resources to Britain. This pile-up of planes for Britain in US depots created shortages for RAF units and, as it transpired, a temptation for the Roosevelt administration to pinch some for its own purposes.

The days were drawing to an end when the British could count on "all aid short of war" to give them priority over the US military for procuring planes. The US War Department was growing restive about yielding to the British, and understandably so. In the last quarter of 1940, the AAC received 66 combat planes, the navy 148, and the British Empire 675.[27] Others in the US government saw the quantity of aircraft stored at American ports or factories and thought that the British had so many planes that surely they could spare some for other deserving Allies.[28] Whether the Tomahawk was an appropriate combat plane to offer to China or Greece was a question of little interest to the State Department and the White House. Planes were pawns in their game to boost the morale of friendly but weak regimes.

In early December 1940, Roosevelt gave the State Department "peremptory instructions" to make available to Prime Minister Metaxas some P-40s as a show of support for Greece in its struggle against Italy.[29] Across Washington, officials felt that the British should support the president's foreign policy objectives because Britain had already received so much. One member of the BPC warned the Ministry of Aircraft Production (MAP) that "the President and the State Department have apparently great belief in the moral and psychological effect that could be obtained from a statement that the United States and Great Britain were assisting Greece by a release of aircraft production capacity by the former, and a deferment of immediate deliveries by the latter."[30]

Henry Morgenthau pressed the British to make friends around town, to knuckle under and release thirty to fifty Tomahawks for Greece. Almost as an afterthought, he asked Sir Henry Self, head of the British Air Commission (BAC), how good a runway was needed for landing a P-40. Self replied that the plane had very heavy pressure and needed "hard concrete runways." He suggested that it would be far better to let the Greeks have some Hawker Hurricanes, which they already knew how to fly: "The Hurricane," he said, "can operate out of cow pastures. The P-40 can't."[31]

The army flatly refused to give up any of its remaining P-40s to Greece: a senior AAC officer, General George H. Brett, revealed to Philip Young that in fact the AAC had no P-40s "fit for combat."[32] But was the British Tomahawk any more fit for the purpose than the AAC P-40? In the winter of 1940–1941, not a single Tomahawk had been tested in battle.

In January 1941 the Air Ministry decided that the first 315 French Mark I planes were to stay in England, while all the Mark II Tomahawks were destined for the Middle East or North Africa. To fulfill this plan, the ministry wanted Curtiss-Wright to ship all the Mark II planes directly from the east coast of the United States to a port on the east coast of Brazil and then on to the port of Takoradi in Ghana.[33] Once the planes were reassembled at Takoradi, the RAF would ferry them to the war zone; at some point between late February and the spring of 1941 the RAF would form Tomahawk squadrons for the campaign in the Eastern Mediterranean.[34]

Thus, at the end of 1940, the Tomahawk was still more of a prototype than a standard piece of equipment. It had yet to see battle in Europe, no less in the rugged climes of the Middle East and North Africa. The new fighter still suffered teething pains in terms of performance, as well as maintenance. If ground facilities in Greece were inadequate for accommodating a Tomahawk, so were airfields in China and the far-flung corners of the British Empire such as Malaya and Burma. In Washington, however, policy makers cared little about the technical aspects of the Tomahawk. Nor were they too bothered about the impact on the British war effort if a few of their Tomahawks were diverted to lesser Allies. In the winter of 1940–1941, the Roosevelt administration was prepared to rob the British in order to pay the Greeks and Chinese.

Robbing Churchill to Pay Chiang   11

On December 23, 1940, the morning after the meeting at the home of Henry Stimson, General Marshall met with his AAC colleagues General Arnold and General Brett. They were to examine Morgenthau's bombing proposal and alternative plans for steering Japan away from Singapore. First, however, they had to take stock of available planes. General Marshall opened by stating that the War Department had supported the president's liaison committee in allotting three hundred "excess" P-40s to the British Purchasing Commission, but he hoped to take some back.[1] These were the extra three hundred P-40s that Curtiss planned to build in the summer of 1941. In his view, only 120 P-40s should go to England, perhaps 30 to Brazil, and 150 to China, where, in Marshall's judgment, "the action of pursuit ships [fighter planes] would have a big result in the vicinity of Singapore."[2] Exactly how fighter planes in China might keep the Japanese from invading Singapore remained unknown. Marshall was prone to such pronouncements.

Marshall outlined the Chinese bombing scheme proposed by Hull and Morgenthau. If it were implemented, the British would have to release twenty-four four-engine bombers, as the army had none to spare. He pointed out that the promoters of the plan believed that the parts could be shipped to the Philippines, where they would be assembled and the planes then flown into China. American pilots and crews would have to fly the bombers.

The generals felt that the plan represented a waste of bombers, which the British could put to far better use than the Chinese. Hap Arnold pointed out that a few years before, the Chinese had acquired some large Martin bombers, but the Japanese had quickly destroyed them on the ground, and they were likely to do so again.[3] Furthermore, it was unrealistic to believe that a scratch crew could fly these big long-range bombers, as only the most experienced pilots could handle them. Finally, the mission would require escorts, but there were no fighters or light bombers with enough range to reach Tokyo from China.

Given this big picture, General Arnold wanted to talk the whole thing over with the British, but Marshall objected: "That is going to be very hard. The British are a peculiar people." He cited numerous examples from the Great War up to the present conflict that illustrated how reluctant the British were to cooperate with allies, especially when it came to sharing military hardware and accepting strategic priorities other than their own. Furthermore, they had no interest in South America, where Marshall and others in the administration feared a "Fifth column situation" might emerge.

Marshall was determined to squeeze planes out of the British. As it might be unlawful to seize their P-40s, he stated, "we must horse trade with the British. I would like to trade big bombers, releasing some pursuit to the Chinese if the legality could be worked out." The rationale for diverting British pursuits to China was clear: "I . . . want to help the situation in Singapore, in order to avoid the pressure to disperse our Navy in that part of the world. They [the British] want us to send 9 battleships to Singapore. I want the British to get pursuit ships [fighter planes] over there to interfere with the withdrawal [of Japanese troops] from China."[4] When Stimson joined the meeting, all agreed that bombing Japan from China was not an option. The Chinese had set off from the wrong end by wanting bombers; they should have started out with fighter planes instead.[5] Yet again, no one at the War Department wanted to acknowledge that this was in fact a "half-baked" American strategy that had started with the president and his cabinet colleagues.

Stimson and Marshall immediately went over to the State Department to meet Hull, Knox, and Admiral Stark about allocating three hundred "excess" P-40s. Hull still wanted to give 30 to the Greeks, 120 to South American countries, and the rest to China. General Marshall, however, thought it best to distribute them in such a way "as to do the most good psychologically."[6] Knox saw no point in supplying South America as long as the war remained in Europe and the Far East. In the end, they split the P-40s equally between

ROBBING CHURCHILL TO PAY CHIANG   77

the British and Chinese: the latter would immediately take their share out
of shipments from the Buffalo factory in the first quarter of 1941.

Then, on second thought, the group decided to improve compensation to
the British through a two-for-one formula: if the British immediately gave
up a hundred P-40s for China from their first-quarter deliveries, they could
have sole rights to buy all the extra three hundred P-40s to be produced in
the summer of 1941. Thus Britain would end up with three hundred planes
in the long run while losing a hundred in the short term.[7]

Later that day, Henry Morgenthau met with Sir Harry Self, head of the
British Air Commission. Self subsequently reported to MAP that Morgenthau made "strong representations" to make the British order immediately
all three hundred extra P-40s because the Army Air Corps did not have the
funds to do so.[8] Worse was to come. In a second meeting that day with the
Plus Four — Morgenthau, Stimson, Knox, and Hull — Sir Harry discovered
that in return for procuring all three hundred P-40s in the summer, he had
to divert a hundred to China then and there: fifty in January, twenty-five in
February, and twenty-five in March.[9]

At a final meeting with Sir Harry on December 23, Philip Young explained
that in the long run, the British would receive "2 planes for every one that you
give up," to which Sir Harry replied, "That is a very welcome statement."[10]
Nonetheless, this was a spurious piece of math: the British had counted
on having four hundred Tomahawks in all — one hundred delivered in the
first quarter of 1941 and all three hundred "excess" Tomahawks scheduled
for production in the summer of 1941. As a result of this horse trading, they
would be out of pocket immediately for three hundred planes that would
not be available until the summer or beyond, and short of a hundred planes
for their delivery schedule in the first quarter of 1941. So there was no gain
at all, from their standpoint.

Sir Harry needed to cover his back with superiors in London, especially
the head of MAP, Max Aitken, Lord Beaverbrook. He wanted three state-
ments to go on the record: that the BPC still required authorization from MAP
for the diversion, that Morgenthau should acknowledge the need for London's approval, and finally that Morgenthau had asked for this arrangement
on behalf of the Chinese government. If officials in London did not approve

the deal, the administration would have to develop another.[11] Morgenthau thought that sounded fine. As he put it, there was no need to add a footnote to the cable that "there is such a place as Singapore": he felt that the point had already been rammed home. The British had to sacrifice planes to China in order to save their colony.[12]

On New Year's Day, 1941, Morgenthau and Young met again with the Chinese delegation to explain that long-range heavy bombers were no longer available but some P-40s were. Morgenthau cautiously sounded out General Mao and Chennault about the number of fighter planes that they might require.[13] Mao suggested thirty-six fighters, enough to make up three squadrons of nine planes each, plus spares.[14] Mao thought of using these to defend the Burma Road from Japanese air raids.[15]

During this meeting Morgenthau stressed the need for absolute secrecy: "If what I am saying to you now ever appears in the paper or you ever say you talked to me about it, I will just say I never saw you."[16] As it happened, Morgenthau had missed a story in the morning editions of the *New York Tribune* and the *New York Times*: a Chinese military spokesman in Washington had suggested that even somewhat outmoded models could "fill the bill" and that "with a little more help the Chinese might be able to nullify the fast developing threats to French Indo-China, Singapore, Burma and the rich Netherlands East Indies."[17] The source was General Mao.[18] As Chennault later told Morgenthau, when Soong found out that Mao had "shot his mouth off," Soong handed him a pistol with the words, "You are a soldier . . . you know what to do."[19]

The generalissimo could hardly believe that Mao had leaked information to the press and stressed to Soong that it must not happen again.[20] Two weeks later, Mao was on the plane back to China.[21] Nevertheless, Morgenthau was so amused by "his Chinese story" that he repeated it to British counterparts as well as Treasury staff.[22] Mao's behavior, however, was hard evidence that the Chinese could not be trusted with sensitive information. The British had already become alive to this problem, but the Americans were just beginning to catch on.

Meanwhile, British purchasing agents were waiting for London to approve release of a hundred P-40s to China. MAP, however, refused to do so because of the impact on aircraft shipments to England starting in mid-January. On

January 3, Arthur Purvis of the BPC and Morris Wilson of the BAC strongly urged Morgenthau to withdraw his request, but the latter was adamant: the president and the Plus Four had promised a hundred P-40s to the Chinese, and "the commitment had to be honored."[23] Moreover, Roosevelt had increased his offer of P-40s to Greece from thirty to sixty. Purvis and Wilson emphasized that it would be "very disturbing" if the administration looked to the British to take care of its promises to Greece.

Purvis explained "really off the record" how the British were building up Tomahawk stocks for operations in the Middle East and North Africa during the spring: the first fifty planes were already being shipped to Takoradi, in Ghana, where they would be assembled and then flown to Khartoum. Purvis hoped to convince Morgenthau that a sudden dip in the flow of planes to England during the critical three months ahead, January to March 1941, would hinder preparations for the spring offensive against the Germans.[24]

Morgenthau had no idea where Takoradi was; in any case, battles in North Africa and the Middle East were of little significance compared to the alleged Japanese attack on Singapore that threatened American interests, especially presidential ones. He reminded Purvis that for the president the "Far East thing" was critical, and therefore he was "very anxious" to give a hundred P-40s to the Chinese.[25] As Morgenthau put it, "This whole thing started with the President," and this decision was not a "thing lightly arrived at. . . . The President is determined that China get something at this time and he has the full backing of his military advisers."[26] The subtext of this statement was that sending planes to China was the only alternative to sending US warships to Singapore: somehow or other planes based in China would keep the Japanese from attacking Britain's naval stronghold and render unnecessary the dispatch of US destroyers to defend it.

Then, for the first time, Morgenthau offered some idea of the tactical operation for which the Tomahawks were required: the Chinese needed "to have enough . . . to do a job on the Burma Road. That is where they are going to go, to keep that thing open . . . and keep the [Japanese] fellows occupied."[27] Harking back to his conversation with General Mao, Morgenthau pressed the point that the Chinese needed thirty-six planes for three squadrons of nine (plus reserves): "With that number they are prepared to defend the Burma Road." Morgenthau had worked it all out: in order for the British to immediately deliver thirty-six P-40s to China, Curtiss-Wright would have to set aside two planes a day for eighteen days; after that, the factory would take one plane a day for ten weeks: so it would take thirteen weeks in all "to complete the thing."

Morris Wilson wondered why this diversion could not be postponed by a month, but Morgenthau babbled incoherently: "The march is to the south by the Japanese. The only way they can get this thing in is through the Burma Road and these people haven't got a thing to keep that Road open. Given these planes, they can keep that Road open and keep these fellows occupied, and we think it is a tremendous influence in the whole Far Eastern picture, and both Hong Kong and Singapore are at stake."[28]

Morgenthau then described the logistics of delivering the planes to China: the Chinese would ship these things by boat to Burma, then take them up the Irrawaddy River to a place where they had a factory and aviators.[29] He was incredulous that the British did not understand how much more was at stake for them than for the United States. He continued: "This isn't an idle gesture. It means a diversion as far as the Japanese are concerned. I can't weigh the military thing, but I know that after very very careful consideration, this is what Mr. Roosevelt wants, with the complete backing of the Secretary of State and the Army and Navy."[30]

This is the only explicit reference to the distraction that either George Marshall or his military planners thought up to keep the Japanese away from Singapore: the CAF would use P-40s to patrol the Burma Road in Yunnan Province not only to keep it open for transport but to attract the enemy into attacking the route as well as its defenders. Morgenthau implied that a display of new P-40s over the Burma Road would lure these Japanese "fellows" like a flock of geese off course from Singapore. Since he and his cabinet colleagues believed that the Japanese were "not naturally airmen," they may have believed that Chinese pilots, if trained by some American instructors, might have more than a fighting chance to survive dogfights with the myopic enemy.

Morgenthau was so carried away by doing the president's bidding that he forgot to tot up the weeks and months it would take to get the P-40s to the Far East: if it took ten weeks to set aside a hundred planes from the assembly line, that task would be finished at the end of February. Then it would be another three months to ship them all to the Far East—if in fact all hundred could be put on one freighter, which was unlikely. At the very earliest, some would arrive in Rangoon at the end of May; they would be transported over the Burma Road up to the CAMCO plant at Loiwing, Yunnan, assembled, and tested. How long might that take—a month, two months? Once there were some planes, American instructors would need to teach CAF pilots to fly them. But these were fast *single-seater* planes. How many would be wrecked on the first flight? Marshall's scheme was even more hopeless than Morgenthau's bombing plan: the Japanese would easily have taken Singapore by the time the Chinese began their "distraction" over the Burma Road.

Purvis and Wilson responded with caution. They could not offer any opinion about the risk of Japanese attack on Hong Kong or Singapore, as they did not have access to the most recent Far East appreciation prepared by the British General Staff. After the meeting with Purvis and Wilson, Morgenthau instructed Philip Young to make sure that two P-40s a day were put aside for China at the Curtiss factory, starting on Monday, January 6. Then he could tell T. V. Soong that the proposal had become an "accomplished fact."[31]

On January 6, Chiang Kai-shek politely thanked Morgenthau for his offer of a hundred planes but reminded him that he needed considerably more than that for a massive counterattack against the enemy and to bomb Japan.[32] In published telegrams from this period, neither Chiang nor Soong ever mentioned the Burma Road: they consistently stressed the necessity of having long-range bombers to destroy enemy targets in China or in Japan, not a handful of fighters for a tactical exercise in Yunnan Province.

As for the British, they were wholly preoccupied at this time with the strategic challenges in the Eastern Mediterranean and North Africa, for which they desperately wanted combat planes. Where Singapore was concerned, the commander in chief for the Far East, Air Vice-Marshal Robert Brooke-Popham, was optimistic about defense capability: if the Japanese attacked Singapore, the British would have five days warning. Brooke-Popham advised the Chiefs of Staff in London that the Japanese would then face tough opposition before the security of Singapore would be seriously jeopardized.[33] In any event, Churchill had already decided that British forces could do nothing about the Far East, as they were tied up in Europe or North Africa. In his mind, Singapore had become Roosevelt's responsibility. He expected Roosevelt to take care of any urgent threat to the Malay Peninsula by dispatching at least nine destroyers.

George Marshall, however, planned to shift this burden back onto British as well as Chinese shoulders. In order to keep the US Navy from being sent to Singapore, Marshall and his team came up with the idea of organizing as quickly as possible an airpower distraction over the Burma Road. Such was the state of play when Bill Pawley and Bruce Leighton, the directors of the Intercontinent Corporation, became involved in the air program for China.

The Private Military Contractor 12

I n January 1941, the us government outsourced a tactical operation to a private military contractor, even if that term did not yet exist. Intercontinent became involved in the China air program for several reasons. First, Bruce Leighton had convinced his friends in the navy that his company could set up an air guerrilla corps without any direct government involvement. Second, the secretary of the navy and his top military advisers probably recognized that neither they nor the army had the logistical experience to conduct a semi-covert foreign air operation in an environment as difficult and remote as China: only Intercontinent, which had facilities on the ground, could do it. Third, Intercontinent inevitably had a hand in the sale of Curtiss planes to China because it had the exclusive right to sell Curtiss planes in China and was owed a 10 percent commission on each contract.

It seems that Intercontinent's active participation in the China air program began in October 1940. In the first half of the month, Bill Pawley was in the United States while his lawyer George Sellett handled new business in India. As Bruce Leighton later recalled, Pawley saw Frank Knox and discussed the proposal for a guerrilla air corps in China before leaving on a Vultee sales trip to Latin America.[1] The conversation may have prompted Knox to seek the advice of Cordell Hull about a "matter which has been brought to my attention and in which I have a sympathetic interest." Knox understood that a number of American pilots would be willing to volunteer for service in China if they faced no penalties for doing so: perhaps the us government could handle volunteers for China in the same way as volunteers for service in Britain.[2]

On October 23, Hull laid out for Knox regulations that might affect the legal status of volunteer pilots: under the new Nationality Act (effective October 14, 1940), a US national would lose his citizenship if he pledged an oath of allegiance to a foreign state, served in its armed forces (unless authorized by the US government), or performed duties for a foreign state usually reserved for its own nationals.[3] Under other statutes, it was expressly illegal to recruit personnel within the territory or jurisdiction of the United States to serve in foreign armed forces. Nevertheless, under other laws still in force, nothing prevented an American citizen from going abroad and signing up in the armed forces of a foreign state. For example, American volunteers who wished to serve in Britain could go to Canada without a passport and enlist. Hull noted that it was State Department policy to refuse a passport to anyone who stated an intention to serve in the armed forces of a foreign state, but he could use his discretion to reassess the policy on passports if there was a sound reason to do so.[4] This was a confusing state of affairs for anyone willing to offer his services to Britain or China. If, however, the recruiters were authorized by the US government to hire pilots on US territory for a mission to China, in principle neither the recruits nor the recruiters would break the law.

At some point, probably at the end of November 1940, the secretary of the navy summoned Bruce Leighton to his office.[5] Knox told him, "*I* have arranged a $100,000,000 loan and got something started on getting planes out there." He asked Leighton if it was possible to make planes at Loiwing, to which Leighton replied, "No can do, must take 'em from production line." Knox then asked him to contact T. V. Soong. At about that time Leighton also talked with Chennault "at length"—probably in December 1940.[6]

On New Year's Day 1941, Pawley returned to the United States and soon became involved in the diversion of British Tomahawks to China.[7] Treasury officials had advised the British Air Commission to sell the hundred Tomahawks back to Curtiss-Wright, which the latter would then sell to the Universal Trading Corporation (UTC). Morgenthau and K. P. Chen had set up UTC in December 1938 to handle strictly nonmilitary acquisitions subsidized by the wood oil loan; on this occasion, however, it acted as a military procurement agent for the Chinese government.

On January 10, however, Philip Young discovered that if Curtiss-Wright sold the P-40s to UTC, it would have to honor its arrangement with Intercontinent and pay the firm its cut on the sale of its aircraft to China. On January 16, 1941, Curtiss-Wright confirmed to Intercontinent its contractual obligation. In objecting to Treasury interference with these commercial arrangements, Pawley's lawyers pointed out a certain hypocrisy: the administration resented the firm's sales commission but not the profit made by the manufacturer.[8]

Such was the anxiety about getting planes to China that Young asked Curtiss-Wright to start shipment "regardless of whether or not satisfactory negotiations had been completed" over Intercontinent's commission.[9] On January 15, Stanley Hornbeck wrote that it was "especially important" for nothing to upset the schedule to take the hundred planes for China out of British production during January–March 1941.[10] The planes had to reach the Far East in time to preempt the enemy's purported spring offensive against Singapore. Thus, negotiations over Intercontinent's sales commission in no way delayed the shipment of P-40s to China.

On January 6, 1941, Curtiss-Wright and the BPC had agreed to a schedule to pull a few planes a day from the assembly line.[11] On January 13, Curtiss-Wright started to earmark two to three Tomahawks a day for the Chinese allocation.[12] By February 5 the factory had dispatched thirty-four planes, with serial numbers ranging from 626 to 736. On February 6, Curtiss-Wright started all over again, and by February 20 it had set aside another seventeen Tomahawks for China, with serial numbers in the range of 742–839. The factory continued to pull planes off the assembly line at the rate of two or three a day until the last eleven planes (869–880) had been taken off the British order in early March.

On January 16, 1941, Captain Mort Deyo from the office of Secretary Knox called Bruce Leighton to give him the "go-ahead" for the full air program "as discussed." Leighton committed nothing explicit to paper about its purpose. He wrote to Pawley that the program included the private employment of personnel and shipment of material from current production. Resignation of *instructors* from the US military would be accepted. Deyo, however, emphasized that the secretary of the navy wanted Leighton to "personally handle personnel selection" and asked him to come to Washington as soon as possible to discuss the details.[13] The reference to instructors suggests that, as far as

Leighton was concerned, he was to organize a training mission; in principle the recruits would teach Chinese pilots how to fly their new Tomahawks.

On January 18, Deyo telephoned Leighton to explain that Knox and the Chinese delegation objected to paying his firm a commission on the P-40 contract: Deyo explained that, at first, everyone had recognized the principle of giving Intercontinent its due, although Knox had felt that 10 percent was "exorbitant."[14] Then it turned out that Soong would not even concede the principle of a commission. Leighton told Deyo that he and Pawley would be willing to discuss the amount, if officials agreed that in principle the company was owed its sales commission.[15]

The current impasse over a sales commission was virtually the same as that which had arisen over the Swedish contract a few months before: at that time Arthur Young had hoped to avoid paying Pawley his commission on the sale of Republic planes to China by trying to arrange a deal between the Swedish and Chinese governments. Knox and Treasury officials went along with the Chinese because they too wanted to reduce the cost.

Although this squabble did not hold up diversion of the planes from the Curtiss assembly line, it was potentially troublesome. There were other clouds hovering over this project, not least one floating from the direction of the White House. At this time, none of the parties knew that Roosevelt was starting to have second thoughts about US policy toward Japan. Whenever the president's perception of the world changed, his advisers had to drop whatever they were doing in order to keep pace with him: suddenly, the China Air Program was out of step with Roosevelt's latest thinking about the Far East crisis.

O n January 16, 1941, President Roosevelt called his top military advisers to the White House for a major review of policy options to prepare for a sudden outbreak of war. George Marshall brought an army perspective to his account of this important conversation.[1] First Roosevelt outlined risks and probabilities. He suggested a one-in-five chance of a coordinated move by Germany and Japan against the United States, which might occur any day. If so, he would have to assure Churchill that Britain would still receive the same level of matériel as before. He estimated that Britain could hold out for six months with existing stocks, and it might be a full two months before the Axis began hostilities in the Western Hemisphere. Thus Roosevelt reasoned that the United States would have about eight months to get up to war strength.

In light of these assumptions, the president felt that "the Army should not be committed to any aggressive action until it was fully prepared to undertake it; that our military course must be very conservative until our strength had developed." As for the navy, Roosevelt repeated the view expressed by Admiral Stark in his Plan Dog memorandum: the armed forces were to remain on the defensive in the Pacific; the US fleet would be based at Hawaii and provide no reinforcement of the Philippines. In case of an emergency, however, the commander of the Asiatic Fleet would be free to decide when and if to withdraw from the Philippines. Nonetheless, Roosevelt advised Knox and Stark that the navy should continue to consider the possibility of bombing Japanese cities. In the context of the discussion, however, the instruction sounded more like an afterthought than an urgent assignment.

Roosevelt advised Stimson and Marshall to focus on getting their air and land forces up to standard. Knox and Stark should continue to manage the broad strategic planning for war in the Pacific. The navy, guardian of Plan Orange, would be responsible for any air operations against Japan, most likely from naval carriers but quite possibly from bases in China. There could be no hint of launching any aggressive activity in the Far East: caution was the order of the day. This was a major about-face. Only a few weeks before, the president and his men had been on the verge of getting the Chinese to bomb Tokyo, and then helping the CAF to use fighters to mount an air distraction over the Burma Road. What accounted for Roosevelt's change of heart?

The answer was the Lend-Lease bill, which the executive submitted to Congress on January 10, 1941. The president wanted to avoid any international incidents in the Far East or Europe that might jeopardize its passage.[2] As had often been the case, whenever the administration wanted to avoid provocation of Japan, it publicly distanced itself from China.[3] This sudden reversal of policy must have thrown the organizers of the China air program into a quandary. Henry Morgenthau had arranged the sale of planes to Chiang's regime; Curtiss-Wright had started to put planes aside for shipment to China. Frank Knox had approached Bruce Leighton about recruiting American airmen as flight instructors for the CAF.

On the one hand, the program could not be dismantled without causing deep offense to the Chinese. On the other hand, it was at odds with new priorities. Roosevelt insisted that the US government should avoid all actions that might provoke Japan at this time, in order to smooth the safe passage of Lend-Lease through Congress. Any leaks about the provision of US combat planes to the Chinese to deploy against the Japanese over the Burma Road would be a disaster on both counts.

In light of these concerns, it seems likely that no one raised the China air program at the White House conference. From this point onward, however, Frank Knox may have realized that the project had become his personal responsibility, and his assistant Mort Deyo would have to handle most of the thorny issues as they arose. Knox may have recognized that he had to sustain the project's momentum just enough to keep the Chinese happy, but he also had to keep it heavily under wraps, lest any leak about its existence undermine the president's agenda. This was a secret to be kept as much from the American public as from the Japanese.

In the week after the White House conference of January 16, 1941, the question of Intercontinent's sales commission and Leighton's role in recruitment dogged the China air program. Leighton talked further with Mort Deyo, and on January 20, 1941, he wrote a lengthy rejoinder to him.[4] He had inferred from their conversation that it was in the vital interests of the US government for China to have an effective air force. Because the US government could not become directly involved in that task, the administration wanted to have it handled through "commercial channels." He understood that Soong had asked for Leighton "as an individual" to hire the volunteers, because Soong did not want to use Intercontinent's services, nor did the Chinese want to pay any commissions to the firm on the sale of airplanes.

Leighton was flattered by Soong's confidence in his abilities but emphasized that no single individual could undertake a task of this magnitude or complexity. He had seen how the Chinese Air Force had tried and failed to manage comparable foreign air missions in the past. He cited in particular the "very sour episode" of the mercenary bomber squadron formed in China during 1937 and 1938. The current initiative required an organization (not an individual organizer) that could manage logistics, transport, and personnel: salaries, insurance, and "inquiries from anxious relatives." Intercontinent and CAMCO were unique in that they could provide such experience and services, thanks to the "outstanding organizing and administrative ability of W. D. Pawley," who had kept the enterprise going despite heavy financial risks and other handicaps. Leighton reminded Deyo that to cover its costs, Intercontinent relied on a single source of revenue: sales commissions. Without commissions, the firm would simply cease to function for lack of funds.[5]

Leighton felt that Soong's offer was an effort to "belittle the value" of Intercontinent and to undermine its long-standing relationship with Curtiss-Wright. He argued that the cost of doing without Intercontinent would outweigh the cost of its sales commission, for if a single individual tried to handle the China project, he would be doomed to failure. Leighton would refuse to participate in it under such conditions.[6]

While the debate over Leighton's future role carried on, so did negotiations about Intercontinent's sales commission. Mort Deyo had made clear to Bruce Leighton that the Chinese did not want Intercontinent to be paid its 10 percent on the sale of a hundred Tomahawks. In an effort to get around this problem, on January 22, US Treasury officials asked the British if they could possibly sell the planes directly to the Chinese procurement agent, UTC, instead of Curtiss-Wright. They did not explain that, as long as Curtiss-Wright handled the sale, it would have to pay a cut to Intercontinent. Treasury officials simply cited "governmental technical difficulties" in making this new request to the British.[7]

The Foreign Office immediately objected that a direct sale to a Chinese purchasing agent might provoke an adverse reaction from Japan.[8] The Air Ministry found it incomprehensible that US officials could "not solve their own administrative difficulties in view of their insistence on this transfer of aircraft to the Chinese to fulfill their own public policy." The contract for resale to Curtiss-Wright had already been concluded, yet the Treasury "assumed we could undo what has been done."[9] It was "all very tiresome of the Americans and slightly mysterious," as no one would divulge the nature of "government technical difficulties."[10]

At the Foreign Office, Ashley Clarke minuted that as long as the British received some credit from the Chinese for their sacrifice of planes, there could be no objection to reversing the transaction with Curtiss-Wright and dealing directly with a Chinese purchasing agent. The foreign minister, Anthony Eden, disagreed: "We are now made to appear to be selling aeroplanes to the Chinese government which in fact the US govt insist upon supplying to that govt to our detriment. Why? Because the US govt do not want to appear in the picture in that guise? But do we? If we had our way, we would buy these aeroplanes ourselves, I can see no reason why we should camouflage this extraordinary operation for the US govt."[11] US Treasury officials refused to admit the true nature of government technical difficulties, namely, that T. V. Soong balked at the idea of a middleman profiting from the sale. This had become a standard sticking point for the Chinese in their previous procurement efforts.

On January 27, Anthony Eden summarized for the War Cabinet all his objections to the administration's airplane deal with the Chinese: the behavior of the Americans had been "extraordinary"; they were fulfilling a promise of planes to China with Britain's allocation, even though they knew full well how urgent Britain's needs were and how incompetent the Chinese were when it came to military aviation.[12] The only possible explanation, he surmised, was fear of US public opinion, should the sale of planes to China appear to give Japan an excuse for hostile action against the United States. Yet the Americans were asking the British to take on that risk in their own relations with Japan. Eden concluded, "Before decision is made we should at least represent to United States Government difficulty into which they have progressively pushed us and stipulate that, if transaction is carried out as they propose and is discovered by Japanese, we should wish it to be made clear that we acted at the request of the US government: I cannot believe that President Roosevelt or Secretary of State would approve way in which matter has been handled if facts were put to either of them squarely. Unless you see objection, I should be glad if you would take this course."[13]

On January 29, the British cabinet agreed that the new British ambassador to the United States, Lord Halifax, should make representations at the highest level to the US government. The British were so indignant that they were willing to have a row with the president despite all the political risks of upsetting the applecart while Lend-Lease was debated on Capitol Hill. Eden, however, was adamant that the Roosevelt administration had to learn a lesson in diplomacy.

The Treasury may well have found out from the BPC that the Foreign Office was scrapping for a fight. On January 29, Philip Young held a daylong meeting with all parties concerned to finalize the sale of the Tomahawks by Curtiss-Wright to UTC. Against his will, Guy Vaughan, president of Curtiss-Wright, substantially reduced the price of the planes: UTC bought a hundred Tomahawks for US$4.5 million. It seems likely that the Chinese drew on funds made available through the tungsten loan that the Federal Loan Administration had arranged in September 1940. At the same time, Curtiss-Wright and UTC agreed to split a fee (in lieu of commission) to Intercontinent: the former came up with $100,000 and the latter $150,000.[14] As Philip Young put it, $250,000 would be enough to cover the services that "this fellow [Pawley] will perform in China for erecting and transporting planes and that sort of thing."[15] Morgenthau was delighted and could not resist a pun; he thanked Young on behalf of the Three Soong Sisters, who should "Sing a Soong of Sixpence."[16] In the meantime, Leighton had ensured a role for Intercontinent and Bill Pawley through his robust defense of both in the letter to Mort Deyo.

On January 25, 1941, T. V. Soong sought Chiang's approval for the following proposals: Intercontinent/CAMCO would engage the volunteers with a contract similar to that for its own employees; the duties would be "explained orally" and set forth in detail after arrival in China, "in view of American law." Furthermore, given the "special character," all American units would be "personally responsible" to Chiang Kai-shek and receive his instructions through their commanding officer, Claire Chennault, because "there must be no division of command or tactical responsibility and authority." Bearing in mind past factionalism, Soong was adamant that the Chinese military must give "whole hearted cooperation to the American personnel"; if there was "no obstruction or sabotage" on the part of the Chinese, then there could be some hope of achieving "very satisfactory results in safeguarding vital communications through Burma and attacking Japanese objectives." Nonetheless, Soong hoped that once American volunteers had instructed Chinese pilots and mechanics how to fly and maintain new equipment, the Chinese could take "an increasing share in operations."[17] On January 27, Chiang replied to Soong that he agreed with everything in his telegram but advised him to make sure that the terms of employment for the volunteers reflected the need to "absolutely obey" orders.[18]

It is inconceivable that the "Plus Four" intended to create an air mission that would subject American servicemen to the generalissimo's personal control and expose them to combat with the Japanese. The airpower deterrent devised by Marshall and which Knox and Morgenthau hoped to implement only required American airmen to train Chinese pilots. On that basis Mort Deyo got in touch with Bruce Leighton to hire flight instructors and to assemble Tomahawks at Loiwing.

Soon after these agreements were forged, Pawley, Leighton, Chennault, and Arthur Young began to work together on recruitment. On February 3, 1941, Pawley and Chennault briefed Mort Deyo in the office of the secretary of the navy about Intercontinent's agreement with the Chinese government to handle personnel: the project would require 100 pilots and 150 enlisted ground crew. Their tasks and objectives at this stage remained undefined, at least on paper. As Deyo noted, the recruiters realized "the necessity for keeping the thing quiet and will take due precautions."[19]

The State Department agreed to issue passports to all the men as bona fide employees of CAMCO. Knox would allow Pawley, Leighton, and Chennault to recruit from navy air bases, even though Admiral John Towers, head of naval aviation, was known to be "not very enthusiastic about the idea."[20] No one as yet had approached the War Department (that is, Stimson, Marshall, and Arnold) about gaining access to army air bases. Nevertheless, Arthur Young was optimistic. On February 13, 1941, he wrote to James McHugh that "the greatest good will" prevailed: he and Chennault were working with Pawley and Leighton on a "good set-up," although there were limits to what they could do without new legislation.[21]

After completing the plane sale to China, Henry Morgenthau left Washington for a short vacation on a dude ranch out west. While he was away, the secretary of the navy found himself lumbered with an old problem: in the autumn of 1940, Roosevelt had promised Prime Minister Metaxis of Greece a few P-40s to boost his country's morale and promote resistance to Italy. In the meantime the US Army and the British had balked at the idea of handing over any of their P-40s to the Greeks; instead Frank Knox offered them some old Grumman planes. Metaxis was outraged. He had been promised the latest models and refused to take obsolescent ones.

On February 5, Knox held a press conference about this fiasco. Almost in passing, he referred to the sale of P-40s to China. The *New York Times* reported "the negotiations for these craft were between the Chinese and British Government, Mr. Knox said, and the United States had little or no hand in them."[22] That was an outright lie. The same day, Morris Wilson of the British Air Commission (BAC) advised the British ambassador that there was no point in making a protest about the way the US government had handled the diversion of planes to China; the matter had been settled.[23]

The British now faced an outcome they had tried to avoid: the Japanese would believe that they were supplying planes to the Chinese. Furthermore, publicity about a Sino-British aircraft deal caused embarrassment with the Greeks, who were bound to reproach London for providing P-40s to the Chinese instead of themselves.[24] At the Foreign Office, J. C. Sterndale Bennett lamented, "The Americans have let us down badly over this aircraft deal with China. To their earlier sins . . . has now been added Colonel Knox's extraordinary and mendacious statement." Bennett wanted to take a stronger line with the administration about American "indiscretions," despite the present dependence on the United States for supplies.[25]

This exercise in plausible deniability stemmed from the new strategy that the president had outlined during the White House conference of January 16. Knox put the monkey on the back of the British in order to avoid the appearance of giving any military aid to China. Again, whenever the US government felt the need to tread cautiously with Japan, it distanced itself from China.

Over the coming months, Roosevelt and Hull turned back to traditional diplomacy for ways to contain Japanese aggression. For some time, they had supported a private initiative by two well-connected Catholic priests, Father Drought and Bishop Walsh, who were based in Tokyo. Known as the John Doe Associates, the priests were discussing a peace settlement with some prominent Japanese civilians who they believed could persuade their government to accept terms to end the war with China.[26] In January to March 1941, Roosevelt and Hull gave a fairly free hand to the John Doe Associates, while Hull also held official talks with the Japanese ambassador, Admiral Nomura. Through these discreet channels, the administration hoped to keep relations with Japan on an even keel while Lend-Lease legislation passed through Congress.

Nonetheless, the president must have still been worrying about the purported Japanese offensive on Singapore. As long as he and his advisers perceived this to be a real threat, he would feel obliged to send some portion of the US fleet to reinforce Singapore. By this stage, military deterrents had been ruled out, but perhaps diplomacy could free him from this onerous commitment to Winston Churchill.

Eugene Dooman was the counselor at the American embassy in Tokyo: a lifelong student of Japanese, he spent most of his diplomatic career in Japan. Ambassador Joseph Grew regarded him as his "co-ambassador"—a faithful Achates to his Aeneas.[27] After a spell of home leave, including consultations at the State Department, Dooman returned to Tokyo. With the permission of his ambassador, on February 14, 1941, he called on his Japanese counterpart, Ohashi Chuichi, the vice-minister for foreign affairs. Dooman made clear that US Far East policy was directly related to the priority of giving all aid short of war to Britain. The administration was intent on securing not only the supply of American arms and aircraft but also the flow of raw resources from British and Dutch colonies in the Far East to England. The United States could not help but be concerned by recent indications of a Japanese advance on Singapore and the Dutch East Indies. If Japan were to threaten the supply lines between Britain and its overseas territories, then, as Dooman put it, "she would have to expect to come into conflict with the United States"; the Japanese could not "alter the *status quo* in Southeast Asia, without incurring the risk of creating a very serious situation."[28]

Ohashi aired his suspicions that the US Embassy, like the British in Tokyo, was sending alarmist dispatches about Japanese moves into Thailand and French Indochina. He had already assured the British ambassador that "Japan had no intention whatever of moving towards Singapore and the Dutch East Indies" unless "pressed by other nations through the imposition of embargoes by the United States or by the sending of an American fleet to Singapore." Dooman pointed out that the United States did not want to interfere in Japan's peaceful commerce, but when Japanese economic relations in the region were accompanied by threats and gunboats, these were hardly "ordinary trade arrangements." Consequently, American anxiety about Japanese policies toward its neighbors was perfectly justified.

As Ambassador Grew later reported, Ohashi became "greatly agitated and distrait" by his interview with Dooman. In Grew's version of the conversation, Ohashi had listened quietly but then suddenly asked, "Do you mean to say that if Japan were to attack Singapore, there would be war with the United States?" Mr. Dooman had replied, "The logic of the situation would inevitably raise that question."[29] At the end of the month, soon after the Japanese foreign minister Matsuoka returned from England to Japan, Grew told him that he "entirely concurred in and approved of all that Dooman had said to Ohashi." To his surprise, Matsuoka also stated his entire agreement with what Dooman had said.[30]

The thrust of Dooman's ultimatum, if not the exact wording, almost certainly came from Roosevelt or Hull.[31] It produced the desired effect: the Japanese Foreign Ministry confirmed to Britain as well as the United States that the military had no plans to invade Singapore. Those assurances dispelled the president's anxiety over being forced to dispatch destroyers to protect the British colony. The relief was palpable. Roosevelt seems to have been so encouraged by the impact of one strongly worded admonition that he delivered another: as soon as the New Japanese ambassador Admiral Nomura arrived in Washington, Roosevelt let him know that the United States would take very seriously any further acts of aggression that might turn "American sentiment against the authors."[32] Diplomacy still had its uses for containing Japan.

By mid-February it seems likely that US officials had realized the folly of the air program for China. In early January 1941, they had presumed that the first thirty-six Tomahawks as well as US instructors would arrive in the Far East just in time for CAF pilots to create an air distraction over the Chinese sector of the Burma Road, which would disrupt Japanese plans for invading Singapore. But given the three-month voyage by sea, the aircraft could never have reached Rangoon before the end of April at the absolute earliest: the Japanese would have already rolled into Singapore and pushed on to the Dutch East Indies as the planes were being unloaded in Rangoon.

Equally untenable was the plan to send flight instructors to China. From the start, the navy took the lead in recruitment. It was an irony that the planes Morgenthau and the liaison committee had offered to China were P-40s and B-17s designed and built for the Army Air Corps. As the navy had no P-40s in its fleet, it had no pilots who could teach the Chinese how to fly them. Knox and Deyo may have hoped that the War Department eventually would go along with the air program for China, but after the White House conference, that seemed out of the question. Marshall, Stimson, and Hap Arnold, head of the AAC, were to concentrate on bringing their forces up to standards for the defense of the United States; they were not to contemplate any offensive operations. In line with that remit, however, they began to reconsider the defense of the US territory most vulnerable to Japanese attack—Hawaii and the Philippines.

The War Department shared responsibility with the navy for Hawaii, but the Philippines, including its naval bases, was entirely army turf. From late January 1941 onward, George Marshall reshaped the entire strategy for this distant American colony. His decisions guaranteed that the Philippines, not China, would become the AAC's future base for bombing Japan.

Reinforcing the Philippines 14

The Philippines lie about seventeen hundred miles south of the southern-most tip of Japan. After the Spanish-American War (1898–1900) they became a US colony, and the War Department became responsible for defending the archipelago, including ports for the US Navy's Asiatic Fleet. By 1940 it faced a problem of divided command and loyalty in the Philippines. In 1935, President Manuel L. Quezon appointed General Douglas MacArthur, the former chief of staff of the US Army, as field marshal of the Philippines Army. MacArthur already had a close connection to the islands because his father had served as governor-general of the Philippines under President McKinley. When MacArthur retired from the army in 1938, he stayed on as military adviser to the Filipino government. At the same time, however, General George Grunert was in charge of the Philippines Department, which was responsible to the War Department. The Philippines Department was made up of US Army units as well as the Philippine Scouts manned by local Filipino American soldiers.

In the Philippines, the War Department maintained a small air force known as the Fourth Composite Group. It was a motley collection of obsolete fighters and bombers, many retired from service in the Hawaiian Air Force, another AAC unit.[1] Up to 1940 there were three pursuit squadrons, which shared twenty-eight antiquated P-26 Boeing Peashooters, but there were only enough crews to put twenty-one in the air at any one time.[2] In November 1940 the group received fifty-two EP-1s (designated P-35As) Republic aircraft: these were the same planes that the Chinese wanted to buy from the Swedish government but the Roosevelt administration had appropriated.[3]

To man these new planes, in October 1940 General Arnold agreed to send out two squadrons, the Seventeenth from Selfridge Field, Michigan, and the Twentieth from Hamilton Field, California; they arrived in the spring of 1941 with about 350 men, more than doubling the AAC personnel in the islands at that time.[4] Therefore at the start of 1941, the Philippines had five pursuit squadrons, an observation squadron, and a bombardment squadron. Nonetheless, the Fourth Composite Group still faced a chronic shortage of modern combat and training planes: of the hundred-odd military aircraft, half were obsolete (such as the B-10 bombers), and the other half (the P-35s) obsolescent.

If the equipment was not fit for the purpose, the ground facilities were even worse: there were no antiaircraft artillery and barely any air warning system. Few airfields in the colony could support the weight of a modern bomber or combat plane. On the northern island of Luzon, Nichols Field had an asphalt runway for fighter squadrons, and Clark Field (the base for the old bombers) had a turf surface that was frequently inundated by heavy rains.[5] Eight hundred miles to the south of the airfields in Luzon was the Del Monte fruit plantation near Mindanao. Del Monte had a naturally level field that could be developed for heavy bombers such as the Boeing B-17 Flying Fortress.[6] Given the small number of airfields, which were surrounded by boggy or exposed terrain, it was virtually impossible to disperse or camouflage aircraft if and when the air warning service kicked in.[7] Major Kirtley Gregg, commander of the Seventeenth Pursuit Squadron at Nichols Field, privately commented that a troop of Boy Scouts flying kites could take the islands without a shot fired.[8] It was Marshall's rotten air force.

Given its responsibility for the Philippines, the War Department felt obliged to develop a program, however unfeasible, for its defense. Lieutenant Colonel Carl Spaatz was chief of war plans for the Air Corps, and his deputy Major Hoyt Vandenberg was a former head of the Air Corps Tactical School. In 1939, Spaatz asked Vandenberg to consider how to defend the indefensible. The latter came up with a radical program that relied on airpower not only to protect the Philippines but to turn the north island of Luzon into a platform for bombing Japan.

In making his case, Vandenberg looked first at the options for defending the Philippines by sea, land, and air. He suggested that a naval blockade combined with large ground forces would not stop the Japanese from taking the Philippines. He argued that airpower alone offered a viable way to deter the enemy. For purely defensive operations, the AAC would need a fleet of five hundred and sixty-five aircraft: at least sixty-four heavy bombers, two hundred medium bombers, a hundred and fifty interceptor fighter planes, and seventy-five reconnaissance planes.[9]

Vandenberg also proposed that preemptive air strikes against Japan might prove to be the most effective strategy for protecting the archipelago against enemy invasion. He estimated that long-range bombers could reach Tokyo from three locations in the Far East: Guam, airfields in the southeast region of free China, and parts of the Philippines. He ruled out Guam because it was too small and vulnerable to Japanese attack. He eliminated China, reflecting the traditional attitude of US Army intelligence officers toward the Chinese: they were militarily incompetent, and their politicians could not be trusted — navy and marine intelligence officers such as James McHugh and Evans Carlson painted the Chinese in a far more sympathetic light for their superiors in Washington than did their counterparts in the army, which in the 1930s included Joseph Stilwell.[10] That left Vandenberg with the choice of Clark Field in Luzon. To bomb Japan from the Philippines, the AAC would require at least 200 B-17s and 150 observation planes.[11] Therefore Vandenberg's ambitious proposal required a total of 915 aircraft for the Philippines: Chiang's call for a 500-strong air armada seemed modest by comparison.

In 1939 and 1940, the War Department turned down this and subsequent versions of Vandenberg's plan because of strategic considerations, lack of funds, and shortage of planes. It had long considered the Philippines indefensible and refused to invest in building up its ground or air forces and facilities. Furthermore, at that time, the AAC had only seventeen B-17 Flying Fortresses, as the rest had been sold to the British.[12] Finally, the cost of reinforcing the Philippines to the degree proposed by Vandenberg was deemed prohibitive: the War Department regarded any investment in relatively small improvements as a waste of money.

Vandenberg did not abandon hope of persuading his superiors to see the Philippines as an asset for deterring Japan rather than a military liability. In 1941 he seems to have been inspired by the success of the RAF in the Battle of Britain, which in his view offered lessons for air defense in the Philippines.[13]

As Churchill famously put it, "Never was so much owed by so many to so few." It was widely believed that even though RAF Fighter Command had been heavily outnumbered by the Luftwaffe, Spitfire pilots had outwitted and outflown the enemy. Perhaps the same could be achieved in the Philippines.

In the autumn of 1940, Morgenthau requested that a British aviation expert come to Washington and advise the liaison committee as well as the BPC about standardizing combat planes for British and US forces: in principle both were to adopt a single model of fighter plane combining the characteristics of an advanced P-40 and the Spitfire.[14] Beaverbrook dispatched Sir Hugh Dowding, who had just retired as chief of Fighter Command during the Battle of Britain. In January 1941, Dowding arrived in Washington to become head of the BPC technical department. The War Department also invited him to give a series of lectures to AAC officers about the tactics of the few against the many.

Hoyt Vandenberg was one of those who listened to Dowding describe RAF fighter tactics: Dowding apparently assured him that his proposal for defending the Philippines was feasible.[15] Thus encouraged, in January 1941 Vandenberg incorporated an expanded role for fighters and interceptors into his original airpower program for the Philippines. Using the Battle of Britain as a kind of template for the air defense of the Philippines against the Japanese, he concluded that even though outnumbered by two to one, a Philippines air force could fend off enemy air invasion. He estimated that the Japanese probably would deploy about half the air strength that the Germans had used against the British. Therefore, the AAC would need a force only half the size of that the RAF used to achieve victory. The data Vandenberg had about the Battle of Britain may have greatly underestimated the air strength of both sides, for he calculated that a fleet of about three hundred P-40Es would be adequate to defend the Philippines and also enough for offensive operations.[16] That implied Japanese deployment of some six hundred aircraft.

In fact, according to the historian Richard Overy, at the start of the campaign in July 1940, the RAF had about 2,000 combat aircraft, of which about 1,500 were fighters. The Luftwaffe had some 2,500 combat aircraft ready for deployment: 1,000 single-seater aircraft, 250 twin-engine fighters, 1,000 bombers, and 280 dive-bombers.[17] So if the 2:1 formula was realistically applied to the defense of the Philippines, the AAC probably would have required some six hundred aircraft to deter twelve hundred enemy fighters. As it happened, production lagged behind ambition and theory: Curtiss-Wright only began to produce the P-40E for the Air Corps in the autumn of 1941.[18]

Owing to shortages of aircraft, as well as strategic considerations, Vandenberg's superiors once again rejected his plan. Nonetheless, they were beginning to come around to the view that more should be done to defend the Philippines. The tide had already started to turn in October 1940 when forty-eight Republic aircraft and ten North American dive-bombers were allocated to the Fourth Composite Group in the Philippines. On December 27, 1940, General Marshall approved a near doubling in troop size (the Philippine Scouts were to be increased from six thousand to twelve thousand) and the dispatch of antiaircraft artillery to bases in the archipelago; a month later he justified this measure on the grounds that the overseas departments (in particular Hawaii and the Philippines) might be "confronted with the execution of combat missions on short notice"—echoing the words of the president during the White House conference of January 16.[19] During that conference, Roosevelt had ordered the army to steer "a very conservative course" while advising the navy to consider the possibility of bombing Japanese cities.[20] Three weeks later, the War Department slowly but surely embarked on a new strategy for the Philippines, which involved a combination of big talk and small investments in reinforcing the islands.

General Marshall, like the president and his cabinet colleagues, relied on rhetoric and bluff to project power into a vacuum created by acute shortages of military hardware. Appearances were all: in October 1940, when Frank Knox was asked if the Philippines could be defended, he insisted that the United States could defend anything.[21] In January 1941, Marshall asked General Grunert to "give evidence" of developing the Scout force in the Philippines "for international effect," by which he meant the effect on Japan.[22] Marshall exaggerated the impact of insignificant measures: for example, by keeping in the Philippines sixty officers who were due for home leave, he claimed that the United States could "impress Japan with the fact that we mean business."[23] Marshall deluded himself and his colleagues in believing that such gestures would deter the enemy.

On February 8, Marshall let General Grunert know that he would soon receive some P-40Bs, which Curtiss-Wright began to build for the AAC in March. These new models incorporated features of the British Tomahawk II that the original P-40 lacked. Marshall vaunted its merits to Grunert: the fighter was the equal of the new Japanese fighter (the Mitsubishi Zero); it had a top speed of 360 mph, self-sealing fuel tanks, two .50 caliber guns in the nose of the fuselage, and four .30 caliber machine guns in the wings.[24] On February 11, General Brett submitted a memorandum that called for the Philippines to have assets not only for air defense but to serve as a "striking force." To that end the Philippines was to have a long-range bombardment wing and modern pursuit groups, as well as upgraded facilities to support all operations.[25]

On February 25, the president agreed to the expansion and improvement of airfields in the Philippines in order to handle a larger air force. On the same day, Marshall authorized shipment of thirty-one P-40Bs as soon as they became available.[26] But as was so often the case in the prewar period, planes could not be converted into air weapons owing to lack of essential items. In April, twenty-five P-40Bs arrived in crates at Manila harbor, but after assembly they could not be flown until supplies of Prestone coolant arrived for the Allison engines. Furthermore, because of inadequate rounds of ammunition, Air Corps personnel never had an opportunity, until after Pearl Harbor, to fire the machine guns that came with the new P-40Bs.[27]

In March 1941, General Grunert asked Marshall to upgrade the Fourth Composite Group to an air force and to give it far greater resources than received to date. On March 28, Marshall agreed that henceforth the group would be called the Philippines Department Air Force (PDAF) and be placed under a veteran AAC officer, Brigadier General Henry B. Clagett.[28] Marshall also advised Grunert that in addition to thirty-one P-40Bs, the new PDAF would receive a squadron of B-18 medium bombers shipped from Hawaii. The B-18 was an obsolete model but better than the ancient B-10s that the Twenty-Eighth bomber squadron used. Marshall indulged in one of his stock phrases: if the Japanese saw new combat planes in the Philippines, they would have "something to think about."[29]

As at least one historian has noted, the principal reason that the army changed its attitude about the Philippines was its exaggerated faith in the Flying Fortress and the tantalizing possibility of deploying it from Clark Field to attack Japan.[30] But first the War Department had to ferry this prized possession from California to Hawaii and the Philippines. The AAC regarded the maiden voyage across the Pacific as a high-risk venture, because any failure en route would be fatal in the eyes of allies and enemies.[31] If, however, the B-17 could reach Hawaii, it could probably reach the Philippines. In May 1941, army aviators ferried twenty-one B-17s from San Francisco to Honolulu. In September, nine of these flew to the Philippines, and in October twenty-six B-17s flew from Hawaii to Clark Field, a total of thirty-five Flying Fortresses.[32]

Thus over the course of 1941 the AAC based the air reinforcement of the Philippines on two principles: the stationing of modern combat aircraft would project power and deter Japan from the Philippines; if the territory was attacked, fighter planes would manage to defend it from the enemy just as the RAF had done in the Battle of Britain. The War Department, however, was not to know that this new air strategy was based, to some extent, on a fallacy. The Battle of Britain had not been a victory of the few over the many: the British had overestimated German airpower, while the Germans underrated British aircraft production, which had been the key to RAF staying power and ultimate victory.[33]

The PDAF had more in common with Chiang's rotten CAF than Churchill's victorious RAF. Marshall thought it would be enough to send some new bombers and fighters to the Philippines without improving airfields, logistical support, and security. The AAC, like the CAF, lacked a well-developed ground organization, not to mention ready access to aircraft and armament produced in or near its own territory. But the CAF had one great advantage over the PDAF: vast spaces and places where it could disperse and hide aircraft. In the Philippines, there was nowhere to hide; planes stayed lined up like ducks on primitive airfields.

In the first six months of 1941, as General Marshall channeled AAC resources toward the Philippines, he rejected all demands to divert army planes to China; he was impervious to pressure on his department from Chinese allies in and out of the White House. Chief among the new friends that the

Chinese made in Washington was the president's administrative assistant, Lauchlin Currie. T. V. Soong and his colleagues were confident that Currie, from his privileged position in the White House, would deliver all the planes and munitions that Chiang required. Currie soon discovered, however, that even if he could occasionally rob Churchill to pay Chiang, he could never squeeze so much as a bullet out of George Marshall.

On December 1, 1940, Henry Morgenthau and T. V. Soong discussed the terms of the $50 million credit from the Export-Import bank that the president had just announced. Morgenthau insisted that this loan required us government supervision, but Soong objected: he had believed that the Chinese would be free to spend the new Export-Import Bank credit as they chose in exactly the same way as the "tungsten loan" of $25 million in September 1940. Morgenthau and his advisers tried to convince Soong that us government supervision was necessary to ensure efficient use of the funds. Soong countered that as long as the Universal Trading Corporation handled procurement, the Treasury would not need any extra oversight, given that the secretary had put old friends at the helm of UTC: the chair was Archie Lochhead, and K. P. Chen was on the board.[1] Morgenthau insisted that the us Congress might not grant further credits to China unless a Treasury representative oversaw the new $50 million credit. On this touchy subject, Morgenthau and Soong reached a stalemate.

In the New Year, Soong launched a preemptive strike. The administration could not complain that the Chinese opposed supervision of the new loan if they invited a prominent member of the administration to advise them on how to spend it. For this mission Soong had in mind Lauchlin Currie, who worked directly for the president and had an office in the White House. Currie had come to Washington in 1935, armed with a PhD in economics from Harvard, to work for the Federal Reserve Board. In 1939 he became the first economic adviser to an American president. His official title of "administrative assistant" belied his influence.

Currie analyzed a range of trade, financial, and fiscal issues for the president. On December 4, 1940, he submitted a memorandum on the Far East crisis that reinforced the mounting sense of anxiety about a Japanese attack on Singapore; he repeated Chiang's argument that if the Japanese took Singapore, they would quickly control most of the Indian Ocean and jeopardize the survival of the British Empire.[2] Currie threw his weight behind Chinese demands for a massive air force to deter Japan from Singapore. In the spring of 1941 he incorporated this memorandum into his short-term air program for China. John Paton Davies, a well-known China hand, found it "odd" that Currie should be regarded as an instant expert on the Far East but noted that "dabbling" in other jurisdictions was "characteristic of the helter-skelter Roosevelt Administration."[3]

After receiving Soong's invitation, Currie saw the wisdom of clearing it with Morgenthau. On January 16, 1941, he rang the secretary to discuss his "little visit" to China: it was a bit crazy and rushed, he explained, especially because he wanted to be back in the White House by March 1. Nonetheless he was tempted, "because it sounds like a nice junket and I would never get out there in the ordinary course of events."[4] He stated that the president had "thought it quite worthwhile." Morgenthau replied that he was "jealous as hell but delighted" about Currie going off to Chungking.

On January 18, at Roosevelt's suggestion, Currie spoke to Sumner Welles about the trip: Welles thought it was an excellent idea for him to go and felt there was no impropriety if Currie took a leave of absence and had his expenses paid by the Chinese.[5] Thereafter no one knew the precise nature of Currie's mission. On January 24, the president announced that Currie was a "special envoy who was going to survey the general economic situation in China"; other sources claimed that he would advise the Chinese about how to spend the loans from the Export-Import Bank and the Currency Stabilization Fund.[6] Briefings along these lines created the impression that Currie was a US government official en route to China to supervise its new loans, but that was not the case: he was a guest of Chiang's regime, all expenses paid.

Different times, different customs. Roosevelt and Welles saw nothing wrong with Currie's little visit subsidized entirely by the Nationalists. To give Morgenthau his due, he seems to have been unaware at the time that the Chinese were footing the bill. A few months later, when he found out that the Nationalists had paid Currie's way, he expressed his deep distress to Roosevelt.[7] In January 1941, however, no one imagined that Currie would leave town as a gamekeeper and return as a poacher.

On January 29, Currie boarded the China Clipper for Hong Kong with three letters in his briefcase.[8] One was a special communication from the president to Chiang. The second was a handwritten letter of introduction by Frank Knox addressed to the assistant naval attaché Major James McHugh. Knox described Currie as a member of the president's administrative staff "in China on an official mission."[9] A third was also for McHugh from T. V. Soong, who wrote that "things in Washington are steadily getting much more favorable to our cause and what had been impossible a few months ago is readily available now."[10] Soong had every reason to feel optimistic. First of all, the president of the United States had personally backed big new loans for China and indirectly the sale of P-40s to China. Second, the administration was willing to let American volunteer pilots go to China. Finally, in Lauchlin Currie, Soong had a new ally based in the White House who he believed would have the president's ear and deliver aid for China in the coming year.

Currie reached Chungking in early February. The Chinese bent over backwards to welcome him, as did Major McHugh. In principle Currie was to advise the Chinese leadership on how to structure a national budget, stabilize the currency, and spend loans wisely. In practice, he gathered evidence to justify a massive boost in US aid to China and the elevation of Chiang Kai-shek to an American ally on a par with Winston Churchill. In conceiving this overhaul of US-China relations, he fell under the influence of McHugh, the Navy's leading China hand.

During separate tours in China during the 1920s and 1930s, James McHugh developed a friendship with the Chiangs' intimate adviser, W. H. Donald, who brought McHugh into the generalissimo's inner circle. Consequently McHugh spent more time with the Chiangs than any other diplomat or military attaché in China at that time. In November 1940, the new secretary of the navy, Frank Knox, wrote directly to Chiang, asking him to let McHugh have full information about the state of Chinese resistance, which McHugh would "personally" report to Knox.[11] Thus McHugh would bypass ONI as well as the State Department in keeping his boss up to date on China. Another marine intelligence officer, Captain Evans Carlson, had an equally privileged arrangement in reporting on China to President Roosevelt. In this respect the navy diverged sharply from the army: no one in the War Department ever went outside official channels to form a special relationship with the generalissimo or to report on China to Stimson.

Given his unique ties to the Chiang-Soong family circle, McHugh was able to influence the debate over US aid to China through Currie as well as Knox. After Currie returned to Washington in March 1941, he and McHugh corresponded regularly about a host of issues that arose during Currie's trip to China. For example, in April 1941, "Mac" wrote to "Lauch" that Chinese morale went up and down like a balloon: it could be inflated by sudden shows of American support but deflated just as rapidly by what the Chinese interpreted as a negative gesture. McHugh advised Currie that the US government should exploit this tendency to the fullest: "kid them along, give them something even though we may feel certain that it will be wasted and keep them in the picture." He firmly believed that the United States "ought to give them planes to crack up *immediately*, ask no questions and merely say 'we are with you to the bitter end, go to it.'" This psychological approach, McHugh argued, would serve US and Chinese interests more effectively than insistence upon a sound military program for deploying the planes.[12]

Lauch Currie returned to Washington on March 10 — the day that Lend-Lease became law. On March 15, he submitted a confidential report to the president. Currie made McHugh's approach to plane aid for China the centerpiece of a new policy toward China: by selling Chiang planes, the administration would inspire his trust in the goodwill of the United States and keep him fighting to the bitter end.

In the realm of military affairs and aviation, Currie dutifully relayed the opinions of the generalissimo. These included the now standard argument to justify a massive injection of military hardware — that if the Chinese were enabled to organize a major military diversion in the mainland or to bomb Japan from China, such actions would keep the Japanese from invading European colonies.[13] Chiang needed the latest and most powerful military aircraft to make deterrence a reality.

The Chinese had recently received fifty new fighters and fifty bombers from the Soviet Union, but they needed even more from the United States.

In the view of Chiang and his generals, the priorities were fighter planes and a few long-range bombers. Although medium-range bombers would be useful, they were not as essential. As Currie pointed out, Chiang expected the B-17 Flying Fortresses that Morgenthau had promised in December 1940: the generalissimo still believed that these would be delivered in March or April. If this was not the case, the misunderstanding needed to be cleared up.[14]

Currie stated that the Chinese were making great strides in building air-fields that could support the weight of a heavy long-range bomber such as the B-17. At Chengdu he saw seventy-five thousand peasants working on a runway: even though they had no mechanized equipment, they had managed to construct adequate foundations and drainage for an airfield. Currie was assured that other fields near the coast were being upgraded in a similar fashion in order to accommodate the Flying Fortresses.[15]

Recognizing his ignorance about aviation affairs, Currie recommended that a senior navy aviation officer come and see for himself the state of the CAF. There were three reasons for such an inspection: to assess the capacity of China to serve as a possible base of air operations; to better understand the current state and tactics of Japanese air forces; and finally to give the Chinese "the impression that we regard them as important potential allies."[16] Not only would the tour produce valuable information, but it would have "excellent psychological repercussions" in China as well as Japan. A high-ranking navy officer rather than a young air attaché at the embassy should conduct the mission in order to maximize its impact in China and the United States.[17]

It seems odd that Currie suggested a senior navy officer instead of a joint army-navy group or a mission led by a high-ranking AAC officer. After all, the B-17s and P-40s that Chiang wanted were in the fleet of the Army Air Corps, not the navy. There was a world of difference, however, between the two services where China was concerned. Officers who served in the Asiatic fleet, such as Admiral Yarnell, openly supported the Nationalists; and Frank Knox and James McHugh went out of their way to build close ties with Chiang Kai-shek. By contrast, the War Department never wanted to encourage Chiang or his supporters to knock on its door in search of army aircraft or ammunition; they were putting all their eggs into the Philippines basket. As Lauch Currie soon discovered, he would get no more equipment out of the War Department for China. On returning to Washington, Currie put the quest for planes aside and focused instead on recruiting some volunteer pilots for China. For the time being, a few men would have to take the place of planes to sustain Chiang's morale, keep him fighting, and make him feel that the Roosevelt administration took him seriously as an ally.

After Eugene Dooman delivered a strong verbal warning to the Japanese Foreign Ministry, the immediate threat of a Japanese attack on Singapore evaporated, and so did Roosevelt's sense of urgency about getting men and planes to China to help its air force disrupt Japan's purported spring offensive. On February 3, 1941, Leighton and Chennault had met with Mort Deyo about hiring pilots, but within a few weeks the recruitment drive came to a halt. This became all too evident on February 21 in a conversation Morgenthau had with Tom Corcoran, an inveterate Washington insider.

Corcoran was a well-known Washington lawyer and one of the original New Dealers: Roosevelt had great affection and esteem for "Tommy." In January 1941, when Corcoran's first child was born, Roosevelt wrote an effusive letter to him in which he emphasized that Corcoran was one of the few men that he could trust; he suggested that Corcoran should continue to put public service ahead of private practice despite his new "family responsibilities." Roosevelt wanted Corcoran to serve in his administration, perhaps at the Justice Department, a job that never materialized.[1] In February 1941, Corcoran was hoping for an appointment as assistant secretary for aeronautics at the Navy Department, but in the meantime he had to earn a living to feed his growing family.[2]

On February 21, Corcoran rang up Morgenthau because he wanted to clear with him a job offer from T. V. Soong. Instead of using UTC to acquire material for the Tomahawks, Soong intended to set up a new military procurement company: he hoped that Tom and his brother David (still in the Far East) would manage it. Corcoran mentioned in confidence that what

Soong really wanted him to do was "to go over and wrangle for him with the Army and with the Navy to have them practically order certain men to enlist in the Chinese Air Force."[3]

Over the years Morgenthau had developed reservations about Corcoran, who in his view exploited Roosevelt's patronage for his own gain.[4] In December 1938, Morgenthau had told Corcoran point blank that unless he stated the purpose of his inquiry, he could not have access to Treasury staff. Morgenthau quipped to his team, "If he's useful to the President, that's the President's business. But when he starts trying to get the Secretary of the Treasury into ward politics in New York—I'm just not going to do it." Other officials agreed with Morgenthau. Guy Helvering, head of Internal Revenue, said, "I'm not just going to let Tommy run my shop."[5]

Three years later, on February 21, 1941, Morgenthau was blunt but cordial to Corcoran. He agreed that UTC should not get mixed up in recruitment or procurement for the P-40s. He also thought it was all right for Corcoran to work for Soong. Nonetheless, he offered one piece of advice: that Corcoran clear his activities with the Chinese ambassador Hu Shih. Relations between Soong and Hu were so bad that the latter might try to undercut Corcoran in some way. Corcoran replied, "I clear all the way around," tongue in cheek perhaps, given his previous history with Morgenthau.[6]

In late February to March 1941, Corcoran evidently did not get the armed forces to release pilots for China. On March 5, Chiang cabled Soong to ask when American air force volunteers would start to come to China; on March 13 the generalissimo complained that Chennault's recruiting of a volunteer group had come to a standstill and Soong should do his best to encourage American volunteers to go to China.[7]

On March 15, Roosevelt told the White House Press Association that China had asked for help and therefore China would have America's help. During the first half of 1941, however, the administration offered no new forms of assistance to the Nationalists. Commitments to China that Roosevelt made in haste before Christmas he repented at leisure afterward. His colleagues were obliged to make good on presidential pledges to release funds, planes, and volunteer airmen to China. While Morgenthau handled thorny negotiations with T. V. Soong about the currency stabilization loan, Lauch Currie worked on plane aid: his March 15 special report on China had made pilots and planes for China the cornerstone of his plan to elevate Chiang to the same status as Winston Churchill.

In March 1941, Lauch Currie managed to get volunteer recruitment back on track. On Monday, March 19, he saw the president for about fifteen minutes, time enough, it seems possible, to obtain verbal consent from Roosevelt to go ahead with the process of hiring pilots for China.[8] This authorization can be inferred because on March 21, T. V. Soong and the directors of Intercontinent drafted an agreement about the role of CAMCO in hiring and managing personnel for "three advanced instruction and training units" the Chinese government intended to establish.[9] It stipulated that the supervisor of the units would instruct CAMCO about the quantity and qualifications of recruits required; CAMCO would hire and manage personnel in line with standard practice for its own employees. There would be no commission for its services, but a special revolving fund of $400,000 would cover all the costs of handling personnel, starting with their travel expenses from the United States to China and their first two months' salary.

In line with its existing contracts for the Chinese government, CAMCO would assemble new planes and maintain the stock of spare parts. When "from time to time" the supervisor requested technical assistance, CAMCO would send mechanics to maintain, overhaul, and repair aircraft or provide any other services to facilitate operations of the units "in the field" in so far as it was practical, given the firm's manufacturing schedule.[10]

On March 22, Currie had lunch with Frank Knox, Mort Deyo, the head of ONI Captain Alan Kirk, and the head of naval aviation Admiral Towers, who in early February had been less than enthusiastic about sending naval aviators to China. As Knox wrote to James McHugh, they decided that in keeping with Currie's recommendation, a competent senior naval aviation officer should go to China to survey its air force and take with him "a very personal credential" from Knox for the generalissimo.[11] Currie and Knox sang from the same hymnal as McHugh about plane aid for China: just give Chiang some men and planes to demonstrate American goodwill and forget about the consequences of their use.

On March 28, 1941, there was a major breakthrough on recruitment. Captain Mort Deyo met with a senior army officer, probably his counterpart at the War Department, Lieutenant Colonel Orlando Ward, who served as secretary to the chief of staff, General George Marshall. Deyo described to Ward the procedure he had worked out with Chennault, Leighton, and Young back in February: as CAMCO would pay the pilots, the US military would have "no financial dealings whatsoever with the Chinese government." Leighton and Chennault would receive letters of introduction to naval air stations and "explain their proposition to the naval reserve officers." The recruits would then send a letter of resignation to Mort Deyo before signing a yearlong contract with CAMCO: either party could terminate it with thirty days' notice. Once it expired, the volunteers would be reinstated and their service with CAMCO treated as a year of duty for eventual promotion.[12]

Deyo and Ward agreed that each air service would provide fifty pilots in order to furnish a hundred reserve officer pilots for the Chinese Air Force. They also would find some enlisted mechanics and clerks for the China mission. The next day, General Arnold wrote to General Marshall that the army would adopt navy procedure in these matters. Soon thereafter Marshall and Stimson authorized the Air Corps to take part in the volunteer program.

The army and navy agreed to release a hundred reserve officers for a year's employment by CAMCO, but they did not commit themselves to a specific operational plan. As Hap Arnold put it, the recruiters would put their proposition to candidates on US bases. But what was that proposition? In the spring and early summer of 1941 there was still no consensus about what the volunteers were supposed to do for Generalissimo Chiang Kai-shek or his air force. The recruiters had one idea about the rights and responsibilities of the recruits, the Chinese a very different one.

When Mort Deyo approached Bruce Leighton to organize flight instructors for China in January 1941, Leighton recalled the "sour" experience of an earlier air mission and suggested that the current effort would end in failure if the Chinese insisted on doing things the same way as before. In Chungking, Major James McHugh thought along much the same lines. In a report to ONI on January 11, 1941, McHugh had pointed out that Chiang's requests for foreign aviation and transportation advisers raised the same old question of "foreign police work in China": all too often, the Chinese mismanaged their own affairs and then turned to foreign advisers whom they would "receive with open arms, encourage them to submit new plans and schemes and then not only . . . fail to follow such advice but . . . permit various cliques to defeat the purpose by indirect resistance and scheming."[13]

In a letter to Arthur Young dated January 14, 1941, McHugh also recalled the mercenary bomber squadron that flew for the Chinese in 1937–1938, as well as the Jouett training mission of 1933–1935. He felt that a new volunteer air group should be modeled on the latter, not the former. The generalissimo had "talked nothing but 500 airplanes and said that he had plenty of pilots to fly anything except . . . Flying Fortresses," but at the same time he wanted a completely American air force to fly planes for the Chinese.[14] McHugh warned Young that imposing an American combat unit on the CAF would be a disaster, because CAF officers would feel as much resentment of this new group of Americans as they had for the foreign bomber squadron at Hankow in the winter of 1937–1938 — the sour episode to which Leighton had alluded. Furthermore, like that earlier mercenary unit, a new American combat group would be "hard to discipline and control. . . . We never could keep their presence as quiet as would be necessary and complications of all kinds would result."

McHugh preferred a "complete American Mission on the order of the first one under [John] Jouett which can take charge of the whole show in cooperation with the Chinese, but who will have full authority to do things." He thought that this new Jouett-style mission should be allowed to "unofficially . . . direct operations and coordinate groundwork; a few pilots might come in advance of the American mission to do some flying for the Chinese."[15]

McHugh saw the Jouett mission through rose-tinted glasses: Jouett had never taken full charge of the Chinese Air Force. In 1932, after a brief but bloody war with Japan at Shanghai, T. V. Soong (still finance minister) arranged through US Commerce Department officials for Jouett and a group of instructors to come to China; he assured Jouett that he would have total autonomy to modernize the CAF. By the end of 1933, however, Chiang became disenchanted with Jouett and bestowed his favors instead on Italian aviators from the Regia Aeronautica: the Italians had been willing to engage in bombing missions against rebels in Fukien Province (in southeast China across from Taiwan). Jouett had refused because the instructors' contracts barred them from engaging in combat. Bitter factionalism ensued. From

1933 to 1937, the Italian air mission was based at the generalissimo's military headquarters in Nanchang and trained CAF officers there. The American instructors who trained Chinese pilots on Curtiss Hawks or other American aircraft were based at Hangchow — they were physically and politically sidelined from the generalissimo and the CAF at Nanchang.[16]

In January 1941, Chiang made clear to Soong that he wanted American volunteers who would be entirely obedient to himself.[17] Such subservience, however, had never been exacted from previous US pilots or instructors, neither in the Jouett mission of 1933–1935 nor the mercenary bomber squadron of 1937–1938. If Knox and Deyo had a model in mind for the volunteer group, it was the Jouett mission. They probably presumed that after completing a yearlong contract, the volunteers either would be reinstated in the army or navy or continue to train Chinese pilots in CAF flight schools on American aircraft. They did not anticipate that the CAMCO employees might be required to sign an oath of allegiance to Chiang Kai-shek, to obey his orders and, in doing so, possibly jeopardize their US citizenship.

Aside from demanding their obedience, Chiang Kai-shek seemed to have no fixed ideas about their duties. In March 1941, Chiang thought that the Americans might fly some Russian planes for which Chinese pilots were lacking; in April 1941, he seemed puzzled about their job description: would one set of volunteers teach at the Kunming Air Force Academy and another train Chinese pilots to fly the P-40s?[18] On May 8, 1941, Chiang told the British ambassador that the volunteers would fly the Tomahawks: in addition to a salary of US$700 a month, a pilot would receive "US$500 for every enemy plane destroyed."[19] This was perhaps the earliest known reference to the bonus that volunteers would earn for each "kill." It also indicated that in early May, Chiang expected some of the volunteers to serve as combat pilots rather than instructors.

In June, however, a situation arose that prompted T. V. Soong to veer back to the idea that the volunteers would form a training rather than a combat mission. On June 2, fifteen Chinese pilots arrived in Rangoon who intended to ferry to Yunnan the first batch of P-40s once they were assembled. This prospect alarmed British officials, who felt that the Chinese, with no experience flying such fast planes, would crash them.[20] T. V. Soong was aware of this risk: on June 6 he suggested to Chiang that American volunteers should keep the planes and train CAF pilots to fly them, so that Chinese could *eventually* take over entirely from the Americans—that had been his original proposal back in January 1941.[21]

In the first six months of 1941, the organizers never reached agreement about the rights or responsibilities of the volunteers once they reached China. Soong and Chiang regarded them more often as flight instructors than combat pilots. If the Chinese were undecided about the function of the volunteers, so were the recruiters, the US military, and other government officials. Whereas Chiang believed that the volunteers would be solely responsible to him, US officials probably thought that, as employees of an American firm, CAMCO, they would be temporary advisers rather than combat pilots obedient to a foreign power. Everyone took the same approach: use air aid in the form of men and planes to fulfill immediate diplomatic objectives with China and leave unanswered the question of their use.

At this stage there seems little doubt that the AVG was plane aid—more psychologically than militarily important. As conceived by Currie, McHugh, and Knox, the presence of American men as well as planes in China would boost Chiang's morale and his trust in the United States; he would appreciate the act of generosity through which Roosevelt expressed his esteem for the Nationalist leader and make him feel that he was the equal of Winston Churchill. Through cooperation on military aviation, Sino-American cooperation could aspire to the same status as the special Anglo-American relationship.

Sooner or later someone would discover that the devil lay in the detail of these proposals. Henry Morgenthau Jr. was perhaps the only man in Washington who had the experience and insight to question what Currie was up to. From 1938 to 1941, Morgenthau had regarded himself as the principal champion of China in the US government. By the spring of 1941, however, he had become resentful of the "China Lobby"—even if that label had not yet been applied to the influence peddling of T. V. Soong.

On April 21, Roosevelt told Morgenthau to act "right away" to release $50 million from the US Currency Stabilization Loan—this was the big credit for China that had been announced on November 30, 1940, but never executed. Morgenthau could hardly contain his irritation at the mention of this loan; he told the president that it "put his back up" to be under pressure by the likes of Tom Corcoran to deliver favors to China. He then revealed that the Chinese were paying Corcoran $30,000 to represent their interests and also had footed the bill entirely for Currie's trip to China. Roosevelt was genuinely taken aback and wanted Morgenthau to raise the matter with T. V. Soong.[22]

Later that day, Morgenthau accused Soong of being a "very smart gentleman" who understood perfectly well what Morgenthau was talking about, even if he tried to change the subject.[23] In referring specifically to Corcoran and Currie, Morgenthau acidly commented that it was hard to know who was on the Chinese payroll and who was on the payroll of the US government.[24] From this point onward, Morgenthau kept his distance from Lauch Currie, T. V. Soong, and the growing China Lobby.

ABOVE T. V. Soong (*left*), special representative of Generalissimo Chiang Kai-shek, and Hu Shih, Chinese ambassador to the United States, at the White House, July 1, 1940. Photo courtesy the Library of Congress.

LEFT Generalissimo Chiang Kai-shek in an official portrait, circa 1940. Photo courtesy the Library of Congress.

Generalissimo Chiang
Kai-shek and Madame
Chiang, in China, circa 1930s.
Photo courtesy Historical
Photographs of China,
University of Bristol.

Lauchlin Currie,
administrative assistant
to President Franklin
Roosevelt, Washington, DC,
1939. Photo courtesy the
Library of Congress.

Admiral Morton Lyndholm
Deyo (USN), at sea, 1943. Photo
courtesy of his granddaughter
Lila Garnett.

Frank Knox, secretary
of the navy designate,
Washington, DC, July 2, 1940.
Photo courtesy the Library
of Congress.

ABOVE Bruce Gardner Leighton, vice president, Intercontinent Corporation, Miami, Florida, circa 1941. Photo courtesy the author.

RIGHT General George Marshall, US Army chief of staff, in an official portrait, 1940. Photo courtesy the Library of Congress.

Atlantic Conference: Prime Minister Winston Churchill and President Franklin Roosevelt, on board HMS *Prince of Wales*, Placentia Bay, Newfoundland, August 9, 1941. Photo courtesy Franklin Delano Roosevelt Presidential Library.

Central Aircraft Manufacturing Company (CAMCO) staff, Loiwing, Yunnan, October 1939. William D. Pawley, president of CAMCO and Intercontinent Corporation, is at far left, in back row. Photo courtesy the author.

President Franklin Roosevelt signing the US declaration of war on Japan, Washington, DC, December 8, 1941. Photo courtesy Franklin Delano Roosevelt Presidential Library.

Cairo Conference: Generalissimo Chiang Kai-shek, President Franklin Roosevelt, and Prime Minister Winston Churchill, Cairo, Egypt, November 25, 1943. Photo courtesy Franklin Delano Roosevelt Presidential Library.

ABOVE Pacific war council, Washington, DC, June 25, 1942: Winston Churchill and Franklin Roosevelt (*seated*); standing (*from center to right*) are Canadian prime minister Mackenzie King (between Roosevelt and Churchill); the British ambassador to the United States Lord Halifax; T. V. Soong; and Philippines president Manuel Quezon. Photo courtesy Franklin Delano Roosevelt Presidential Library.

RIGHT Henry L. Stimson, US secretary of war, 1940, Washington, DC. Photo courtesy the Library of Congress.

Air Vice Marshal Arthur Travers "Bomber" Harris (RAF) in an official portrait, 1941. Photo courtesy the National Portrait Gallery, London.

Air Vice Marshal John Slessor (RAF), circa 1943. Photo courtesy of Anthony Slessor.

Claire Lee Chennault (*far right*) and Olga Greenlaw, the future secretary of the Flying Tigers, Hengyang, Hunan, China, October 1938. Photo courtesy the author.

Anthony Eden, British foreign secretary, in an official portrait, June 1941. Photo courtesy the National Portrait Gallery, London.

Cordell Hull, US secretary of state, Washington, DC, 1940. Photo courtesy the Library of Congress.

Henry J. Morgenthau Jr., US secretary of the treasury, and Franklin Roosevelt at the wheel, February 9, 1934. Photo courtesy the Franklin Delano Roosevelt Presidential Library.

US Navy consultation, Washington, DC, October 10, 1940: (*left to right*) Admiral Harry E. Yarnell (retired); Admiral Harold R. Stark, chief of naval operations; Secretary of the Navy Frank Knox; and Admiral James O. Richardson. Photo courtesy the Naval History and Heritage Collection.

Meeting in Burma, March 1942: General Lancelot Dennys (*far right*) with General P. T. Mao (*middle*) and General Sir Archibald Wavell, commander-in-chief, India (*left*). (Dennys died in a plane crash two weeks later, on March 16, 1942.) Photo: Harrison Forman. Courtesy of Nicholas Dennys, QC.

I n his March 28 memorandum to General Marshall about recruitment, General Arnold stated that the specific amount of flying experience was not discussed, although it was known that the Chinese wanted pilots who could fly a P-40 type plane.[1] Arnold suggested that ten of the P-40s bought by China should be retained in the United States at a civil airport some-where to allow volunteers to learn how to fly them.[2] By the end of March, however, it was too late to hold back any Tomahawks: all had long since been loaded onto freighters for the three-month voyage to Rangoon. The volunteers would have to wait until they reached the Far East to fly a P-40, most for the first time.

In 1941, the P-40 was still the fastest and most challenging aircraft that had ever entered the AAC fleet. In 1942, when the P-40B was used for train-ing rather than combat, an Army Air Forces manual stated, "The P-40 is no cinch to fly; it's fast and skittish and responds like lightning to controls." The army concluded that if a pilot could learn to fly the P-40, he could handle any other fighter.[3]

It was standard practice for military pilots to undergo "transition training" between advanced and operational training. From 1940 to 1942, AAC pilots who had already gained their wings required seventy hours of "transition" training under experienced AAC instructors to familiarize themselves with their new combat plane; thereafter operational training required another forty hours. AAC instructors and staff officers kept a close watch over pilots in a tightly regulated environment: the daily schedule was packed with courses, physical exercise, and chores.[4]

As the navy had no P-40s, all fifty volunteers from this air service in principle would require transition training. The situation was not much better in the army. By March 1941, the fleet of P-40s in the AAC had suffered heavy attrition due to accidents and difficulties to do with maintenance: Curtiss only started to produce improved P-40s for the army in mid-March 1941, and most of these were destined to either Hawaii or the Philippines.[5] Consequently, in the early spring of 1941, there were relatively few airworthy P-40s at US Army bases and too many AAC pilots waiting to fly them. As one Flying Tiger later recalled, most Air Corps volunteers had never even sat in a P-40.[6] It seems likely that only fourteen army recruits had any experience on a P-40 before joining up.[7]

Colonel Claire Chennault may not have known exactly what the volunteers would do, but he knew precisely what sort of men he wanted. On April 1, 1941, three days after the army and navy agreed on recruitment, he drafted a detailed list of job specifications and matériel, which T. V. Soong approved.[8] In this document, Chennault drew up his "dream team"—the ideal manpower composition for the special air unit. He estimated that 264 American volunteers were required to form and operate the 101st, 102nd, and 103rd Pursuit Squadrons in China.[9] In page after page, he described the types of machinery (apart from airplanes) needed for operations, as well as job profiles not only for pilots and armorers but also for technical, clerical, and medical staff.[10] He asked for a hundred pilots who had already served in pursuit (fighter aircraft) units: at least eight officers with over five years' active duty who could serve as commanders, forty-two with three to five years' active duty for the role of flight leader, and fifty with one to three years' active duty to be wingmen (flight pilots).[11]

Chennault also wanted the Chinese government to supply six hundred additional personnel to bring the squadrons up to "war strength." Most Chinese would be in noncombatant support roles, but some might serve as armorers.[12] So, if Chennault had his way, he would have an air corps under his command made up of at least eight hundred men.

Conspicuous by its absence from this memorandum was any provision for transition training. Neither Chennault nor his old friends who served as AVG "executive officers" had flown a P-40 or were qualified in any way to train a pilot for it. Chennault may have been under the impression that the volunteers would receive some training on P-40s in the United States before going to China — that, after all, had been Hap Arnold's idea. For months thereafter the British also presumed that the pilots would be fully trained to fly their Tomahawks before reaching the Far East.[13] Nor did the terms of the CAMCO contract allow for standard procedures in military flight training, the right to dismiss a pilot if he "washed out" and wrecked planes in the process.[14] The lack of transition training was to have foreseeable consequences: accidents, sometimes fatal, reduced the number of planes and pilots in the volunteer group well before it faced the enemy.

On April 15, T. V. Soong and Bruce Leighton signed the CAMCO agreement (unchanged from the March draft).[15] The same day, Intercontinent finalized the wording of the employee contract with the volunteers.[16] All the elements were in place to start the recruitment drive on US air bases, thanks largely to Lauch Currie's determination.

Intercontinent employed a retired AAC officer, Colonel Richard Aldworth, to manage a team of recruiters. From spring to autumn 1941, Aldworth submitted almost weekly reports to Currie. In the first, dated May 3, he logged seventy-three applications from pilots, of which he endorsed eighteen, evidence of a relatively selective process.[17] The recruiters followed to the letter the instructions received from "the supervisor," Colonel Chennault, about the categories and numbers of men to be hired.[18]

That same day, Lauch Currie drafted a stock response to use in case reporters picked up rumors about the Chinese government hiring pilots: with the full knowledge of US military officials, CAMCO was taking on personnel for its assembly and commercial airline operations in China; none of the recruits would fly military aircraft for the Chinese government.[19]

Over the summer Aldworth and his associates continued to receive on average sixty applications a week for pilots, and by September 6, CAMCO had engaged just over a hundred pilots, as specified by Chennault. In the end there were 59 navy pilots and 43 from the AAC; 117 technical experts were hired, as well as 55 administrative staff and 7 medical personnel. By October 18 the roster came to 289 volunteers.[20]

As Chennault's biographer Martha Byrd noted and the volunteers themselves admitted, they knew little about the politics behind the project.[21] Recruiters told candidates that they were going to China to defend the

Burma Road or a Chinese aircraft factory. Occasionally they stated that the volunteers would keep Japanese bombers from attacking Chungking.[22] The young men paid little attention to these pitches. Some signed up for adventure; others were in debt and needed the money. The salary on offer was at least three times better than wages in the military: a pilot would receive $600 a month from CAMCO, compared to $210 from the Air Corps.[23]

Skip Adair, who later became an AVG staff officer, recruited Chuck Baisden, an armorer in the AAC Sixty-Fifth Pursuit Squadron at Mitchel Field, Long Island. Adair told members of his squadron that CAMCO needed pilots to protect a Chinese aircraft factory and would pay $350 a month, compared to his AAC monthly salary of $72. Baisden knew nothing about the Far East but suspected that the Japanese were the bad guys. He was willing to take a gamble. After receiving an honorable discharge on May 14, he went to the offices of Intercontinent in New York and signed a yearlong contract.

Another recruit from Mitchel Field was Robert Brouk, a pilot in the Thirty-Third Pursuit Squadron who kept a diary of his time with the AVG. Skip Adair explained that CAMCO needed pilots to protect the Burma Road: eleven from Brouk's unit signed up. After resigning from the AAC, they were told to go to Los Angeles by June 12. The muster station turned out to be Harlow Aircraft in Alhambra, northwest of Los Angeles. Brouk probably did not know that Harlow was wholly owned by the Intercontinent Corporation. At that time it was producing training planes that were shipped to Bangalore for use by the new Indian Air Force — all part of a contract that Bill Pawley had recently negotiated with colonial authorities in India.[24] The head of Harlow was Ernest Allison, a former commercial pilot who had been chief of operations for the national airline of China, the Chinese National Aviation Corporation (CNAC). In 1919, Allison had taught Chennault to fly and kept him from being washed out of the air service.

Adair made his way to Selfridge Field in Michigan and approached the Forty-First Pursuit Group: Lieutenant Estes Swindle signed up, and like Robert Brouk was part of the second contingent that arrived in mid-August. No one knew where they were heading when they disembarked at Rangoon on the morning of August 16. A few hours later the men were on a train to Toungoo (Taungoo), 170 miles north of Rangoon, where they took up quarters at an RAF airfield outside the town. In the spring of 1941, the RAF had built an airbase at Kyedaw, nine miles to the northwest of Toungoo. It had an asphalt runway about fifteen hundred meters long.[25]

From Adair, Swindle (who soon resigned) had understood that the job in China was to patrol the Burma Road; there would be no night flying and no operations against enemy fighter units. Swindle felt that Adair had not misled any of the volunteers on this point, because when Adair interviewed him, the Japanese were not yet in Indochina and Thailand. Furthermore, given the limited range of their fighter squadrons, the enemy could not yet reach targets in Burma or Yunnan.[26]

On June 9, 1941, Chuck Baisden and twenty-nine other technicians were the first group of recruits to travel to the Far East. At San Francisco they boarded the *President Pierce* and spent about five weeks at sea, stopping at Hawaii, Australia, Manila, and Hong Kong, where they transferred to a Dutch ship to carry on to Singapore. There they spent ten days at the famous Raffles Hotel, where their antics made them less than popular with the locals.[27] They finally reached Rangoon on July 29. That day, Walter Pentecost, the Allison engine specialist who was assembling the Tomahawks in Rangoon, marked "first A.V.G. arrival" in his Royal Dutch Mail calendar.[28]

After the first group of volunteers left San Francisco, Lauch Currie became anxious that Japanese intelligence would find out about the departure of others and sabotage their ships. On June 21, he asked the president to request a naval convoy from Admiral Stark for the Dutch passenger ship *Jagersfontein*: on June 26, Knox agreed to assign some cruisers once the ship reached Hawaii.[29]

On July 6, Brouk and thirty other recruits left Los Angeles and spent twelve hours traveling to San Francisco. There, on July 10, they joined other volunteers on board the *Jagersfontein*. As Richard Aldworth put it, this was the "core" shipment, containing fifty pilots and seventy-three mechanics; seventy-six volunteers came from the army and thirty-eight from the navy.[30] They spent the next six weeks at sea before reaching Singapore on Monday, August 11; they finally docked at Rangoon on August 16. A third contingent of pilots left California on July 22 and turned up on September 15.[31] The very last group left San Francisco on September 24 and arrived in Rangoon November 12.[32]

Currie and McHugh had predicted that high-spirited young men on a junket to the Far East might attract attention. On June 1, the *Washington Post* reported that the US Navy and Army were letting pilots and mechanics serve in the Chinese Air Force and that a Chinese recruiting agency based in Washington was busy hiring them. The State Department immediately denied the story, while the War and Navy Departments claimed that any Americans currently fighting for China had "no official American status."[33]

The Japanese had every opportunity to track the progress of the volunteers. On August 27, 1941, Admiral Stark complained to Lauch Currie that any notion of secrecy had become an "utter laugh." Stark had heard that the young men had stayed in the best hotels in Singapore, where they talked openly about going to Chungking to anyone who would listen. They had no idea that they might have ended up as "a fine bag for the Japanese Navy." He pointed out that the situation was made worse because the American President Lines (owners of the *President Pierce*) issued short bulletins about their passengers, including the pilots heading to China.[34]

Typical was an item in the *Straits Times* of Singapore, which on July 19, 1941, let the world know that "Col. Chanault, leader of the American pilots who will train Chinese aviators to fly United States bombers and fighters in Chungking left [Hong Kong] for the Chinese capital by plane today."[35] In Shanghai, *China Weekly Review* reported that "Lieut.-Col. Chennault of US Army Air Corps" had arrived in Hong Kong on July 18 and was soon due in Chungking: he would supervise training of Chinese pilots and the handling of new fighter planes and bombers recently sent to China from the United States.[36]

On Monday, July 28, Chennault met the first thirty men when they arrived in the harbor and had supper with them that night.[37] The future secretary of the American Volunteer Group, Olga Greenlaw, was also there to greet them. In the lobby of the Minto Mansions Hotel at Rangoon she spotted a group of young men who were "having themselves a time." Olga asked her husband Harvey if he had seen the group; he surprised her by stating that they were part of "our gang." "Why they're just children," she said. Harvey replied, "It's a young man's war."[38]

Also at Rangoon to meet the volunteers was Boatner Carney, an old colleague of Chennault from the flight school at Kunming. In *Way of a Fighter*, Chennault stated that Carney was "hastily pitching camp" at Toungoo in advance of the volunteers. It seems that on July 29, Carney actually stayed in Rangoon for a party after he saw the volunteers onto the train for Toungoo.[39] Carney was with the AVG off and on through the autumn but also spent time at the flight school in Kunming. He was a less than ideal staff officer; he was eventually convicted of manslaughter in Kunming in 1943, the last case ever tried by a US judge in China.[40]

As Chennault had no staff officers to take charge of the first or second group, the volunteers were left on their own to get on with it. Through a fellow armorer, Chuck Baisden received an order from Chennault, "the old man," to drive all the baggage up to the Kyedaw field near Toungoo. It turned out that living quarters were another couple of miles from the runway. When Baisden arrived, the barracks were totally deserted and extremely primitive; he spent an "uneasy" first night alone there.[41] The rest of his party arrived by train the next day. They all agreed that this was not the sort of accommodation to which they were accustomed.[42] It was better for the second contingent; both Brouk and Swindle felt that conditions were not too bad in Burma.[43]

Nearly all the men had been told that they were going to China, where they would patrol the Burma Road, defend an aircraft factory, or possibly protect Chungking against Japanese bombers. So why were they pitching camp on an RAF base in Burma?

In *Way of a Fighter*, Chennault blamed Bill Pawley and the weather for keeping *his* group in Burma. He wrote that Pawley only became involved in the AVG when he demanded his 10 percent cut on the sale of the P-40s. The dispute over Pawley's commission dragged on for months, until Henry Morgenthau called a daylong conference on April 1, 1941, and forced Pawley to accept a much-reduced fee of $250,000. Only then were the P-40s loaded onto an old Norwegian freighter.[44] This account was a fabrication, as the problem of Pawley's commission had been resolved in January 1941 and in no way impeded the mission. Nevertheless, Chennault (or his editor Hotz) insisted that the "wrangle in Washington" so delayed the departure that by the time men and planes reached the Far East, the monsoon had already "transformed the grass-covered airfields of Yunnan into quagmires." Chennault claimed that once he arrived in Burma, he and Pawley made a deal with local British authorities to borrow a paved RAF airfield where the volunteers could train during the rainy season.[45]

This distorted narrative served two purposes: to savage Pawley's reputation and portray Chennault as sole master of the group's fate. Over the years, chroniclers of the Flying Tigers have toned down the stigma attached to Pawley but accepted that the monsoon was to blame. This makes no sense. Chennault could not have just turned up in British sovereign territory and negotiated on the spot (with some help from Pawley) the loan of an airbase for the volunteers. Imagine the reverse: a group of Chinese coming to California to undergo military training without giving any advance notice to US authorities.

It is sheer mythology that the Flying Tigers were a strictly Sino-American affair, created by Claire Chennault and T. V. Soong with the backing of the Roosevelt administration. From the start, the British were closely involved in the project, and by the summer of 1941 they were becoming the key decision makers in shaping the group's fate. In late January 1941, British and Chinese officials in Chungking started discussions on Sino-British military cooperation, which became more meaningful as time went on. In the late spring of 1941, Chiang's generals and British military representatives in China reached an informal understanding about mutual security that included a role for the American volunteers.

With a hundred Tomahawks, the AVG more than equaled all the modern aircraft that the RAF had in Singapore and Burma. Consequently the AVG represented the most important single air asset based in the Far East. If and when the Japanese declared war on the British Empire, the AVG and the RAF would coordinate their efforts to defend Yunnan and Burma. Even though the British knew remarkably little about the AVG, they backed it to the hilt. By the summer of 1941, a few men and planes in Burma had become the backbone of Sino-British cooperation.

The International Air Force 18

I n October 1940, Chiang had called for a Sino-Anglo-American alliance and a vast air armada to deploy against Japan. At that time, the US and British governments decided against trilateral action and turned down Chiang's requests: it was too risky to project the impression that the three allies were working closely against Japan. Nonetheless, to boost his morale, Hull, Stimson, and Morgenthau tried to find a few modern planes for the generalissimo while the British separately considered their own response to his demands.

British officials recognized that Far East defense depended on the coordination of the RAF and whatever naval forces were already in Singapore until the Royal Navy arrived.[1] In November 1940 the Singapore Defense Conference recommended an ideal air strength of 582 modern combat planes for the region but accepted that a minimum of 336 first-line aircraft could provide a fair degree of security.[2] At that time, the RAF in Singapore had eighty-eight military aircraft, of which at least a third were obsolete. In Burma there were no planes or personnel to speak of.

In February 1941, the British Chiefs of Staff transferred No. 60 Squadron with its thirty-two Bristol Blenheim bombers from India to Mingaladon near Rangoon. At the same time, the RAF in Singapore began to receive from the United States Brewster Buffalo fighter planes — 167 were due there by the end of the year. Some of these aircraft, however, remained for months in their crates because there were not enough pilots. Thus, for much of 1941 the commander in chief Far East (C-IN-C), Air Vice Marshal Robert Brooke-Popham, had about 250 first-line aircraft, divided among fourteen squadrons, to defend all British territory in the Far East against Japanese attack.[3] When combined with the AVG, that made just under 350 planes. By contrast, the combined air forces of the Imperial Japanese Navy and Army had 3,500 combat planes to deploy against British and European colonies in the Far East.[4]

The RAF was thus outnumbered by 10 to 1 versus the Japanese, and that ratio explains why it was so vital for the British to keep the Japanese bogged down in China. With so few air and land forces of their own in the Far East, the British had to find ways within limited means to bolster Chinese resistance. They looked for ways to work with the generalissimo that would both boost his morale but also develop some genuine if low-cost forms of military assistance.

In November 1940, the War Cabinet decided to transfer from India Brigadier General Lancelot Dennys, to serve as the new military attaché in Chungking. In that capacity, Dennys was to head the "204 Mission"; its objective was to "encourage the Chinese in their struggle against Japan," and its first tasks were to train the Chinese in guerrilla warfare, improve lines of communications between Burma and Yunnan, and explore the scope for further cooperation.[5]

In mid-January 1941, Brigadier General Dennys arrived in China.[6] He held his first "unobtrusive discussions" with General Ho Yao Tzu, a senior officer in the generalissimo's personal headquarters.[7] Among other subjects, Dennys and General Ho explored the role of military aviation to defend their territories, although, at first, this seemed the least promising aspect of cooperation. Ho asked if the British could sell aircraft and man them with British volunteers, "provided America agreed to do the same." Such airplanes, he insisted, would have "Chinese markings and since they would operate only over Free China, there would be no possibility of British or American pilots falling into Japanese hands." Dennys thought such a scheme was out of the question, but General Ho reverted to it again and again. The generalissimo wanted the British government to take seriously the concept of an international air force.[8]

Dennys rapidly concluded that the Chinese were incapable of mounting an offensive that would keep the Japanese from withdrawing forces to deploy against the British elsewhere. Although skeptical about offering any prewar air support, he recommended that as soon as war with Japan broke out, British squadrons should move into China, as this would be the most effective way to "stiffen" Chinese resolve.[9] Such operations, however, required an advance supply network for fuel, ammunition, and food between Burma and Yunnan.[10]

Dennys transmitted his ideas to Brooke-Popham in Singapore, who became responsible for organizing "Chibase" in Burma to coordinate logistics for 204 Mission. Dennys advised his counterpart in Malaya that Chiang really wanted fighter planes manned by British volunteer pilots, as well as a British agreement to divert to China arms and aircraft that the British Purchasing Commission had on order in the United States.[11]

While General Ho and Dennys discussed military cooperation in Chungking, T. V. Soong approached British envoys in Washington. In February 1941, Soong was in touch with his old friend, Jean Monnet; they had worked together on economic aid for China in the early 1930s.[12] In the winter of 1940–1941, the BAC was offering cover for British officers who had come to Washington for the America Britain Canada talks about future American participation in the European war; they wore civilian dress and pretended to be BAC technical advisers.[13] A leading figure in the delegation was Air Commodore John Slessor, former head of plans for the Air Ministry. Monnet introduced T. V. Soong to Slessor, and on February 11 Slessor sent a cable about their discussion to the Air Ministry.[14]

As Slessor reported, Soong emphasized that the Japanese were bound to make an early attempt on Singapore while the British were preoccupied by the war in Europe. The fall of Singapore, Burma, and the rest of British territory in the region to the Japanese would be fatal for China. Therefore, the generalissimo wanted an international air force composed of five hundred planes and volunteers that would help the army attack the enemy in China, but "above all, if Japanese attack Singapore, the Chinese could bomb cities in Japan and thus create an important diversion."[15] Thus weeks after the Roosevelt administration had dropped the idea of the Chinese bombing Tokyo, the Chinese continued to embrace it.

A few months before, Slessor had heard something about a Chinese international air force from James Buckley of the president's liaison committee, but at that time he had rejected it as unfeasible. After the discussion with Soong, however, he conceded that it had become "more practical": the

Chinese had given up on trying to acquire bombers and were prepared to make a start by forming a fighter unit from the hundred Tomahawks diverted from British contracts. Furthermore, Soong claimed that he had secured "enthusiastic support" from the administration to release AAC reserve officers for the initiative, when in fact the president and his colleagues had put the project on the back burner by mid-February 1941.[16]

Slessor felt that the Air Ministry could not provide volunteer squadrons because of poor lines of communication from Burma to China, as well as the acute shortage of British servicemen. Nonetheless, he and others in the British delegation regarded Soong's plan as "strategically very important," especially if the P-40 squadron proved to be a success. He probably did not need to remind the Air Ministry that in Burma there was only one squadron (RAF No. 60), with thirty-two Blenheim bombers, while in Malaya/Singapore there were eighty-eight "first line" aircraft.[17] Slessor complained that the US government refused to reinforce the British in the Far East in the event of war with Japan but were doing this for the Chinese. As the administration supported this scheme, the British should also take it seriously.[18]

Since the Chinese had made a start on a fighter unit with the Tomahawks, Slessor wondered if the British could offer the 144 Swedish Vultee Vanguards (the 48-C interceptor), which were "much more likely to be useful in China than anywhere in Europe."[19] In August 1940, the Chinese had their eyes on these planes, but British purchasing agents had edged ahead of them and acquired them from the Swedish Purchasing Commission. In principle, they were destined for use in Canada, but the manufacturer had not yet built and delivered them.[20]

While waiting for a response from London, on February 21 Slessor discussed the "International Air Force" (IAF) with Bill Pawley, who seemed "an able and sensible person with great experience of China." Slessor noted that, having built the Loiwing factory, Pawley was now building one in Bangalore and would eventually assemble the Chinese P-40s in Rangoon. Thereafter the American volunteers would take possession of them.[21] Pawley suggested that the volunteers would form three squadrons of eighteen aircraft each (plus reserves). He claimed not only that the US military would release ground personnel but that he was making progress in hiring volunteers. In fact, precisely at this time, the recruitment drive was at a standstill, despite support from the navy.

Pawley also planned to line up fifty administrative and a hundred technical staff for the group. He already had a large workforce in the Far East: his organization had 350 Chinese ground staff with good English as well as engineering degrees, and there also were three thousand Chinese mechanics who provided "a solid basis of experienced ground personnel on which to build up the force."[22] Pawley understood that Slessor had doubts about lines of communications from Burma to China but argued that this was not an insurmountable problem. His company had proved that a capable group of foreigners (not Chinese) could handle logistics in this difficult area. Furthermore, although the factory at Loiwing had been bombed, it continued to receive materials via Burma. Pawley felt that the volunteer project could do without British administrative staff officers, but he hoped that the British government would send some pilots with war experience to serve in the group.

Slessor, in cables to London, betrayed a keen interest. He advised his superiors that it would be important for the volunteers to form squadrons and undergo some operational training as units in Burma before going into China. He understood that the airfield at Mingaladon (near Rangoon) had been enlarged and would be suitable for this; he wondered if the British ambassador in Chungking could arrange for the C-IN-C Far East, Robert Brooke-Popham, to discuss the matter with Pawley's brother Ed.[23] In these suggestions, he laid the foundation for accommodating the AVG in Burma several months hence.

Detailed as his report was, it was remarkably lopsided and unquestioning. Slessor relied entirely on Soong and Pawley to form his view of the IAF and US government support for it. British files about the IAF and aid to China contain no evidence that in February–March 1941 Slessor spoke to any US officials (for instance, Philip Young or Mort Deyo) about the so-called IAF. Had he done so, he might have detected weak support for it on the part of the administration. The only reasons that Roosevelt did not abandon the volunteer program altogether were political and psychological: it would have dealt a demoralizing blow to Chiang Kai-shek.

The Air Ministry naively relied on Slessor's summary as an accurate re-flection of US policy. On March 6, 1941, Sir Charles Portal, chief of the air staff, forwarded to Lord Beaverbrook, head of MAP, Slessor's suggestion to divert 144 Vultee Vanguards to China. Portal seemed to accept outright that the Roosevelt administration had endorsed the IAF: "The question of giving assistance to the Chinese has also been exercising the Americans and as a result, a scheme for setting up an International Air Force for China has been adopted in the U.S.A. Recruitment of volunteers is proceeding satisfactorily, a number of bombers are on order and a fighter force of 3 squadrons is to be formed from the Tomahawks already allotted." Portal then asked Bea-verbrook to support the diversion of 144 Vultee Vanguards to China. The Vultees, he noted, were "not of a sufficiently high standard for our own use. We therefore propose to allot these aircraft to the Chinese."[24] Beaverbrook readily agreed.[25]

Across Whitehall, officials immediately if prematurely added their sacrifice of 144 Vultees to the balance sheet of piecemeal measures that constituted British material aid to China. Exercising caution, they decided to say nothing just yet about the Vultees to the Chinese. Rightly so, as it took months for the US government to buy back the planes and reallocate them to China.[26] In April, Slessor as well as T. V. Soong consulted Frank Knox and Admiral Towers, head of naval aviation, in an effort to push progress this reallocation. Knox was in favor of sending the Vultees to China, but Towers, "as is his habit [was] less so . . . because it would be premature to offer them more aircraft at present."[27] The Vultee Vanguards did not reach China until mid-1942.[28]

Slessor's reports on the IAF also elicited enthusiasm from the C-IN-C Far East, Brooke-Popham.[29] He and Lance Dennys had already agreed that in the event of war with Japan, some British squadrons based in Burma and Singapore should immediately relocate to airfields in Yunnan: they intended to set up fuel dumps and other supplies to provide for air operations in China after war broke out.[30] Brooke-Popham felt that Soong's IAF should be "coordinated with our organization in China" and wanted "some central authority to ensure cooperation between the R.A.F. and the IAF."[31] Although all the matériel and personnel might be American, Brooke-Popham thought that the term "international" would be useful for propaganda reasons: it in-dicated that operational control was in "English or American hands and not

Chinese." He stressed that a few foreign advisers alone would not guarantee effective Chinese use of the aircraft. For the sake of Chinese prestige, the CAF should have "nominal command," but the "real control must be in the hands of some non-Chinese," ideally an RAF officer.[32]

In early March, the Air Ministry advised Brooke-Popham to maintain "effective liaison" and "closest coordination in event of war" but reminded him that the basis of Far East policy was still avoidance of war with Japan. Therefore, it vetoed the idea of a senior RAF officer at the head of the IAF. Nor was it keen for Mission 204 to be visibly associated with the IAF, despite discreet coordination between them.[33] The Air Ministry was anxious that the IAF, once established in China, should alert the British of any plans to bomb targets in Japan. Officials countermanded Slessor's recommendation about IAF training in Burma: they insisted that the pilots should get their training on P-40s in the United States. Nonetheless, Pawley and CAMCO would be allowed to assemble and test a hundred P-40s at Rangoon.[34]

In mid-February 1941, T. V. Soong sought yet another favor from the British. The first lot of thirty-six Tomahawks was on board the *Nidareid*, and the remainder would follow the same route on Norwegian vessels in March and April. Soong feared that the Japanese might sabotage the freighter but presumed that they would not dare attempt to intercept cargo that they believed to be British.[35] Therefore he asked the British ambassador, Lord Halifax, if the aircraft could be consigned to the RAF in Singapore or Rangoon.

Halifax dismissed this new demand as excessive. Not only had the British been forced to give up their planes; they were now expected to assume the risk of transporting them to the Far East. The Japanese might regard it as a provocation if they found out that the British were directly shipping aircraft for China to a British Far East port.[36] At the Foreign Office, Berkeley Gage minuted, "In view of the fact that we consider it an absurd waste of good material to send these ultra-modern machines to the Chinese, who are unlikely to have pilots trained to fly them, I think it a lot to ask us to use the subterfuge suggested by Mr. Soong to protect them on their way, especially as the Japanese know all about the transaction. I think we should refuse to do so." His colleague Ashley Clarke added, "There is something to be said for our taking over the aircraft in spite of the exasperating features of this whole matter."[37]

Another crucial favor that the Chinese demanded of the British was to provide guns for the Tomahawks. On March 10, Sir Arthur Blackburn in Chungking cabled the Foreign Office about this deficit for the planes shipped from Buffalo. The Chinese claimed that they could not obtain the appropriate guns for the planes in the United States and therefore wanted the BAC to release these from British stocks.[38] Once again the British "reluctantly agreed" to do what they could, "despite the extreme urgency of their own needs."[39]

In the spring of 1941 Chiang tried to extract more from mutual cooperation than the British could offer. The signing of the Soviet-Japanese Neutrality Pact on April 13, 1941, raised Chinese anxiety that the Japanese would no longer be worried about war with Russia; then they would be free to divert troops into China, either to control the Burma Road or to mobilize for expansion southward.[40] The generalissimo wanted a commitment that if Japan were to launch a full-scale attack on Yunnan from Indochina, the British would deploy RAF squadrons from Singapore to Yunnan.[41]

The British faced a dilemma: on the one hand, they feared that their military intervention in Yunnan would precipitate war with Japan, but on the other, they did not want to undermine Chinese confidence in their desire to develop genuine security cooperation. In mid-May 1941, they finally turned this request down but only after giving Chiang their most sincere assurances of support.[42] Rhetoric again had to save the day. The generalissimo responded by sending a very personal message to the prime minister on May 20, in which he pointed out, "I know that you are hard pressed but believe me, so am I," a moving translation perhaps by Madame Chiang.[43] In Churchill's reply, advisers suggested that he refer to China as one of the democracies. So he assured Chiang, "Your cause too is that of democracy . . . the cause which inspires both our nations is just. We need not fear the outcome."[44]

Chiang's demand for British intervention in Yunnan heightened British anxiety about the security of communications with the Chinese high command. As a Foreign Office expert pointed out, none of the Chinese generals, with the exception of the generalissimo, could keep a secret. Furthermore, as Japanese intelligence had broken the Chinese cipher, the enemy tracked every new development in Sino-British cooperation.[45]

From December 1940 to April 1941, British representatives in China and London plugged away at building up military and air cooperation with the

Nationalists. Some measures were thrust upon them, but others they adopted willingly, albeit after careful deliberation. In December 1940, the British took a big step, by their standards, in removing all barriers to assembling and testing planes in Rangoon; if the planes were unarmed, Chinese pilots would be allowed to ferry them into Yunnan. In January 1941, the British were virtually blackmailed by Morgenthau into giving up a hundred Tomahawks to China; in March they released machine guns for the Tomahawks, while their aviation authorities also sanctioned the diversion of 144 Vultee Vanguards for use by the IAF.[46] On balance, in the first quarter of 1941, British material aid to China actually surpassed that of the Roosevelt administration.

By far the most important decision for Sino-British cooperation was the agreement to transfer RAF units from Singapore, Malaya or Burma to Yunnan *if and when* the Japanese declared war on the British Empire. Brooke-Popham was authorized in principle to set up "unobtrusive" coordination between his RAF squadrons and the IAF after the latter was installed in the Far East—probably somewhere in Burma. In the spring of 1941, he and Brigadier General Dennys were already trying to improve lines of communication, establish fuel dumps, "RAF stores, bombs etc" near the Burmese border in anticipation of wartime air operations in Yunnan.[47]

While forging its own relationship with Chiang, the British government nonetheless felt that it had to stay in step with the US administration about aid to China. It soon became evident to the Foreign Office that the Air Ministry had put the cart before the horse by promoting the IAF when its officials (Slessor and Portal) knew almost nothing about the administration's actual involvement in it. On March 13, the Foreign Office began a cable to Lord Halifax with the syllogism, "If it is clear the United States administration are in favor of the scheme outlined by Slessor for an International Air Force to assist Chinese, we should wish to support it."[48] But was it clear? Not at all. London asked Halifax to discover more about the US "attitude towards a scheme for an International Air Force."[49] Two months later, in May 1941, the Foreign Office was still waiting for Halifax to provide a clear answer about the US government's stance on the mysterious volunteer group for China.

19 Staying on in Burma

From March to June 1941, the British struggled to secure details from the administration about air aid to China. It was like getting blood from a stone. What little British diplomats learned about the IAF/AVG circulated like Chinese whispers around the empire. Misconceptions abounded about how the Chinese might use the P-40s and the volunteers—separately or together.

On April 29, the Air Ministry wanted the air attaché in Washington, Air Commodore George Pirie, to find out about "Pawley's International Volunteer Air Force for China," such was the enduring influence of Slessor's name for the project in his original reports.[1] Pirie set the record straight a few days later: the IAF had nothing to do with Pawley but was under the command of Claire Chennault, who would "operate directly under Chiang Kai-shek." He added that "the U.S. Admin have no official knowledge of [air] force, which is expected to reach Rangoon about mid-July."[2] On May 13, the secretary of state for Burma repeated the gist of this report to the governor of Burma: "U.S. Administration disclaim official knowledge of Force which is under command of Col. C. L. Chennault who will operate directly under Chiang Kiashek [sic]."[3]

As the volunteers were about to turn up in Burma, the Air Ministry urgently wanted "fullest information" from US officials or Chennault about the number of men, the state of their training, and the date of arrival.[4] According to Pirie, only a few men would need flight instruction at Rangoon, and their operations would start in late July or early August.[5] On May 8, Chiang informed Ambassador Clark Kerr that the US government had approved the recruitment of reserve officers who would receive US$700 a month and

"US$500 for every enemy plane destroyed."[6] On May 20, 1941, the Foreign Office complained that information provided thus far had been "meagre and disjointed" and pressed Lord Halifax for more.[7] That day, the British Chiefs of Staff also sent Admiral Alan Kirk, the head of ONI, a summary of British aid to China that highlighted progress on guerrilla training of the Chinese and "unobtrusive support" for the IAF. They asked Kirk for more information about US policy toward the project, since "the position as regards the development of the scheme is obscure"; the British Chiefs of Staff would "welcome energetic action by the United States to further it," as long as it did not detract from the European theater.[8]

ONI, however, left this British questionnaire about the IAF and aid to China unanswered for several weeks. On July 8, Kirk wrote to the CNO, Admiral Stark, that "in view of the Navy's lack of information on this subject," it would be better to postpone discussion with the British until officers had spoken to Lauchlin Currie.[9] Kirk's assistant, Lieutenant Commander Arthur H. McCollum, was blunt in characterizing US aid for China as "largely talk, with very little concrete help having been given other than the lending of money on rather favorable terms." They could not discuss aid for China with the British, "as we do not know what the extent of our own actions are."[10] McCollum was head of the Far Eastern Division in ONI; for him to make such a confession revealed how little ONI knew about the volunteer scheme for China, even though Frank Knox had been its chief proponent. It seems likely that, at this stage, the navy's man in Chungking, James McHugh, was equally in the dark. There is no mention in McHugh's papers at Cornell University of Sino-British discussions about the IAF. Nor did he receive any information that summer from his friend Lauch Currie that he might have passed to ONI.

There are several possible explanations for ONI's ignorance about either British or American air aid for China at this time. First, the Chinese and British succeeded in keeping their plans secret in order to avoid any interference from the enemy. Second, the White House (through Lauch Currie) did not want to foster any Anglo-American-Chinese military cooperation because Japan might have interpreted any hint of trilateral interaction as proof that a formal alliance was in the works. Furthermore, at a later stage, the Americans made no bones about wanting to influence military aid policies for China in the long run. They were not prepared to share control with the British.

In the year before Pearl Harbor, there was no such thing as trilateral consultation between the United States, Britain, and China about the AVG or any other form of military aid for China. The three powers operated like furtive couples — Sino-British, Sino-American, and Anglo-American, each of them dancing to their own tune.

In May 1941, the War Cabinet was baffled by the situation regarding the volunteer group. Since the US government pretended to know nothing about it, officials in London felt obliged to follow the American example and "disassociate themselves publicly from this force."[11] Privately, however, departments across Whitehall were already deeply committed to the venture about which they knew so little.[12] In Singapore, Brooke-Popham complained that it was difficult for him to maintain "effective liaison" with the IAF and "closest co-ordination in event of war" if he was not fully informed about the latest developments. It was all the more urgent for him because he was about to receive Brigadier General Dennys and "one General Mao of the Chinese Air Force," with whom he wanted to discuss IAF "command and organization."[13]

On May 26, Lord Halifax finally came through with a few details about the IAF. It was under the command of Colonel Chennault, USAAC (retired). A hundred Tomahawks were on their way to Burma, and a hundred ex-army and navy pilots were due to travel there. It was understood that the force would be in action in China by mid-August 1941 — truly an exaggeration, but how were they to know better? Halifax also reported that the US government had finally appropriated the 144 Vultees for China, for which crews were being recruited. The IAF was receiving "active assistance" from Lauchlin Currie, although the US government was "not publicly associated" with it. Yes, Currie was the only official in the entire administration who was looking out for the group. Furthermore, Currie stated that no British or Allied pilots were required for the unit, yet surely the group needed all the help it could get. This perhaps was evidence of Currie's anti-British bias, for he soon revealed how keen he was to keep the British at arm's length where the AVG was concerned.[14]

This latest news from Lord Halifax revived debate in the Foreign Office.

On June 6, 1941, officials gathered to review aid for China, including the Dennys 204 Mission and support for the IAF. They considered whether or not the 204 Mission should have a few RAF officers who could assess air facilities in Yunnan. One thought led to another: perhaps some RAF officers should also carry out "covert liaison with the IAF." From Currie's communication, however, it was far from clear that the US government wanted any British assistance for the force and, if so, "what sort." Before embarking on the next step, "a discussion with Colonel Chennault, the commander of the International Air Force, was the first essential."[15]

At the same time, the Foreign Office was not "altogether happy" about the proposed talks between Brooke-Popham and General Mao. On June 6, Ashley Clarke of the Far East Department asked the War Office to remind the C-IN-C Far East that "it was the military attaché Chungking who has the primary job of dealing with the Chinese in this matter": he advised against discussions on such a sensitive matter in two places. Brooke-Popham was to exercise caution and be fully aware of the "increased danger of leakage" should more Chinese than necessary find out about British plans.[16]

Brooke-Popham protested that even if Chungking remained the center of Sino-British discussions about the IAF, he had to be kept abreast of all discussions because its maintenance and operations affected his command "very closely." He pointed out that the Tomahawks would be assembled in Burma and probably be stationed on RAF aerodromes in Burma—an indication that by early June 1941 Dennys and the Chinese had already decided that the AVG should be kept in Burma and not proceed to Kunming. Brooke-Popham desired consultation about sharing facilities and supplies sent over the Burma Road between the IAF and the RAF. Also, in his view, there had to be coordination on "operations of International Air Force and our plans in event of war between Japan and us."[17]

The C-IN-C's message implied that in Chungking, the British and Chinese were already consulting about cooperation between the RAF and the IAF in the event of war between Britain and Japan: discussions covered the disposition of airfields, logistics, supplies, and operations. So sensitive were these plans that Dennys and his Chinese counterparts were forbidden to dispatch cables on these subjects. Therefore, Brooke-Popham had no access to information unless he met Dennys or his adjutants in person.

On June 20, General P. T. Mao, the CAF chief of operations, descended on Brooke-Popham for a six-day visit. Mao believed that Chennault was arriving in Chungking that very day and carrying on to Rangoon. Brooke-Popham fired off a telegram to Clark Kerr to see if anyone on the diplomatic circuit knew of Chennault's whereabouts in order to direct him to Singapore.[18] Clark Kerr replied that he had no idea where Chennault was: the embassy in Washington "professed to be equally in the dark" and thought that he had not yet left the United States. Clark Kerr added that the Chinese were preparing in two to three weeks' time to receive 246 Americans in Kunming.[19]

While in Singapore, General Mao repeatedly asked for British volunteers to join the IAF. Brooke-Popham surmised that Mao was under orders from Chiang to press this demand, but he flatly refused to offer pilots. The C-IN-C argued that British capacity to help maintain the IAF in Burma or to send any RAF units into China would depend entirely on improvement to the Burma Road. On June 25, Brooke-Popham wired London to request a meeting with Chennault in Singapore to discuss the IAF's organization and operations: he would let the Chinese know loud and clear that he regarded Chennault, not Mao, as the "executive commander of the International Air Force."[20]

Chennault was already preparing to leave Washington. On June 21, he finally met the British air attaché, George Pirie. For the first time a British official spoke directly with the "supervisor" of the volunteer group. During their conversation, a particularly significant detail emerged that has never surfaced in subsequent narratives about the Flying Tigers. Chennault told George Pirie the following: the US naval attaché in Tokyo had reported that the Japanese were fully aware of the formation of a so-called international air force for China. For this reason, "the P-40 fighters would not leave Rangoon until everything was ready for them to go into action in China. Previous intention had been to send them into China immediately they were erected and tested." Chennault now felt that the volunteers — some two hundred to three hundred — should stay in Burma to be fully trained in operating and maintaining the Tomahawks before moving into Yunnan; Chennault wondered if accommodation could be readily found for this number of men.[21]

This cannot have been a decision taken by Claire Chennault in Washington, DC. By this stage, the British were committed to organizing the air defense of Yunnan and Burma in the event of war with Japan. They were well aware of how vulnerable Yunnan was to Japanese air attack, as were the Chinese: in Singapore, General Mao had confessed to Brooke-Popham that the CAF was "quite ineffective" as a fighting force.[22] It seems likely that Lance Dennys and Chiang decided that to protect the AVG and its assets from being destroyed by the enemy, the group should be based in Burma. There the volunteers would be safe to train and establish coordination with the RAF. Once Britain was at war with Japan, the group would be better prepared to mount joint operations in defense of Burma and Yunnan.

In the meantime, a hundred Tomahawks finally began to arrive in Burma. On May 23, the Norwegian freighter *Nidareid* finally docked at Rangoon and disgorged thirty-six aircraft in huge crates. To oversee the assembly of planes, Intercontinent had hired Walter Pentecost, a specialist in Allison engines, and Byron Glover, a test pilot from Curtiss-Wright: they too reached Rangoon on May 23.[23] Two days later, Pentecost, with a team of Indian and Chinese laborers, started to unpack parts and embark on assembly operations. On July 12, another Norwegian freighter, the *Gunny*, docked at Rangoon with thirty planes; by the end of July the final lot of Tomahawks had arrived.[24]

One engineer and one test pilot, aided by a few Chinese mechanics, were bound to make slow progress on putting together one hundred planes. In the first eight weeks, Pentecost and Glover assembled and certified six planes. In the following weeks the pace picked up but then slackened because of the weather, ill health, and lack of parts.[25] The monsoon sometimes made it impossible to work or fly. Walter Pentecost marked "rain" in his calendar nearly every day in August. Byron Glover fell seriously ill twice during the autumn of 1941 and suspended test flights. Extreme humidity caused engine trouble: rusty thrust bearings were the most common culprit. It took weeks for replacements to arrive from Singapore or Calcutta; on two occasions all planes were grounded while Pentecost checked the thrust bearings. In this challenging environment, Pentecost and Glover "sold" planes at an average rate of only three to four a week; the very last Tomahawk was tested and certified on November 28, 1941.[26]

Chennault reached Chungking on July 18 and soon met Brigadier General Dennys and the British air attaché, Major James Warburton. Chennault informed them that he alone had complete command of the force—which may have been a surprise to them. Chennault also stated that forty-one pilots and ninety-eight ground staff would soon arrive at Rangoon and another sixty pilots by the end of September. At Rangoon he intended to train the recruits in "practical flying by day and night flying" as well as "air to ground individual gunner practice." Chennault also had big plans for bombers: by the end of the year he expected to have sixty-six Lockheed Hudson type 414 aircraft with a range of three thousand miles "for direct action against Japan." That was something of an exaggeration, as the range of the Lockheed Hudson was closer to two thousand miles. Curiously, the British officials did not ask how the Chinese had managed to secure these bombers.

Chennault seemed oblivious of the diplomatic dimension of operating in British territory: Warburton pointed out that training at this level would require "Foreign Office sanction."[27] In fact, consultation about AVG operations in Burma extended across Whitehall. On July 19, the governor of Burma, Reginald Dorman-Smith, received instructions from the War Cabinet about the IAF: its officials advised him that after conferring with Chennault and Brooke-Popham, he would be the judge of how far the American volunteers could go on British territory. The War Cabinet suggested that he should allow the volunteers to fit their aircraft with armament before the planes were ferried to China; he also could "permit instruction in the use and maintenance of the aircraft while they were in Burma."[28]

The Air Staff, however, had some reservations about these orders. Its experts reminded their colleagues in the War Cabinet that the facts before them about the IAF now differed substantially from earlier information. They had previously understood that the volunteers would be fully trained in the United States to fly Tomahawks (or Vultees), and, if necessary, they would receive some further training in China. As things stood, the War Cabinet was under pressure to consider a demand by the IAF to run an operational training unit in Burma. Although the Chiefs of Staff had regarded the successful establishment of the IAF in China as "strategically desirable," they also had been "nervous" about Japan's potential reaction to British assistance for it. For that reason, it had been necessary "to cloak as much as possible the extent of the overt assistance being rendered in Burma." The British were "accepting considerable risks in assisting the International Air Force" while also trying to avoid provocation of Japan.[29]

But the traditional argument that the British should do nothing to provoke

Japan was beginning to break down. A few years before, the British government would have regarded the presence of American men and planes in their Far East colonies as a red rag to a Japanese bull. In the summer of 1941, however, the Air Ministry conceded that "Japan will decide the major issue of undertaking open hostilities against the British Empire on bigger issues than the International Air Force."[30] The Air Ministry was still reluctant to allow the volunteers to use guns and live ammunition for operational training on British territory, but this message got lost in the cable traffic and never went through to Reginald Hugh Dorman-Smith, the governor of Burma.

On July 23, Chennault arrived in Rangoon, where he discovered that Intercontinent had already started to assemble and test airplanes at the nearby Mingaladon airfield.[31] The same day, he met with Hugh Dorman-Smith. As Chennault later wrote to Madame Chiang, the British had a sincere desire to cooperate fully in matters to do with the American Volunteer Group and aid for China. The governor of Burma offered him nearly everything that he wanted: the training of pilots in squadrons; installation of machine guns in the planes and gunnery practice for pilots; suspension of customs barriers for US goods and personnel; permission to set up observation posts across Burma for enemy aircraft; the full use of an RAF base at Toungoo, as well as one at Magwe, although the latter as yet had no facilities apart from an airfield.[32] In fact they were one and the same thing—Magwe was the airfield several miles outside Toungoo.

On July 26, Dorman-Smith communicated to London roughly the same details that Chennault reported to Madame Chiang: the governor was "anxious to meet Chennault's wishes . . . and anticipate[d] no opposition from my Ministers."[33] Dorman-Smith had interpreted the War Cabinet's instructions as permission for him to let the American volunteers conduct operational training "without further reference to London."[34] On that basis, he told Chennault that the pilots could start training in squadrons before going to Yunnan.

The governor had overstepped the mark. On July 27, the C-IN-C Robert Brooke-Popham reminded him that according to the War Cabinet's instruction, the pilots would be allowed to receive enough instruction to learn how to fly the planes and ferry them to China. However, they would not be permitted to train in methods of attack or camera gun practice while in Burma. This was a difficult decision for Brooke-Popham, who urgently sought clarity about this policy from the War Cabinet. For he was about to receive Chennault in Singapore. He posed a straightforward question: Would the War Office allow the IAF to set up an operational training unit in Burma or not?[35]

That same day, July 27, 1941, Chennault started his three-day visit in Singapore: Brooke-Popham found him to be "tough, active and forceful," with "sound ideas on training and operations. . . . [He] should be easy to work with especially in War." In his cable to London, the C-IN-C reported the following details provided by Chennault: All hundred P-40s were now in Rangoon and twenty already constructed; after training in Burma, the squadrons would operate from Kunming to protect the Burma Road. Chennault expected 144 Vultees to start arriving in October and to be used by the CAF. Republic P-43s also would be delivered starting in January 1942 and distributed between the CAF and the IAF. The only drawback was that spare parts would not be available before January 1942.

Chennault also offered details about the deployment of light bombers that were to be delivered to China: his volunteer group would keep the Lockheed Hudsons somewhere in central China; from there they would refuel at airfields in East China before conducting air raids on Japan—perhaps he had revised his estimate of this bomber's range. There also were Douglas DB-7s with considerably less range: these would go to the CAF. It seems not to have occurred to Brooke-Popham to find out how or when the Chinese had acquired these bombers.

Chennault told Brooke-Popham that the three P-40 squadrons would not be "operationally efficient" until October. Furthermore, because of rain and the risk of enemy attack, he could not possibly train his men on Chinese airfields, so they would have to stay in Burma. He seemed determined to give the C-IN-C the impression that these were all his decisions: easy enough, as Brooke-Popham remained somewhat in the dark about the deliberations of his colleagues in Chungking. Nonetheless, Brooke-Popham made it absolutely clear to Chennault that his masters in London forbade operational training in Burma.[36]

Before leaving Singapore, Chennault pointed out to Brooke-Popham that the International Air Force forthwith would be officially known as the

American Volunteer Group.[37] The British, however, never got out of the habit of calling the group the IAF and continued to do so right up to Pearl Harbor.

On July 30, the War Office responded to the C-IN-C Far East about allowing the AVG to undergo operational training in Burma. Their answer was no.[38] If it was an awkward response for Brooke-Popham, it was even more so for Chennault. Having concluded all his meetings with British authorities in Singapore and Burma, he reported to Madame Chiang on August 5, 1941, that local British representatives could do nothing about the prohibition on operational training imposed by the British government. For the time being, the volunteers would only be allowed to train in groups of three, with no gunnery practice. He counted on the Chiangs to exert pressure on the British to reverse the ban.[39] But it was a moot point: the volunteer pilots had yet to even arrive; there was still plenty of time for the British to change their mind.

20 *Squabbling over Bullets*

I n *Way of a Fighter*, Chennault contended that the AVG got off to a slow start because the British prevented his men from gunnery practice: he or Hotz alleged that in the view of the British, firing live ammunition at the ground would alarm the natives and possibly provoke the enemy. Therefore, it was "late in October [1941], long after the AVG arrived," before the British authorized full combat training but only on the condition that the AVG did not attack the Japanese from bases in Burma.[1]

This version of events is sheer make-believe. Chennault (or Hotz) distorted dates and decisions to make a scapegoat of the British when the fault lay elsewhere. If the volunteers had a slow start in combat training, the responsibility lay entirely at the door of the US War Department: its army generals refused to release bullets for the machine guns mounted on AVG fighter planes.

Although some of the Tomahawks had been shipped with armament, no one had filled out the necessary paperwork to obtain ammunition. That was part and parcel of the wholly incompetent approach by policy makers in Washington to plane aid: they assigned a huge political value to selling the latest combat planes to China but could not be bothered to deal with all the accessories required to convert them into genuine weapons.[2]

On July 3, Lauchlin Currie went to Harry Hopkins and President Roosevelt in the hope that they might put pressure on the War Department to release some ammunition: Currie insisted that there would be "an international scandal" if the US government could not come up with some bullets. On July 12, Hopkins wrote to General Burns that the president had proposed a "token amount to show them [the Chinese] we mean business."[3] Such phrases had become stock-in-trade in the administration in describing relatively minor gestures aimed at Japan or China. The army received this order from Hopkins and placed it at the bottom of the in-tray.

On August 5, the British Embassy in Washington reported that the War Department was aware that the lack of ammunition would keep the IAF from going into operation; after several weeks of delay, however, the department was willing to send a month's supply to Burma. In the meantime, Lord Halifax wondered if Brooke-Popham could also spare a few rounds, but the C-IN-C barely had enough for his own squadrons in Malaya.[4]

In Chungking, Brigadier General Dennys threw his weight behind Chennault's request for 1.5 million rounds of .50 caliber ammunition. He hoped that the British War Office could intervene to "put this deplorable situation right" by either providing some of its own or putting pressure on the US Army to release some. He emphasized yet again the psychological significance of the IAF: from the standpoint of Chinese morale, "Chennault's force must be given every possible chance to win . . . first battle."[5] The British nonetheless recognized that the group had to perform in a meaningful military way in order to stimulate a sharp boost in morale on the part of the Chinese.

General Dennys sided with Chiang and Chennault against Brooke-Popham and the War Cabinet about operational training. He felt that the volunteers had to start functioning as squadrons before they went into China. He stressed that the Chinese were "pinning highest hopes on these squadrons," and if they met with early reverses, the moral effect would be very bad.[6] Unlike the US government, there was nothing ad hoc about the British government's planning process; however meager their resources might be, they debated each and every aspect of policy that might apply to the AVG long before the group was up and running.

James McHugh separately echoed Dennys's sentiment in a letter to Lauch Currie: "It is highly important that his force not meet the Japs until they are ready. The first encounter will be very important *psychologically*."[7] On August 12, Brooke-Popham suggested a compromise to the War Office: if the Japanese attacked the Burma Road, the group could go ahead with operational training in Burma; otherwise the ban should remain in force.[8]

At this stage, however, the question was still moot. There were not enough planes or pilots to even start training. On July 28, the first thirty volunteers had arrived, but no pilots figured in this passenger list. On August 15, the second group of volunteers arrived, with thirty-seven pilots. By this time, Pentecost and Glover had assembled and certified only seventeen planes.[9] Therefore, in mid-August 1941, the group was still a long way off from having the resources to start flight or combat training.

The British and the AVG organizers rightly regarded ammunition as essential for AVG training. To their relief, in early August 1941, General Gerow of the army's War Plans Division finally had approved release of nine hundred thousand rounds of ammunition for the group, and on August 14 the cargo left the Raritan Arsenal in New Jersey.[10] As the voyage would take up to six weeks, the British prevailed upon the US government to get some ammunition to Burma sooner than that. The War Department agreed to a diversion of ammunition from the US (Asiatic) fleet in Manila if the British arranged the transport.[11] On September 16, the *Iran* left Manila for Rangoon with six hundred thousand rounds of ammunition destined for the AVG.[12]

As soon as 1.5 million rounds of ammunition were secured for the AVG, the British immediately settled the question of operational training that had dragged on since July 17. The Chiefs of Staff advised Winston Churchill that that "operational training would not add appreciably to [the] provocative effect [on Japan] already inherent in presence of IAF aircraft in Burma."[13] On August 21, Churchill wrote to Anthony Eden, "Do you approve? If so I agree." Eden replied, "I agree." Thus Churchill gave his personal approval for the volunteers to start gunnery practice once they had the ammunition to do so.[14] The Chiefs of Staff attached one caveat to Churchill's authorization: the squadrons should not launch any action against the Japanese from airfields in Burma. Thus by mid-August — *not* in October 1941, as claimed by Chennault in his memoir — British authorities had lifted all restrictions on operational training. Full combat training began only in October, once ammunition had arrived from New York and Manila, and by that stage, about two-thirds of the volunteers had reached Burma.

From mid-August to October 1941, the volunteers who had arrived in Burma found that they had time on their hands because of the slow pace of aircraft assembly and the lack of ammunition for artillery practice. During this slack period, what sort of training did Chennault and his executive officers establish for the volunteers? The answer is very little.

In *Way of a Fighter*, Chennault claimed that he had established a "kindergarten" at Kyedaw—the RAF field outside Toungoo—to teach bomber pilots how to fly fighter aircraft. If there was ever such a play group for bomber or fighter pilots, the infants seem to have been in charge of it. In the history of military aviation, no contingent of pilots, *before or since*, has ever been left to learn how to fly an advanced combat aircraft with so little formal instruction or supervision. The volunteers seem to have made up their own instruction at the RAF Kyedaw airfield, apart from lectures on fighter tactics by Chennault. Their routine bore no resemblance to the rigorous training required by the US military or that which American volunteers received from the RAF when they joined the "Eagle Squadrons" in England.[1]

The recruits could not possibly have relied on their "supervisor" or any of the "executive officers": Chennault, Harvey Greenlaw, Boatner Carney, and Skip Adair were too old and inexperienced to have mastered the temperamental nature of the P-40; none of them, including Chennault, were qualified to run transition training on the P-40. There was another executive officer, the columnist Joe Alsop, who had never even flown a plane. The command of the AVG was pretty much a joke.

So the volunteers taught themselves how to fly the Tomahawk. As AAC pilots might have put it, "oldies" who knew how to fly the plane instructed "newies." Given the challenges of flying the Tomahawk, it is remarkable that the rookies did not suffer more accidents. That was a credit not only to them but to their prior AAC training. It had nothing to do with Chennault and his thin organization in Burma.[2]

In early September 1941, Pentecost and Glover had twenty-seven Tomahawks ready for the volunteers to fly. Pentecost's ferry records reveal that AAC pilot Erik Shilling was the first volunteer to fly a plane up to Toungoo on September 4. Shilling stated that he had twenty hours of flying time on a P-40. He had come from the AAC's Eglin Field, which had no P-40s but had bomber squadrons in which he had served; somehow he seems to have racked up these hours at Kyedaw.[3] Other volunteers had far less time in their hot new planes before starting to fly them from Rangoon to Toungoo. For example, on September 5–6, four navy pilots claimed to have two to three hours' experience in a P-40 before taking them up to Kyedaw.[4] It is impossible to know how the ferrying operation was implemented. It seems likely that decisions were ad hoc; Pentecost and the pilots somehow decided who would man the planes. For not only were there no competent staff officers at Toungoo, but in August–September 1941, the AVG "supervisor," Claire Chennault, was absent much of the time.

In his postwar memoir, Chennault stressed his passion for establishing his own air force in the Far East, yet at the time he greatly preferred to spend his days with the great and the good instead of the rookies. For his diary and British reports reveal how little time he spent with the new recruits in Toungoo during August–September 1941.

From 1937 to 1941 Chennault kept a five-year diary off and on that had space for very short entries; the last was November 22, 1941. On its own, the diary tells us little about his life with the volunteers in the months before Pearl Harbor. Nonetheless, the entries reveal what he found important enough to write down. In 1941, he recorded the names of nearly every British, US, or Chinese government official that he ever met. If and when Chennault commented on the volunteers, he highlighted their complaints, resignations, accidents, or fatalities while flying—nothing positive. Otherwise he commented on his bouts of ill-health (chronic bronchitis), or victories at cards, volleyball, or baseball games with the volunteers. In short, Chennault was considerably more interested in his peers and superiors than his young subordinates.

On July 16, Chennault disembarked from the Pan Am Clipper in Hong Kong, the first of many stops to confer with officials across the region. On July 23, he came to Rangoon and met the governor of Burma as well as British military officers. A few days later, on July 28, the first thirty volunteers who had crossed the Pacific on the President Pierce were in the harbor at Rangoon. At a dinner offered by two senior Chinese officers, Chennault met this first contingent. The next day, he was off to Singapore to meet Robert Brooke-Popham and then went on to Chungking. Three weeks later, on August 21, Chennault returned to Toungoo. The following day, for the first time, he met the second and third contingents—some 160 volunteers, of which 50 were pilots. According to his diary (August 22, 1941), he did not much like what he saw: "agitators" had stirred up resentment about military discipline and combat service; that night he explained the setup to them.[5] Soon thereafter, however, Chennault took off again: for the rest of August and part of September he was in orbit between Rangoon, Chungking, Kunming, and Singapore, conferring with military men of every stripe.[6] In the meantime, the volunteers, left to their own devices, had adventures, some of them fatal.

At 9 a.m. on September 8, Chennault left Toungoo by plane for Kunming with a small party on board. Because of bad weather they did not reach their destination until well after dark. Meanwhile at Kyedaw, a navy aviator, John Armstrong, died in a crash. It seems that Armstrong had a thousand hours of flying but not much experience in a Tomahawk. He collided midair with another navy man, Gil Bright, who managed to escape, while Armstrong, strapped into his plane, spun down to his death.[7]

According to his diary, Chennault learned of Armstrong's death later that night of September 8. The following morning, the group buried Armstrong in the English churchyard at Toungoo. Chennault carried on to Chungking for meetings: he had tea with Madame Chiang on September 11 and lunch with her on September 15—always a high point of his existence. After all, she would always be a princess to him.[8] A third contingent of pilots arrived at Rangoon on September 15. Chennault was in Chungking and flew on to Kunming for appointments with Chinese officers. On September 18, he returned to Toungoo via Rangoon, where he conferred with Bill Pawley. The following day, September 19, he was back in Toungoo. He noted that six men wanted to resign, and everyone was complaining about the food.[9]

The same day, Air Vice Marshal Robert Brooke-Popham arrived with a party of Air Ministry officials in Rangoon and flew up to Toungoo, where the volunteers put on a show flying in an eighteen-ship formation. This was the first of several demonstration flights for visiting British dignitaries in September–October 1941: as Chennault had spent only a few days in Toungoo during the previous six weeks or so, he could take no credit for the AVG's performance.

On September 22, Air Vice Marshal Conway Pulford arrived at Toungoo from Singapore. This proved to be another "black Monday." Army pilot Maax Hammer was killed while flying a Tomahawk: he went into a tailspin and could not come out of it. The plane was a write-off. In his diary, Chennault noted in two short sentences the death of Hammer and the arrival of Pulford.[10] On Thursday, September 25, after the rain let up, the pilots put on another demonstration flight for Pulford.[11]

The assistant secretary of war for air, Robert Lovett, regarded the AVG pilots as the "cream of our fighter squadrons."[12] As far as Chennault was concerned, however, they were the dregs in a half-empty glass. In early November 1941, full combat training with live ammunition had finally gotten under way. Chennault sent two blistering letters of complaint to CAMCO because the recruiters had misrepresented the mission: they had created the impression that there would be no night flying and that operations would be confined to defending the Burma Road against enemy bombers without fighter escort. As Chennault put it, "Most pilots volunteering under a misapprehension of the Group's real nature are quite useless to me."[13]

In a second letter to CAMCO, on November 7, he condemned the entire recruitment process and singled out for particular sanction ten navy recruits who came to Toungoo on October 29. He was particularly scathing about a navy flier called Ed Conant who cracked up three planes in the first week of flying: Chennault conceded that since he was a young man of "some spirit" he might still prove to be of some use, but under the terms of the contract he could not send Conant home: in fact Conant stuck it out to the very end.[14] Chennault asserted he was "willing to give a certain amount of transition training to new pilots but we are not equipped to give a complete refresher course. It is too much to expect that men familiar only with four-engine flying boats can be transformed into pursuit experts overnight."[15]

The most important service that Chennault might have incorporated into his planning was transition training for the P-40, but he failed to do so. It would not have taken much for an old AAC officer like Chennault to find out that in 1940 and 1941 there was a chronic shortage of P-40s and consequently of competent P-40 pilots in the army. Many of the fliers had been trained to fly single-engine combat aircraft but *not* the tricky P-40 Tomahawk. If Intercontinent had received orders from Chennault to hire instructors for transition training, they would have provided a tempting salary to instructors in order to fulfill his specifications. But in April 1941, Chennault omitted this essential job profile for instructors competent in advanced or transition training on a Curtiss P-40.

It could have been otherwise. In 1941, CAMCO was asked to recruit some advanced flight instructors for service in China—unfortunately, not for the AVG. This matter arose in the summer of 1941 when Lauch Currie entered into discussions with the War Department about training CAF pilots in the United States. On August 7, Robert Lovett turned down the idea of bringing Chinese to the United States, because there were not enough instructors to train AAC pilots, no less CAF ones. By contrast, he suggested that some fliers in the AVG might be used to train the CAF in China.[16]

On August 18, Lovett gave Richard Aldworth permission to hire ten instructors; he recruited them within only two days. One instructor left for Rangoon on September 24, and the other nine on October 14.[17] Unfortunately they did not arrive in Burma until the very end of November, too late to have been of any real use to Chinese pilots or indeed any of the American volunteers before the Pacific war broke out. On this key issue of transition training, Chennault refused to acknowledge his own errors in planning the mission and instead pinned the blame squarely on CAMCO.

On November 12, the last group of volunteers arrived in Burma. This included Charlie Bond, an officer in the AAC Ferrying Command. In his diary, Bond noted that discipline was entirely up to the individual and seemed to be a matter of respect between the men.[18] Bond also commented that Chennault enjoyed the company of the volunteers whenever his "administrative duties" allowed.[19] For the first two weeks in Toungoo, Bond found nothing to criticize. Then toward the end of November he noted how low the mood of the men had suddenly become. Many were complaining that Chennault or the recruiters had misrepresented the mission to them.

On December 5, Bond had a heart-to-heart with Chennault. As a military man, Bond found it difficult to accept the lack of discipline and such freedom from rules and regulations. In his diary, he wrote, "Poor discipline! I believe that is what is happening to the morale and I told him so." Chennault ducked the issue and spent the rest of the conversation saying nice things about Bond and building up his ego.[20]

The AVG was totally unorthodox and relatively privileged. To grasp its exceptional status, let us compare the group to the Philippines Department Air Force (PDAF), the other US air force unit in the Far East that happened to fly P-40s. From July to November 1941, pilots and mechanics arrived in waves to reinforce the Philippines. They were crammed into old army barracks with leaking roofs and intermittent electricity and water supplies. Some lived in huts without doors, several without walls.[21] Ted Fisch, commander of a bomber squadron, described his living quarters as a "rat's nest."[22] There was nowhere to disperse equipment and hide aircraft, if and when the Japanese attacked.[23] In the Philippines, members of P-40 squadrons could not fly their planes for three months until, in July 1941, coolant for their Allison engines finally arrived. Many pilots never fired their machine guns before Pearl Harbor for lack of ammunition. Experienced pilots of the Seventeenth Pursuit Squadron who were transferred to the Philippines in October 1941 found the more advanced P-40Es complicated, difficult to operate, and still prone to ground-looping.[24] Ted Fisch found it nearly impossible to bring newly qualified pilots up to operational standard. He complained to his wife about "90-day wonders" because all they did was "get drunk and crack up airplanes."[25]

By November 1941, the AVG was far better off than the PDAF: the volunteers had ammunition with which to practice gunnery (some of it diverted from the Philippines); they fixed up their rustic living quarters to their liking; they had decent drinking water and had hired their own cook for the mess hall. They were virtually in charge of their own training. Furthermore, Kyedaw airfield was relatively secure from enemy attack: it was surrounded by bomb-proof shelters and dugouts for planes in the event of an emergency, whereas the aircraft and facilities of the PDAF were horribly exposed to enemy attack.

In the autumn of 1941, if army analysts had compared the AVG to the PDAF, they might have concluded that, under the circumstances, the unconventional AVG was performing at least as well if not better than air corps units in the Philippines. But no one made that evaluation. Furthermore, the liberal regime at Toungoo did nothing for the group's reputation. As the autumn wore on, observers in and out of the US government grew skeptical about the AVG's prospects as a tactical unit and the competence of Claire Chennault as a military commander.

On July 15, George Marshall had asked Lauch Currie for a "proviso" to do with the volunteer scheme. He suggested that an "appropriate American Government representative" should decide when and if the American volunteer air unit was ready for combat.[26] In this and other ways, the chief of staff revealed his ambivalence about US air aid for China. On the one hand, he was reluctant to release any army aircraft or ammunition to the group, but on the other, he wanted control over the group and its equipment. The reason for Marshall's revived interest in the AVG was entirely to do with aircraft that it might eventually receive: 144 Vultee Vanguards, as well as 66 medium-range bombers.

When Chennault met British officers in the Far East, he referred to sixty-six bombers expected by the end of the year. Neither the British air attaché James Warburton nor the C-IN-C Far East Brooke-Popham posed the crucial question of how the Chinese had managed to extract *any* bombers from the US Army. Soon enough, the British were to discover that, like the group's hundred Tomahawks, the sixty-six bombers heading for China came from British allocations. Lauchlin Currie was nothing if not resourceful in championing the cause of China. To get a few bombers for Chiang, Currie once again had resorted to robbing Churchill.

22 The Short-Term Air Program for China

After Currie took care of the volunteer recruitment program, he turned his hand to the much trickier problem of obtaining more combat planes for China. On May 9, 1941, Currie sent a "tentative" air program for China to the president and Harry Hopkins, labeled as "Lendlease" for China. He proposed 112 bombers, 340 trainers, 22 transport planes, and 147 Republic P-43s (diverted from the AAC), in addition to the 244 fighter planes released by the British (the hundred P-40s and 144 Vultee Vanguards) — 865 aircraft. Currie also surmised that the army could release a hundred P-40Bs to replace and extend the Chinese ones, because the Air Corps would soon receive more-advanced P-40s — the model Ds and Es. As for bombers, since the army had 258 outdated B-18 bombers, he presumed that it could spare 40 for China. Finally, over the next eight months, another 72 bombers, currently under construction, should be set aside for China — diverted from British as well as US Army orders.[1]

On May 9, 1941, in a memorandum to the president about this "tentative" program, Currie emphasized the "psychological importance" of giving Chiang an air force on which he could rely. The proposed quantity, he presumed, would be as much as the Chinese could handle that year. He assured the president that this modest allocation for China would not detract from either army or British procurement plans.[2]

Roosevelt replied on May 15 with little enthusiasm: Currie could negotiate about "the air program or any other thing that the Chinese request but I don't want to imply that I am at this time in favor of any of the proposals"; these could "only be finally worked out in relationship to our whole military problem and the needs of ourselves and the British."[3] Roosevelt seemed to have finally recognized that military hardware was too precious to be frittered away on morale-boosting gestures.

Where the Vultees were concerned, Currie had counted his chickens before they were hatched. For months the British had tried to resell these planes to the US government for release to China, but the US military and Harry Hopkins were taking their time to authorize the deal. On April 25, Lord Beaverbrook asked Sir Harry Self of the BAC to approach Hopkins about this issue; on May 2, Self passed the proposal to the War Department. On May 5, General Arnold responded by arguing that money spent on buying back the Vultees would reduce available funds for producing planes that the British actually wanted. On May 19, Sir Harry wrote to General James Burns of the War Department to find out the state of play. Burns replied that he had passed Self's letter to Currie, who was preparing a "general plane-aid program for China which might include the Vultees."[4] Thereafter the British heard nothing further about them.[5]

As for the B-18 bombers, General Arnold wanted these for training. The story might have ended there, but Robert Lovett, the War Department's special assistant for air affairs, tipped Currie off about another source: the British had a hundred Lockheed Hudson 414 light bombers that had not yet been shipped to England. Lovett felt that the British were piling up more planes in the United States than they could use "at once." He pointed out that the British also had bought some Douglas DB-7 bombers, which, given their "low priority rating," could be spared for China.[6]

Officials in Washington kept forgetting that Britain was at war, while their own country was at peace. "All aid short of war" was disintegrating as a slogan and a policy. Lovett did not bother to consult with British procurement agents before offering their war weapons to China.

With Lovett's backing, Currie revised his tentative program to include sixty-six bombers "taken over from old British commercial contracts," which, he argued, would relieve financial pressure on the British but still allow delivery to the Chinese under the umbrella of Lend-Lease. Currie knew full well that the British had already bought these planes with hard cash back in 1940 and that Lend-Lease technically did not apply to this equipment. On May 21, Currie sent a brief and formal letter to Henry Morgenthau in which he asked the treasury secretary for advice on obtaining aircraft for China under Lend-Lease. Currie thought it would be best to induce the British to release some planes from their "old commitments rather than any new supplies under Lend lease." Given his growing suspicions about Currie, Morgenthau was in no hurry to answer him, but on June 10 he finally replied.[7]

Morgenthau was in sympathy with what Currie was doing and agreed that it might be possible to take some planes off British contracts for China, by which he meant the Vultee planes that the British had pledged for China. Morgenthau, however, did not want anyone to pressure the British into giving up any equipment other than that which *they chose to offer.*[8] He was not about to support Currie's ruse to expropriate British planes and pass them off as Lend-Lease supplies for China.

For this new airplane program, Currie targeted thirty-three Lockheed Hudson 414 bombers that the British had bought but not yet taken delivery of—twelve to be released immediately by the British and then three a month until the end of the year. The same release schedule was to be applied to thirty-three Douglas DB-7s to China, twelve immediately and then three a month starting in June.

The AAC, however, also had its sights on the Douglas DB-7s. On May 23, General Arnold wrote to Sir Charles Portal and asked for thirty-seven DB-7s—twenty-five "urgently" needed for the Philippines and twelve for Brazil. The "urgently" was particularly questionable. If the Air Ministry turned these over to the War Department, would it accept "deferred delivery" under Lend-Lease? Portal politely turned down the request because the "transfer of even 37 D.B.7's will place us in immediate difficulties": there were shortages of every type of aircraft across all theaters, and the DB-7s would have to "fill the gap" in the Middle East created by the loss of light bombers.[9]

Chennault had ambitions for these Douglas and Hudson bombers. On June 11, he and Currie visited General Arnold and told him that the Douglas bombers could be deployed to attack Japanese supply lines, while the Lockheed Hudson had "ample range to perform missions against targets in Japan." Chennault stated that the distance from advance bases in Eastern China to industrial Japan was thirteen hundred miles. He claimed that he could fit the Lockheed with incendiary bombs to attack targets there.[10]

Could the Lockheed have been used as Chennault suggested? In principle, it had a range of thirty-three hundred miles.[11] In practice, with a full bomb load, it had a range of just under two thousand miles, enough for a round trip from a base such as Chuchow (Quzhou) in southeast China to Taiwan or Nagasaki (a major industrial hub) but not to and from Tokyo. There was another drawback. Fighter escort would be required, but the P-40 Tomahawk had a maximum range of 950 miles. Without fighter escort, these bombers could never have gotten past Japanese air defenses to raid Nagasaki or Tokyo: enemy fighters would have brought them down before the bombers approached the coast. As for the Douglas DB-7 (also known as the Havoc), it had a range of just over a thousand miles, so it could have raided Taiwan but no other targets in Japanese territory.

Both medium bombers, however, could reach Japanese bases in Thailand or northern Indochina from bases in Yunnan with P-40 escorts. But the Chinese already had Russian medium bombers that could accomplish such a mission. So in tactical terms, the diversion of these British aircraft to China provided nothing new. By contrast, the British needed medium-range bombers to field against the Germans in Europe, but Currie was too focused on his own agenda to ever think through the strategic implications of his scheme for either China or Britain. All that mattered to him was the psychological impact of plane aid on Chiang Kai-shek.

On May 19, Currie sent his revised air program to the Joint Aircraft Committee (JAC), which was composed of representatives from army and naval aviation, as well as the British purchasing agents. Soon thereafter, the JAC met in his office. The British made clear that they could not sacrifice the sixty-six bombers, because they were needed in Australia and elsewhere. On May 23, the chief of the air staff, Charles Portal, sent a personal message to General Arnold: much as the British wished to help, they could not give up any of the Douglas DB-7s; heavy reinforcements for the Middle East had created a shortage of light bombers.[12] A few days later, Portal confirmed his refusal in a cable to the embassy in Washington.[13] The British air attaché George Pirie then sent a letter about Portal's decision to Lauchlin Currie, with a copy to Harry Hopkins.[14] Pirie hoped that Currie might persuade his government to hand over some of their own bombers to China.[15]

As far as the British were concerned, the dossier was closed. They had acted in accordance with a procedure established in the conclusions of the America Britain Canada (ABC) staff talks: at the end of March, all the delegates produced an agreement known as ABC-2, which enshrined the following principle: the US chiefs of staff, in consultation with the British military mission in Washington, would "jointly advise the president on the allocation of air equipment" among all the different air forces of the United States and the British Commonwealth.[16] Between the lines, ABC-2 was designed to protect the British from unilateral decisions by their American supplier about the allocation of planes. Therefore, when Portal rejected the request for the sixty-six bombers, the British believed that they would hear nothing more about it.

The matter was not settled for Lauchlin Currie. On May 28, he submitted another version of his China air program directly to Knox and Stimson, which they eventually forwarded to the Joint Army Navy Board composed of General Marshall and Admiral Stark. In a cover letter to Knox, Currie referred to a revised "Short term Aircraft Program for China under the Lease-lend act," but the actual document was titled "A Short-term Aircraft Program for China" and labeled thereafter as Joint Board (J.B.) 355.[17] As the archival record makes clear, the British never received a copy.[18]

The Joint Planning Committee, composed of General L. T. Gerow for the army and Rear Admiral R. K. Turner for the navy, agreed with Currie's proposal, and on July 9 they submitted J.B. 355 to Marshall and Stark for approval. Included in their assessment was a significant recommendation. By this stage, the US military knew more than previously about Sino-British cooperation in the Far East. Gerow and Turner pointed out that the British were maintaining liaison with the Chinese in the Burma Road area and establishing a "military mission for employment in aid of China in case of war between Japan and Great Britain." The army and navy analysts did not believe it "advisable to turn over control of equipment and personnel provided by the United States [to the Chinese] to the British, until some understanding can be reached. . . . The supply of equipment and personnel from the United States can best be handled by the United States government through the Army."[19]

This passage must have referred to discussions between General Dennys and his Chinese counterparts about developing Mission 204: that included deployment of the AVG and the RAF once the Japanese had declared war on the British Empire. In this memorandum, Gerow and Turner revealed their priorities: the US military should maintain control over American hardware provided under Lend-Lease and not entrust it to some combination of Chinese and British officers. They betrayed not only their mistrust of British influence over the Chinese, but also a desire to diminish it. Thereafter it became their goal to increase the influence of the US military, especially of the army, over security arrangements with China.

On July 18, the secretaries of the navy and army recommended J.B. 355 to the president, who on July 23 put his signature to it. A month later, on August 18, British purchasing agents attended a JAC meeting and learned for the first time that the president had authorized the reallocation of sixty-six British-owned bombers to the Chinese.[20] It fell to a senior RAF officer to find out how this request had bypassed his colleagues and reached the president.

In June 1941, Air Marshal Arthur Travers Harris—later known as "Bomber" Harris—had arrived in Washington with a naval delegation.[21] In July and August, other British officials turned up before the secret talks between Roosevelt and Churchill in Placentia Bay near Argentia on the coast of Newfoundland (August 8–11, 1941). After this famous first encounter between the two leaders, most of the participants returned to Washington.

On August 21, "Bomber" Harris related a sorry tale to Sir Charles Portal about the loss of "66 priceless and irreplaceable aircraft" for which, nearly two years before, the British had paid hard cash. He turned to every man of influence in Washington to unravel Currie's work and persuade the president to give the British back their bombers.[22]

23 Currie Gets in a Jam

On August 18, Lauch Currie suddenly realized that there was a flaw in his near-perfect ploy to deliver bombers to China. As he explained to his boss, Harry Hopkins, the Joint Board had approved his plan to divert to China sixty-six bombers, which, he alleged, were "at the bottom of the British list of requirements." Once the president had endorsed the program, Currie had assumed it would be done forthwith. He had just learned, however, that the army needed a waiver from the British; but "in the meantime," as he wrote to Hopkins, "I had told the Chinese that the President had approved the recommendation . . . you can see what a jam I am in."[1]

It was all too true: Currie was in a jam right up to his neck. On August 19, General Arnold formally requested the Air Ministry in London to release the sixty-six light bombers.[2] Harris, on hearing what had happened, explained the situation to Sir Charles Portal: the British purchasing agents had no idea that the Joint Board would recommend to the president the dispatch of these bombers to China. In contravention of ABC-2, the British had been denied an opportunity to present their case against the diversion.[3] As Harris put it, Marshall and Stark had approved Currie's plan without knowing or caring about British air requirements; they had recommended the transaction to Roosevelt on the basis of a general declaration (as stated in the air program) that Britain had "a predominant interest in maintaining China as a belligerent."[4]

Harris recounted this subterfuge to General Arnold, who was sorry and "ashamed of the way the matter had been handled." Arnold admitted — perhaps disingenuously — that the British case had never reached him. Although the whole thing was a "headache," he had to ask Harris and the BPC to give up the planes, since he could not go against a presidential directive.[5]

Harris went to Lord Beaverbrook, who was then in Washington; the latter agreed that the British should mount resistance. Beaverbrook protested to Harry Hopkins, to the director of British-Lend-Lease Averill Harriman, and apparently to Roosevelt himself, but to no avail.[6] In the meantime, Currie leaned heavily on Hopkins, the army's General Burns, and Harriman to obtain a waiver from the British.[7] When Harris spoke to Harriman, the latter advised that the British would have no choice but to release the planes in order to avoid "unpleasantness" for the president.[8] Harriman felt that Roosevelt was "irrevocably committed" to this course because the Chinese had already been informed that they would receive the aircraft. He wondered if some other bombers could be "raked" up in England: perhaps if the British gave up these medium bombers now, they could receive half of all heavy bombers produced in months to come. Harris accepted that this might be the basis for a compromise but still wanted to impress on everyone that the British would make things "thoroughly uncomfortable" for Currie or anyone else who tried to impose this sort of unilateral decision on the British again.

Harris appealed to Roosevelt's son James, who served as a US liaison officer with the British on the staff of Colonel Bill Donovan, head of Special Operations. James promised to raise the matter with the president and agreed that his father appeared "to have been led up the Garden path by Currie": in his view Roosevelt must have presumed that the bombers were Lend-Lease or US Army planes rather than paid-up British contracts.[9] After all, Currie had originally referred to his plan as a short-term program under Lend-Lease.

When Harris confronted Currie, the latter "confined himself to covering a guilty conscience by a rapid descent from a pseudo strategic harangue to schoolboy abuse of the British in their conduct of war in general and their abandonment of China in particular."[10] In the view of Harris, Currie was covering his tracks after creating a crisis "by his high handed and misconceived assumption of dictatorial power over . . . our property. He is unrepentant and even at present engaged . . . on similar action to extract Tomahawk spares for China at expense of M.E.'s [Middle East] desperate need."[11]

Even Harris could not have imagined how high-handed Currie was.

When the British would not give in, on August 26 Currie sent a memorandum to the president pointing out that the army required the British to release the sixty-six bombers back to the army before it could in turn reallocate them to China. Currie then drafted for Roosevelt a telegram to send to Churchill: the president would explain that since Chiang had been notified earlier about the bombers, he, Roosevelt, was "embarrassed by their not being available"; he would also request full armament for these planes, as well as a hundred tons of incendiary bombs from the British, as the US government did not have any.[12]

This was an extraordinary situation: Currie, with the rank of administrative assistant, was holding the president to ransom, by asking him to go cap in hand to Churchill in order to cover up his own mess. If senior US officials failed to make the British cave in, Currie would make the president send the cable to Churchill, in order to get the bombers and bombs for China.

If someone was going to lose face over Currie's jam, however, it could not be the president. Harry Hopkins and Averill Harriman began to soothe the ruffled feathers of Bomber Harris and to pin all blame on Currie. On August 28, Hopkins finally confessed to Harris that the British had been treated in an intolerable manner. Echoing Currie's own words, Hopkins admitted that "the U.S. personnel concerned" had gotten everyone in an "inescapable jamb"; he admitted that Currie had taken it upon himself to wire directly to Chiang Kai-shek about the availability of bombers for China.[13] Hopkins must have been embarrassed by the prospect of Roosevelt being forced to beg equipment from Churchill. He explained to Harris that since the US military had no bombers, the Americans were now "suppliants" for British assistance. Employing a veiled threat, he suggested that if the British did not allow the medium bombers to go to China, some portion of the heavy bombers that the Air Ministry had already ordered might be diverted to the AAC. Hopkins told Harris that he was "staving off" the president's cable to the prime minister, since "that would be merely an unfair transfer of the headache from the President to the Prime Minister."[14]

On August 31, the Air Ministry gave in: the vice chief of the air staff, Sir Archibald Sinclair, felt that it would be better to hand over the sixty-six bombers, which were still in the United States, than to divert to China any aircraft already in RAF service. Sinclair advised Harris that the loss of the sixty-six bombers would be unwelcome but unlikely to jeopardize the fleet's expansion.[15] He then waited for the Americans to make the next move.

On September 2, Hopkins told Currie that the president did not want to send a note directly to Churchill. So Hopkins leveled with Sir Archibald Sinclair: Chiang Kai-shek had been "advised inadvertently" that sixty-six medium bombers were to be released to the Chinese; the president was anxious to deliver these bombers, but as the US Army did not have any to take immediately from production, he earnestly hoped that the British would find a way to give the Chinese the bombers, as well as ammunition and a hundred incendiary bombs.[16]

On September 5, the Air Ministry agreed to send to China fifty thousand four-pound incendiary bombs (totaling a hundred tons), and by September 12, 1941, it was preparing to transfer all sixty-six bombers as well as accessories — bombs, guns, and ammunition — to the US government for the Chinese.[17] Given the hopeless state of logistics, however, none of the bombers ever reached Rangoon before Pearl Harbor.

As regards the hundred tons of incendiary bombs, Currie revealed a genuine desire to stick it to the British. In September 1941, Currie pointed out to the British that the US government, not the Chinese government, was asking them for these munitions; he reminded them that this was "a reciprocal measure. In the light of the overall picture of the billions of dollars of articles being lend-leased to the British government, we believe that the particular items requested which are not immediately needed for the defense of Great Britain should be furnished this Government . . . we would remind you that we are purchasing defense articles in Canada to lend-lease to your Government."[18]

In October 1941, the British government suggested that the Chinese should pay for the incendiaries out of an unspent pound sterling credit dating back to 1939 — not an unreasonable demand, given the subterfuge to which they had already been subjected. Currie rejected the British proposal. In his view, the Chinese should not have to pay the British directly for the incendiaries, which instead should be part of British Lend-Lease: the British Treasury would include this item in the big bill to be settled eventually after the war. Once again, an armchair general in Washington was prescribing what the British did or did not require to fight the war with Germany.

Furthermore, by forcing the British to channel this matériel through the

US government, Currie was depriving the British of any credit for supplying some matériel to China. To the fury of Lord Beaverbrook at MAP in the autumn of 1941, Currie also managed to draw on Lend-Lease funds to obtain machine guns and ammunition from Canada to deliver to China.[19]

In hindsight, the dispute over bombers may seem like a storm in a teacup, but it revealed troubling trends in Roosevelt's style of governing, his command over Far East policy, and the organization of Lend-Lease. The summer of 1941 was a significant transition period. When the president appointed Harry Hopkins to direct Lend-Lease, Henry Morgenthau dismantled the liaison committee through which he had previously matched the supply and demand of airplanes and armament for foreign procurement agents. Meanwhile, Hopkins juggled assignments between London, Moscow, and Washington, which interfered with his ability to develop a new organization for Lend-Lease. Lauch Currie exploited this bureaucratic vacuum.

Roosevelt had much on his mind: the imposition of an oil embargo on Japan and preparations for the secret conference with Churchill in August 1941, to name just two items on the agenda. He probably did not keep track of each new stage in the evolution of Currie's bomber program for China after he commented on the earliest draft in May 1941. Given the title of Currie's proposal—"Short term Aircraft Program for China under the Lease-lend act"—a busy president was bound to presume that the bombers were an entirely new Lend-Lease allocation to China, not in effect the expropriation of aircraft that the British had already owned since 1940.

That this was the case can also be deduced from the wording of Roosevelt's approval for Currie's program. On July 23, 1941, he scribbled on the cover page of J.B. 355, "O.K.—but restudy military mission versus the attaché method FDR."[20] What exactly did he mean?

In July 1941, the State Department and the War Department had crossed swords about the status of the liaison officer who would handle Lend-Lease in China. Lauch Currie later described this turf war to James McHugh in Chungking: The State Department wanted a military attaché who would be responsible to Clarence Gauss, the US ambassador in China. The War Department, however, wanted its own man to head a full military mission that would be responsible for Lend-Lease supplies in China—that preference was in line with Marshall's insistence that a US government official should have some control over the AVG and its equipment. In early July, General Marshall proposed Brigadier General John M. Magruder to lead the American Military Mission to China (AMMISCA). His principal assignment was to serve as the Lend-Lease liaison officer between the Chinese and US governments, but other objectives might shelter under that umbrella — such as keeping an eye on the AVG.[21]

In August 1941, Currie ought to have been fired for getting himself and Roosevelt in a jam over US relations with Britain, as well as with China. One can only speculate about the reasons that may have persuaded the president and Hopkins to save his skin. First of all, there might have been embarrassing speculation about his sudden departure from the White House, which would have invited journalists to probe into a squabble among allies over planes. Second, even if he had made a mess of things, Currie was hardworking, extremely clever, and articulate. On reading J.B. 355, R. K. Turner, the navy's chief of plans, congratulated Currie on "his fine command of ideas, language and expression. . . . If he is out of a job I would like to have him work for the Navy . . . to express the thoughts that we are so dumb about."[22] Since 1939, Currie had been the president's amanuensis to draft memorandums on a range of topics. In 1940, he became the chief analyst of plane aid for China, which fit in with the broad theme of US-China policy as defined by Roosevelt. China, having called for help, would get America's help in the form of aircraft. Finally, in August 1941, the president's men gathered around to prevent any embarrassment to Roosevelt caused by Currie's faux pas. The president may never have been fully aware of the jam that Currie had created for everyone.

The fracas over bombers for China also marked the start of testy relations between Bomber Harris and his American military counterparts: over the next three years, the wary attitude of Harris toward Americans hardened into opposition to any efforts on their part to interfere in his bombing strategy against Germany.[23] Currie, however, could have cared less about ruffling British feathers, especially those of Bomber Harris.

In mid-August 1941, T. V. Soong observed that Chiang had never been happier than when he heard the news about the sixty-six bombers.[24] The generalissimo apparently had no idea that the aircraft had been diverted from the British. On September 16, he finally expressed "keen appreciation" to Clark Kerr for the release of bombers from consignments destined for England: this appears to have been the only sign of gratitude to the British by Chiang on this score.[25]

But Soong and Chiang were running out of patience with American charity. On September 18, in a cable to Chiang, Soong commented that thus far the administration had offered matériel "out of comradeship": it was time to convince them that they had to engage in military cooperation with China and not just send supplies "to express friendship."[26] As the Chinese had made clear, they wanted fighter planes and the long-range Flying Fortress; the medium bombers were no substitute for these. In terms of quantity, sixty-six light or medium bombers constituted only a third of the 150 bombers that Chiang had demanded. The range of the Lockheed Hudson was insufficient for bombing Tokyo. Finally, nothing could make up for the slow pace of delivery. The Lockheeds would not be shipped until October and were only due to arrive in the spring of 1942.[27] Currie also had not factored into his calculation that all the munitions for these bombers were in England and would have to be shipped from there to the United States. As it turned out, these were not loaded onto freighters until late November 1941.[28]

General Marshall and the Air Corps went along with Currie's air program primarily because it did not impinge on their stocks of aircraft and armament. By the summer of 1941, Marshall regarded army rearmament and reinforcement of the Philippines as a greater priority than all aid short of war for the British and a small amount of air aid for China. No great fan of the British, those "peculiar" people, Marshall had recommended the diversion of a hundred British Tomahawks to China in order to fend off any claims on AAC aircraft. As long as the War Department did not have to release its precious bombers to China, it endorsed the efforts of Lauch Currie to divert as many planes as he liked from the British.

When Marshall's chief of plans General Gerow approved the short-term aircraft program, he revealed the army's mistrust of Sino-British military cooperation, especially where the AVG was concerned. Marshall now wanted to exercise the "proviso" designed to extend the army's control over the AVG. After John Magruder reached the Far East, he was to judge the state of the AVG's combat readiness, based on his inspection of the group in Burma and his consultation with the Chinese government.[29]

O n August 26, Roosevelt announced the appointment of John Magruder
to lead AMMISCA, which the president compared to the Lend-Lease
mission on its way to Russia; both were in keeping with "the world effort
in resistance to movements of conquest by force."[1] In late August, Cordell
Hull advised the British Embassy that the purpose of the new mission was
to make China feel that it was being kept in the picture and to deliver a
kind of "backhander" to Japan — another morale-boosting gesture rather
than genuine military advice or delivery of material aid.[2]

The War Department defined the mission more narrowly: Magruder
should establish a "detail" for Lend-Lease — that is, a regional office in
Chungking. He and his group of some twenty-five officers would coordinate
Chinese requests with another detail inside the War Department that would
report to the new Lend-Lease organization led by Harry Hopkins.

Now that Currie had obtained some bombers for China, Chennault
wanted a second volunteer group to man the Lockheed Hudsons, while
instructors hired by CAMCO would train CAF pilots to fly the DB-7s. On
September 11, Currie sought permission from the president to authorize this
second volunteer bomber group. He referred to the president's "earlier authorization" under which the Intercontinent Company had hired 101 pilots and
181 ground personnel. If there was such an authorization, no written version
exists; perhaps Currie was referring to the verbal permission Roosevelt gave
him in March 1941 to kick-start recruitment for the first volunteer group.
Currie recognized that there was a shortage of military pilots at that time,
but he presumed that the AAC would have some to spare by October when at

last it reaped the rewards of the training expansion program started in 1940.[3]

On September 15, Roosevelt told Currie to "get in touch right away with General Magruder and work this out with him."[4] On September 18, however, Currie confessed to the president that he could not "work it out" with Magruder: the latter would not take up the issue of bomber crews with his department. Magruder advised Currie that the president would have to issue another directive to the services. Currie asked the president if he would "mind signing the rather mildly worded directive attached?"[5] Roosevelt duly did so.

Chennault and Richard Aldworth of CAMCO worked out in detail, down to the lowliest clerk, the personnel requirements for new bombardment groups and came up with a total of 359 personnel, of which 82 were staff officers.[6] On September 29, Chennault forwarded this list to Soong, who passed it on to Currie. Armed with these job specifications and the president's authorization, Currie once again approached Robert Lovett at the War Department.

This time Lovett was far less willing to part with the "cream" of the Air Corps than he had been in August 1941. On October 17, he wrote to Currie that AAC training centers had already been canvassed for personnel and "lost many experienced officers." Furthermore, the department was preparing units for overseas duty (a reference to Hawaii and the Philippines), and any reduction of personnel from the main training schools would disrupt this program. Nevertheless, Lovett offered a list of smaller airfields across the country where Aldworth could go in search of candidates for the bomber group. By November, however, the navy was so short of personnel that it refused to take any part in this recruitment drive.[7]

When the British found out about the Magruder mission to China, they wondered how best to respond to this latest move by the administration. Should they set up a comparable mission, independent of Brigadier General Dennys, or try to coordinate Sino-British with Sino-American programs, or simply maintain informal liaison with the Magruder mission?[8] The British chose the latter option. They began by holding a meeting with Magruder in Washington before he left.

In July 1941, the War Department had expressed its displeasure with Sino-British military cooperation in comments on J.B. 355. On September 9, Magruder met with British officials in Washington and again made clear that he and his army colleagues took a dim view of cooperation between

Britain and China. During this briefing, Magruder intimated the British were "adopting a somewhat unsympathetic attitude towards China and . . . do not fully appreciate consequent unfavorable reaction on Chinese morale."[9] The British tried to set the record straight about aid for China and gave him a list of arms and ammunition released to date: the largest single item was the fifty thousand four-pound incendiary bombs.[10] Furthermore, they were setting up an aircraft factory and depot in Calcutta to store all airplanes or parts destined for China.[11] In a second meeting on September 12 with the British military attaché, Magruder asserted that the American policy toward China went further than the British because it aimed for a gradual buildup of China's armed forces over the long term so that they could eventually carry out full-scale operations. The short-term goal of US policy was to improve the Burma Road.[12]

In his meetings with the British, Magruder reflected the discomfort about Sino-British relations that his superiors in the War Department had expressed earlier in the year. His gloss on the superiority of US policy toward China was based solely on the premise that US aid was long term. The Chinese and British could not help but have a different perspective. The former were already at war with Japan, and the latter sensed that they soon would be. Neither had time for the long term: they had worked for months on measures they could deploy as soon as Japan declared war on the British Empire.

Perhaps it was awkward for US officials to accept that two countries who were both at war had more in common with each other than either had with the United States, which was at peace and determined to remain so. Once John Magruder left Washington for the Far East, however, he began to spread his wings and departed from the narrow guidelines that his superiors had set for his mission.

On his way to China in September, Magruder stopped in Manila to confer with General Douglas MacArthur, whom George Marshall had recently appointed as commander of the US Army Forces in the Far East. MacArthur outlined a scheme for intelligence gathering. He wanted Magruder to stay close to Brigadier General Dennys and make contact with Vasily Chuikov, the head of the Russian military mission in Chungking. The three should meet regularly and make sure that any advice that each gave to China had been agreed beforehand by all of them. Moreover, MacArthur told Magruder to investigate the possibilities of using B-17s to bomb Japan, possibly by re-fueling at landing grounds in Eastern China and returning via Vladivostok and Central China, whereas George Marshall had rejected this option in favor of the Philippines as the platform for bombing Japan. Macarthur knew firsthand all the drawbacks of his air bases and seemed willing to entrust B-17s to the Chinese.

Magruder went on to Singapore and met Brooke-Popham on October 7.[13] Brooke-Popham applied much the same terms to Magruder as he had to Chennault: he was a "strong character" and would be a good man to work with; he felt that Magruder understood the need for secrecy in dealing with the Chinese. The C-IN-C noted what a poor opinion Magruder had of Chinese aviators. As Magruder had yet to visit China, he presumably retained impressions he had formed in the 1920s and published in *Foreign Affairs* in 1931. Magruder told Brooke-Popham that the United States and Britain needed to help Chiang develop the CAF and hoped that the British might be able to train some Chinese pilots in India—possibly a reference to the development of air facilities at Calcutta.[14]

Three weeks later, on October 30, Magruder reached Chungking and had his first interview with the generalissimo and Madame Chiang, who, as so often, interpreted for her husband. In this conversation were echoes of others between the Chiangs and foreign military attachés over the years. It was as if Madame Chiang had a tape in her head that she switched on whenever the subject of their rotten air force came up.[15]

Magruder reported to Marshall and Stimson that Chiang regarded his air force as a "complete wash-out." The generalissimo contended that AMMISCA should reorganize every aspect of the CAF and place a senior American air officer in command who would have "full and absolute authority, free from any and all existing [Chinese] Air Corps interference or politics."[16] That was almost exactly what they had asked of the British air attaché Robert Aitken three years before.

Based on this conversation with Chiang, Magruder outlined for the War Department a plan to take over the AVG as well as the CAF. Magruder empha-sized that in its current state the AVG was not likely to improve substantially, even if it received the parts and personnel planned: the pilot training of the AVG in Burma and the CAF in China was not up to standard. These observations, he claimed, were in no way a reflection of Chennault, but it had to be acknowledged that "this outfit is . . . a suspended organization and . . . has no sound composition or basis for moral[e]. It lacks . . . firm feeling or attachments for either the U.S. or to any foundations in China."

Magruder proposed that a senior US Air Corps officer with a staff of at least five officers take charge of the Chinese Air Force and also "immediate command of the A.V.G." This same commanding officer would gradually assemble a Chinese force formed from the best of the CAF. With integration of the command of the AVG and the CAF, a substantial air force of five hundred planes could "without doubt" be realized. Magruder recognized that the US Army would inherit huge difficulties if it became responsible for these different air units in China. Therefore, he regarded such intervention as an emergency measure.[17]

There is no reason to believe that the generalissimo himself had made any of these points about the AVG; Magruder was expressing his own views. Nonetheless, in reports to Stimson and Marshall, Magruder implied that Chiang would have allowed an AAC officer to supersede Chennault and make him redundant as AVG commander. That would have suited Chiang because, in doing so, the US military would inevitably have become entangled in the war with Japan.

Rumors about Magruder's ambitions soon got back to the State Department and Lauch Currie. Stanley Hornbeck, chief political adviser to Secretary Hull, feared that Magruder would end up on a collision course with Chiang if he tried to take total control of China's military aviation and made his mission solely accountable to the War Department.[18] On November 12, Currie wrote to Chennault, "It has been suggested that we supply personnel for the reorganization and operation of the whole Chinese air Force including the A.V.G."[19] Currie assured him that this would be impractical and offered some ideas for preempting Magruder: Chennault should select the best Chinese pilots to serve under his tactical command, while Currie would try to dispatch some American staff officers to help Chennault in his "larger duties," releasing more planes to the CAF or letting the Air Corps assume responsibility for CAF operations. Currie wondered if there were facilities in Burma that would be adequate for training Chinese as well as American units. However unsatisfactory the AVG might be, Currie, with support from the State Department, was determined to keep Chennault in charge and the War Department at bay.

US officials were not alone in worrying about the AVG. At precisely the same time, General Dennys and Air Vice Marshal Brooke-Popham were expressing doubts about the capacity of the volunteer group to function as a combat force alongside RAF units once war was declared. By the end of November, however, one man in the British War Cabinet was prepared to throw his weight behind Chennault and the volunteer group: Winston Spencer Churchill.

n late August 1941, the C-IN-C Far East, Robert Brooke-Popham, had reorganized the No. 60 Squadron based at Mingaladon near Rangoon: one half retained sixteen Blenheim bombers, while the other received sixteen Brewster Buffaloes "with generous reserves," as well as eighty thousand rounds of .50 caliber ammunition—a drop in the bucket, but it was all that could be spared from stocks in Singapore. He intended to send another squadron of Brewster Buffaloes to Burma as soon as one became available. Finally, he dispatched to Burma a large consignment of bombs, including 960 bombs each weighing 250 pounds.[1] In the weeks before Pearl Harbor, this redistribution of assets left the RAF in Malaya with four Buffalo squadrons, one Blenheim bomber squadron, and a few units with obsolete planes—in all, about two hundred first-line planes.[2]

In mid-October 1941, Brooke-Popham also secured a pledge from Chennault that if Rangoon came under Japanese attack, three AVG squadrons with eighteen Tomahawks each would defend the city. They agreed that two AVG squadrons would use a base at Zyautkwin, twenty-five miles to the north of Rangoon, and the third would be at Mingaladon.[3]

That was the long-term plan, but within a few weeks the Chinese and British became convinced that the enemy was about to make its long-awaited move. Chiang's discussions with John Magruder about the AAC possibly managing the CAF and the AVG were related to this new threat perception. Chinese intelligence suggested that toward the end of November, the Japanese would seize Kunming in order to cut off the Burma Road. The generalissimo wanted air support to reinforce his troops in the defense of Yunnan.[4]

In Washington, on October 30, 1941, T. V. Soong pressed Roosevelt to immediately deliver the "modest allotment" of airplanes and ordnance already promised to China: Chiang still wanted 350 fighter planes, whereas only 100 P-40s had been delivered. He also expected 150 bombers, of which 66 had been promised but none shipped.[5] On this memo Soong added a hand-written note that aircraft were urgently needed "to meet attack on Burma road through Indo-China." Roosevelt added his own note, "to H.H. [Harry Hopkins] please hurry, FDR." For at least a few days in early November, Roosevelt took seriously the threat of a Japanese enemy offensive against Kunming from Indochina.

In Chungking, the British ambassador, Archibald Clark Kerr, suspected that the Chinese were crying wolf. On November 1, he listened politely to Chiang's "well-worn but cogent arguments" that Kunming was now "the key to the Pacific" and the Allies had to intervene to defend it.[6] Chiang stressed to Clark Kerr that if the Japanese took the Burma Road and Kunming, it would mean the end of Chinese resistance: the enemy would then push south to take Malaya. He insisted that "only British air support for Chinese ground troops could save the country and preserve peace in the Pacific."[7] Furthermore, the United States would have to supply the RAF in Singapore and Malaya.

But the British had in hand a telegram by John Magruder dated October 28, which revealed how seriously Magruder took this new Japanese threat. In his words, there were "strong indications" of a Japanese air attack on Kunming that would put an end to Chinese resistance. In his view, the CAF was useless, and the AVG would not be combat-ready for months to come; therefore the only way to provide air support for the Chinese army was to deploy British or US air units from Singapore or Manila in time to keep the Japanese from seizing the capital of Yunnan.[8]

Magruder's telegram may have influenced the War Cabinet to ignore Clark Kerr and take the threat to Kunming seriously. The British, however, were not to know that Magruder's communications fell on deaf ears at the War Department. For George Marshall, reinforcement of the Philippines continued to take precedence over any US Army Air Corps involvement in China. A few weeks later in November, Marshall refused to allow the diversion of antiaircraft guns to China, stating that it would be an "outrage" to deny General MacArthur this matériel and send it instead "on a round-about uncertain voyage up into China."[9]

In Chungking as well as London, British officials now accepted that a crisis in Yunnan was on the horizon and pinned hopes on the AVG to have some deterrent value. Brooke-Popham concurred that intelligence reports pointed to "preparations for action somewhere in South West China." On November 5, the War Office contacted Brooke-Popham and stated categorically that, in light of this threat, "the only hope of helping Chinese in time repeat in time would be in affording assistance to Chennault"; Brooke-Popham should send some experienced officers as volunteers to serve in the group and "expedite operational readiness of International Force."[10]

On November 5, Brooke-Popham had referred to a recent inspection of the AVG by RAF staff and assured the War Office that, by the end of the month, Chennault would be ready to transfer his squadrons to China. Brooke-Popham stated that once he was satisfied that the AVG was up to combat standard, he would form another squadron of Brewster Buffaloes for Burma and suggested that the pilots—mostly New Zealanders and Australians—should have the same volunteer status as the AVG pilots. Before committing himself to this course, however, Brooke-Popham intended to assess Chennault's "exact status" and needs.[11]

On November 8, Group Commander Darvel and Wing Commander Tuckey, two RAF staff officers from Singapore, went to Toungoo to inspect the AVG. Chennault gave them all the "dope" and wrote up a candid assessment of his group's deficiencies, which he sent to Currie and T. V. Soong: seven planes had crashed, twenty-three were disabled, and twenty-six were grounded for lack of tires, which tended to have a very short life because of the climate in Burma.[12] There was a laundry list of parts the group desperately needed to keep the Tomahawks airborne; Chennault hoped that these could be dispatched from the Philippines, the United States. or the Middle East, where the RAF also operated Tomahawks. Joe Alsop alerted Currie that if the AVG could just get an adequate number of tires, the group could put sixty-eight planes into the air. If Manila or Hawaii could immediately supply tires and other parts for the P-40s, they would be compensated later by supplies off the AVG's December orders. Alsop warned Currie, as Chennault had done before, that if for lack of tires the combat group could not operate, "American prestige and Chinese morale will drop"[13]

RAF observers summarized all of Chennault's dope for Brooke-Popham: The AVG had only forty-one planes available for operations. Neither oxygen nor synchronized guns were functioning correctly. Given the lack of spares, the group could not repair damaged planes and bring them back into service; shortages of tires and undercarriages were particularly severe. In fact, no spares would reach Rangoon before February 1942.

In light of such acute maintenance issues, Brooke-Popham estimated that the AVG could field one squadron of eighteen aircraft to sustain "intensive operations" for about a week. He came to the conclusion that the AVG should not move into China until it could deploy two fully functional squadrons. Until that time, he would refrain from forming another squadron of sixteen Brewster Buffaloes on a volunteer basis to cooperate with the AVG in Burma. To accelerate the delivery of spare parts to the AVG, he sent requests to General MacArthur in the Philippines and to all Commonwealth missions for spare tires as well as undercarriages to supply the AVG Tomahawks.[14]

On the ground, Brooke-Popham was pulling one way, but in London, Winston Churchill was pulling the other. On November 2, Chiang Kai-shek wrote one of his most heartrending appeals to the president of the United States and the British prime minister: he needed their help immediately to keep the Japanese from taking Kunming and Chinese resistance from collapsing: "I have nothing that I can call an Air Force to pit against what the Japanese would bring to bear upon me. . . . If, however in this battle Japan's Air force can be checked or even smashed, her power to enter upon what I have called fresh enterprises will be much diminished." Chiang pointed out that "the American volunteer air force now under training is good but very small. Our only hope is that British air force in Malay with American co-operation may come into action and support American volunteer and existing Chinese Air Force. The British Air Force could cooperate as a part [of] Chinese Air Force or assume the role of an international volunteer force. The result would be to save China and to save the Pacific."[15]

This plea from the generalissimo made a profound impression on the prime minister. On November 5, in a cable to Roosevelt, Churchill stated that he shared Chiang's anxiety about the alleged Japanese plans to take Kunming and was receptive to his call for air assistance. Chiang almost certainly was "crying wolf." Nonetheless, Churchill gave every sign of believing him and was "prepared to send pilots and even some planes if they could arrive in time." This was a curious formulation. In an earlier draft he had written, "Nonetheless I should be prepared to send pilots and aeroplanes, if they could possibly arrive in time—But they cannot. The crisis is likely to be upon us before then."[16]

In fact, Churchill and his advisers knew that there was no way to transfer RAF squadrons from Malaya to Burma in time to preempt the purported attack on Yunnan. Therefore, he wanted Roosevelt to "remind" Japan that any such aggression would be in "open disregard" of US policy. As in February 1941, there was still some hope that a stiff diplomatic warning might postpone the crisis.

On November 7, the president responded to the "Former Naval Person," as Churchill styled himself in correspondence with Roosevelt. Only a week before, Roosevelt seemed to have accepted that the Japanese were planning an offensive against Kunming, but now he dismissed the possibility. He pointed out that there were no signs of mass mobilization in Indochina for such an operation. Nor, given "Japan's present mood," did he feel that there was any point in delivering new "remonstrances," which might have just the opposite effect of a deterrent. Instead Roosevelt seemed to side with George Marshall about denying matériel to China that was needed for the Philippines. The president stated that continued reinforcement of the Philippines in parallel to British measures to strengthen the defenses of Malaya would "increase Japan's hesitation." He confirmed that he would do what he could to "facilitate the building up of the American volunteer air force" in terms of personnel and matériel.[17] He indicated that he would reply to Chiang in the following week but took his time to do so.

For years the Foreign Office had cautioned that the British should stay in lockstep with the Americans on Far East policy. On this occasion, however, Churchill ignored Roosevelt's dismissive assessment of the latest Japanese threat to the region. The Chiefs of Staff drafted but did not yet send instructions to Brooke-Popham about setting up a volunteer squadron formed of Brewster Buffaloes and ANZAC pilots: they had already laid the groundwork to ask the governments of Australia and New Zealand to release pilots to serve as volunteers in this new unit on the same terms as the AVG.[18]

On November 9, Churchill sent a brief note to the chief of staff, General Ismay: "Let us hurry up the arrangements for sending volunteer pilots and airplanes to join Chennault's party."[19] Such was his impatience that when he heard nothing further from Ismay, Churchill wrote again to the Chiefs of Staff on November 11. As he bluntly put it, there was no longer any point in weighing the pros and cons of sending another squadron to Burma from Singapore: "Surely we ought to make up our minds and give some definite lead to the C.-in-C. Why do we not say, 'We should like you to send BUFFALO and BLENHEIM squadrons at once unless you have any serious objection to raise.'"[20]

That day Churchill also cabled a forthright message to Chiang: even though he was unsure that Kunming was the next target, he felt certain that South China was in the line of fire. Therefore, Churchill assured Chiang that he was trying "with all speed" to strengthen the International Air Force—that is, the AVG.[21]

True to his word, Roosevelt bided his time in replying to Chiang's letter of November 2. He left this task to the State Department and on November 11 approved its draft response. On November 14, Stanley Hornbeck handed to Ambassador Hu Shih a letter for Chiang from the president. Whereas Churchill got straight to the point about supporting the AVG, Roosevelt put his signature to a set of anodyne and evasive arguments.

State Department scribes drafted the following excuses for the president to give to Chiang for not offering greater assistance: There were competing demands on matériel that prevented the US government from doing much more for China. Furthermore, the Japanese attack on Yunnan was exaggerated, for there were no obvious signs of troop mobilization in Indochina. The president urged Chiang to continue reinforcing Yunnan, while the United States would do its best to speed the flow of Lend-Lease supplies for China, as well as more equipment and personnel for the "American volunteer air force." By way of reassurance, the president highlighted reinforcement of the Philippines and Hawaii, which he regarded as "an ever present and significant factor in the whole situation"—whatever that was supposed to mean.[22] Here was further evidence of how well the War Department deluded itself and

COUNTDOWN TO WAR *181*

possibly the president about the dysfunctional state of its ground and air forces in distant Pacific colonies.

On November 16, Ambassador Clark Kerr reported to the Foreign Office that Chiang was in "high spirits," thanks to the encouraging cable from Churchill and a heartening message from Roosevelt, who, in Clark Kerr's words, had reassured Chiang that "the American Air Force in Manila was much stronger than the Japanese had any idea of. Chiang Kai-shek was therefore not to worry."[23] Nothing was quite so explicit in the president's letter that State had so carefully crafted. It is impossible to know how Chiang or Clark Kerr reached this happy conclusion. Nevertheless, their impression was an accurate reflection of the propaganda about airpower in the Philippines that General Marshall was personally orchestrating.

On November 5, 1941, twenty-four B-17s had landed at Clark Field in Luzon. On November 15, General Marshall gave a secret briefing to a select group of reporters about plans to bring air strength in the Philippines up "to a level far higher than the Japanese imagine."[24] He claimed that, if necessary, the United States would "fight mercilessly" and send out the B-17s to set Japan's "paper cities" on fire with no qualms about harming civilians. Marshall admitted to journalists that the B-17 did not yet have the range for the round trip to Japan, but in the short term, B-17 units could use staging posts at Vladivostok in the Soviet Union. Furthermore, the B-17 would be soon replaced by the more powerful B-24, which could make a nonstop trip to Japan, unload missiles, and return to the Philippines.[25]

The entire point of this briefing, as Marshall then revealed, was for reporters to ascribe leaks about the Flying Fortresses to the White House or the State Department. He presumed that, on hearing about the big bombers in the Philippines, the Japanese would think twice about their ambitions to expand across Asia.[26] Marshall knew full well that the B-17 could not reach Tokyo, but nothing could shake his blind faith in large metal scarecrows: the sheer presence of the Flying Fortresses in the Philippines would intimidate the Japanese and make them think twice about invading Europe's Far East territories.

At the end of October 1941, Marshall had rechristened the PDAF "the Far East Air Force" (FEAF). In November, he entrusted to the FEAF's new commander, General Lewis Brereton, secret plans about air operations in the Philippines to pass on to General MacArthur. MacArthur was ecstatic about the transformation of his domain into a base for "offensive air operations in furtherance of the strategic defense."[27] General Brereton, however, had deep reservations about stationing B-17s on deficient bases, which in his view were wholly vulnerable to enemy attack: the archipelago had insufficient fighter squadrons, inadequate air force personnel, and virtually no air warning system.[28] On the eve of Pearl Harbor, there were thirty-six B-17s, seventy-two P-40s, and eighteen P-35s, which were no match in terms of quality or quantity for the combined Japanese army and navy air forces.[29] Nobody in Washington was willing to admit to Roosevelt the real state of the FEAF; consequently he ended up with a completely misleading picture of air assets in the Philippines as a shield against Japanese expansion across the region. On November 11, Churchill sent instructions to the C-IN-C Far East to form a new squadron and send two others to Burma to serve under Chennault in the so-called IAF. Two days later, the War Office also authorized Brooke-Popham to send incendiary and other bombs into China under cover of being supplies for the AVG.[30] Brooke-Popham, however, refused to follow orders. On November 15, he informed the War Office that he could not send two squadrons to Burma to fight with the AVG because "at present I.A.F. is not capable of sustained effort. Until our combined efforts can get this satisfactory I do not propose to send either volunteer squadron into China."[31] Nonetheless, he would go ahead and arrange three months' worth of supplies for the three squadrons, which he would eventually send to Burma. These measures included reserve aircraft kept in crates, as well as bombs, ammunition, and spare parts. As for getting RAF units to Burma, he could not offer a "time table as the limiting factor is maintenance of I.A.F.," that is, the AVG.[32]

On November 19, 1941, the Chiefs of Staff forwarded this cable to Churchill, accompanied by a note in which they defended Brooke-Popham's position: "It is clear from paragraphs 3, 4 and 5 that the C.-in-C. is doing all he can to help Chennault." Next to this passage Churchill wrote "so proceed"—his way of saying *get on with helping Chennault.*[33]

Cables between the Far East and London were always subject to delay. On November 17, Brooke-Popham had indicated to the Air Ministry that he would try to establish volunteer squadrons on the same terms as those of the

AVG: CAMCO would handle the project.[34] It seems that even before Churchill ordered him to help Chennault, Brooke-Popham had decided to do so.

Since October 31, CAMCO's president Bill Pawley had been in India looking after new business with the Indian air force in Bangalore. He returned to Rangoon on November 18, but the next day took off for Singapore.[35] In a letter to Bruce Leighton (November 18, 1941), Pawley described an urgent call from the C-IN-C Far East, who had explained that the generalissimo had wired Churchill for air assistance, and so it was now proposed to set up a new British volunteer squadron under cover of employment with CAMCO. Through this arrangement, Chennault would command two additional squadrons (one fighter and one bomber) composed of British personnel and planes.[36] Pawley told Leighton that he had already contacted T. V. Soong about paying all salaries and expenses for the British squadrons from the "revolving fund" in the same way as the AVG.[37] If so, then US loans to China would be used to subsidize British as well as American volunteers under the command of Claire Chennault.

Pawley was deeply worried about the scarcity of supplies for the volunteer group. Although he had been getting on well with Chennault and admired him as a "thoroughly capable officer," he felt that Chennault had rebuffed all his offers of help, especially to recruit staff officers for the group. In the spring of 1941, Pawley had suggested that CAMCO find and hire at least ten staff officers who would start out in New York and line up all necessary materials to ship to Burma in advance of their own departure for Rangoon. Chennault had turned Pawley down and insisted on using his own flying officers on a part-time basis to handle each task (communications, transportation, finance, and the like). Consequently, as Pawley put it, Chennault had ended up doing the work of ten men. In Pawley's view, inadequate staff was "his greatest handicap" and had now resulted in the unit's inability to move into action.

Pawley felt that CAMCO had hired a great bunch of men, but delays in getting the group into action was causing "alot of disgust, unrest, disappointment and in general an unhealthy situation." In his view, CAMCO was working overtime to help Chennault and could do a great deal more if only he would turn the entire job on the ground over to CAMCO so that he could devote his attention to "the very necessary military end of the task."[38] One of Chennault's staff officers, Skip Adair, seems to have felt the same way. In private correspondence, he pointed out that everyone who worked in the AVG was doing the work of ten men.[39]

On November 21, Brooke-Popham clarified to the Air Ministry that CAMCO would set up a one-year contract for the ANZAC volunteers. However, if the British were at war with Japan, this contract would be canceled and the volunteers would revert to being RAF personnel. Nonetheless, the squadron thus formed would continue to serve under "Chennault's direction" even if they were an RAF unit.[40]

By the end of November, anxiety about a Japanese attack on Kunming had focused the minds of British officials as well as John Magruder, who bombarded the War Department with requests for matériel for the AVG, which he felt should be flown rather than shipped to the Far East.[41] Marshall and Arnold, however, turned down his appeals for air assistance for the AVG.[42] They had long since decided that scarce air assets should go to the Philippines and Hawaii rather than China.

The status of the American volunteers in Burma now became ambiguous. On arriving at Rangoon, some of the men, including Chuck Baisden, had signed an attestation about their service in the Chinese Air Force: they promised "to render loyal service to China and to obey the orders of my superior officers and the military laws and regulations of China."[43] In his diary on November 21, Charlie Bond also described a meeting in which Chennault described how their life would change once the group moved to Kunming—another sign that Chiang and his British counterparts thought that a Japanese attack was in the works.[44] Once in China, the volunteers would be under the command of the generalissimo and in effect have the same status as Chinese officers. It may never have occurred to any of the young men exactly what an oath of loyalty meant: nothing along these lines had been inserted in their CAMCO contracts. Yet back in January 1941, these were precisely the terms and conditions that Chiang and T. V. Soong had wanted to impose on the volunteers. It is not inconceivable that Chennault was easy on the volunteers to keep them happy and unsuspecting during their stay in Burma because once he had delivered them to China, they would be in thrall to the generalissimo.

Right up to Pearl Harbor, the volunteers enjoyed the summer camp atmosphere at Toungoo. At the end of November, they were painting sharks' teeth on the cone of their planes, playing cards, and having picnics. Chennault gathered them around for lectures on tactics. They fired the machine guns installed on their Tomahawks, flew in formation, and got in dogfights with each other. There was the occasional "match" of the AVG versus RAF Squadron No. 60: in these encounters, the AVG pilots came out on top and proved once and for all that a Tomahawk was superior to a Buffalo.[45]

Before Pearl Harbor, most officials regarded the volunteers as youngsters who might never be fit for battle. In October 1941, James McHugh heard disparaging reports from his army colleague in Chungking about the lack of discipline in Chennault's outfit: an army mess sergeant was constantly drunk; pilots had wrecked airplanes; and two pilots had been killed since training started. By this stage, McHugh had known Chennault for several years, and in the past had expressed his reservations about him.[46] Nonetheless, he believed that "the old man" would get the best out of the AVG. With exceptional prescience, he went on to say, "The kind of men who voluntarily leave their organization at home for adventure are naturally those least amenable to discipline and there is very little control that can be exercised over them in a situation like this except what they naturally feel for a leader."[47]

On December 7, 1941, the Japanese attacked Pearl Harbor. No one in Washington alerted Chennault and his group in Burma. The men woke up on December 8 and heard the radio report like everyone else. It took another week before their orders came through from Chungking. After consulting with the British, on December 16 Chiang Kai-shek decided that since Burma did not have an adequate warning net, the squadrons should finally move to Yunnan: if and when the Japanese attacked Burma, he was prepared to let them return to defend it.[48] In London, the British felt that they had no authority to overrule Chiang's decision, even though the transfer of the squadrons to Yunnan would cut in half the air defense of Burma.[49]

On December 17, the first and second AVG squadrons flew from Burma into Yunnan, where the Japanese had already dropped the first bombs on the provincial capital, Kunming. On December 20, 1941, the squadrons saw combat over Yunnan for the first time, but three days later both units were back in Burma to join the third AVG squadron as well as the RAF in defending Rangoon against the enemy. The squadrons fought their most stunning air battles on December 23 and Christmas Day, when they brought down about thirty enemy aircraft.[50] By the time the group was disbanded on July 4, 1942, they had destroyed at least 283 Japanese aircraft, 215 in the course of aerial combat: these are the figures that were compiled for Claire Chennault in the summer of 1942.[51]

This book began with questions: Who founded the Flying Tigers, when, and why? For over seventy years their story has resembled a Russian doll: Claire Chennault is painted on the outer shell, and all other participants have been crammed inside. According to the standard version of events, Chennault came to Washington in November 1940; with help from T. V. Soong, he persuaded men of influence, including the president, to adopt his plan for American combat pilots to fight the Japanese in China even before they declared war on the United States. As a wealth of new sources reveal, this was a myth that served various purposes during World War II and in the postwar era.

From beginning to end, the organization of the AVG suffered from a lack of consensus about its purpose among the Americans, British, and Chinese. Equally damaging was the absence of coordination among the three governments about strategy in the Far East. In this diplomatic minuet, there were always three pairs: Anglo-American, Sino-British, and Sino-American. Each kept the results of bilateral consultations to themselves. The couples occasionally stepped on the each other's toes and inadvertently discovered what the others were up to. Sometimes separately, sometimes acting with another, the three allies shaped the destiny of the Flying Tigers.

In 1941, the Roosevelt administration did more to undermine than facilitate the planning of the volunteer group. Over the course of the year, shifts in Far East policy, odd ideas about airpower, and turf wars within the US government interfered with the timely procurement of supplies and personnel to make the group fit for combat before Pearl Harbor. US officials never took the AVG seriously as a military outfit, because for the most part they regarded it as a morale booster in the framework of "plane aid" for China.

Soon after the Munich crisis of September 1938, President Roosevelt came up with his own concept of air assistance. I have referred to this as "plane aid"—a label that at the time was occasionally applied to the admin- istration's aircraft sales to allies. Roosevelt became convinced that France and Britain would feel far more confident about resisting Germany if they had a big fleet of planes. Thus reinforced, they would make Hitler "think twice" about attacking his neighbors. What mattered to the president was the psychological impact of airplanes on friend and foe alike, rather than their military value for actual operations.

"Aid" was a misleading term for this policy. Roosevelt gave France and Britain priority over the US military to acquire the limited supply of combat aircraft produced by US manufacturers at that time; nonetheless, they still had to pay hard cash for all military hardware. In this diplomatic game, the Curtiss-Wright P-40 became the highest token of the president's esteem for allies. As Britain and France had competent air forces, neither Roosevelt nor any of his advisers ever asked how the equipment would be deployed.

Plane aid was based on a fundamental misconception, that air strength was equivalent to airpower. As one historian pointed out, Roosevelt was interested in planes and lots of them: the ground organization required to deploy aircraft had no bearing on his strategic thinking. The outbreak of war in September 1939 and the German invasion of France and the Lowlands in May 1940 demonstrated that, on its own, a fleet of modern aircraft would not keep a determined enemy at bay. Nonetheless, Roosevelt and his colleagues continued to exaggerate the deterrent value of modern military aircraft. George Marshall insisted on stationing B-17s and P-40s in the Philippines and Hawaii on the grounds that the presence of these war weapons would make the Japanese "think twice." This was a static and misguided approach to deterrence: right up to Pearl Harbor, he and others failed to see that one man's scarecrow was another man's sitting duck. Such complacency about the alleged air deterrent in the Philippines contributed to the false sense of security that blinded analysts across the US government to the possibility of a Japanese attack on Hawaii.

In 1940 and 1941, the Roosevelt administration continued to use "plane aid" to boost the morale of weaker allies such as Greece and China. In October 1940, Cordell Hull wanted a few planes for China, the more the better, within limits, to express support for Chiang Kai-shek and keep him fighting. The same applied to Prime Minister Metaxis of Greece. Whether their air forces could handle the planes and whether the planes might go to waste was of no great concern to the president and his advisers. As had been the case with France and Britain, the us government did not get involved in "after-sales care."

In October and November 1940, plane aid shaped the proposal to sell perhaps fifty P-40s to China as an expression of American support for Chiang. In arranging this transaction, Treasury Secretary Henry Morgenthau Jr.—the aviation czar since 1938—expressed no views about the eventual deployment of the planes. In December 1940, however, he and others in the administration departed from this traditional approach to air assistance. For the first time ever, they prescribed air operations that the Chinese should execute in order to suit the strategic interests of the United States.

In the winter of 1940–1941, Roosevelt and his cabinet became convinced that Japan would invade Singapore in the spring of 1941 and thus force the president reluctantly to honor a pledge to Churchill—if there was a genuine threat to Singapore, Roosevelt would dispatch some part of the us fleet. This new crisis might well entangle the United States in a war with Japan at a time when none of the us military believed that the armed forces were ready to wage one.

Morgenthau came up with a bold but impractical solution to keep the Japanese from invading Singapore: he wanted to sell a few heavy bombers to Chiang, with which his air force would bomb Tokyo and thus disrupt the enemy's plan to break out of China and head south. The War Department, however, soon stepped in and put an end to Morgenthau's pipe dream: George Marshall refused to give up any of the army's B-17 Flying Fortresses for this mission. Marshall suggested an alternative: the P-40 Tomahawks reallocated from the British to the Chinese could be used to create a "distraction" over the Burma Road that would have the same effect of deterring the Japanese from Singapore. All that was required was a team of us instructors to teach the CAF how to man and maintain their new P-40s. In mid-January 1941, Frank Knox renewed contact with Bruce Leighton of Intercontinent and asked him to hire the instructors. This was the seed from which the Flying Tigers emerged through a series of haphazard decisions during the rest of the year.

In February 1941, the Japanese threat to Singapore evaporated and with it the rationale for sending a hundred planes and some instructors to train CAF pilots for an operation over the Burma Road. US officials seemed prepared to let this project wither on the vine, but by this stage they could not do so without damaging relations with Chiang: the planes were already on the way to China, and some volunteer instructors had been promised.

The man who rescued the project was the president's administrative assistant, Lauchlin Currie. In March 1941, Currie returned from a boondoggle to China as a complete convert to the Nationalist cause. He revived the lapsed China air program and made it compatible with the president's notion of "plane aid." The volunteer group was to become an element of an expanded aircraft program that would not only boost Chiang's morale but make him feel like the equal of Winston Churchill in the eyes of the president and the American people. The Short-Term Aircraft Program for China became the platform for transforming US-China relations. Through future deliveries of airplanes, allegedly under Lend-Lease, Currie would give Chiang a reliable air force, inspire his trust in US support, and build up his status as a world leader.

With these aims in mind, in late March 1941, Currie resuscitated the recruitment drive that the secretary of the navy had already delegated to Leighton and Intercontinent. How Chiang might ever use American men and planes was not Currie's concern: like the president and his cabinet colleagues, he was interested only in the psychological and diplomatic effect of American largesse on the generalissimo.

Was this the kind of US assistance that Chiang wanted? Not really. The generalissimo politely thanked Roosevelt for whatever he received but saw through the rhetoric and gestures; Chiang wanted hardware, not soft power, from the US government. From October 1940 onward, he had dreamt of a vast international air force formed of foreign volunteer squadrons. Under his command they would smash the Japanese in China and quite possibly in their homeland. The volunteer group would be just one small unit in this glorious air armada.

High expectations led to deep disappointment. Unable to obtain the big loans to acquire a thousand planes and pay at least as many pilots, the generalissimo was perpetually frustrated by inadequate American plane aid. Furthermore, he pinned little hope on the volunteer group, which he suspected could not withstand the Japanese air forces. For that reason, by June 1941 Chiang and his British counterparts decided that after arriving in the Far East, the volunteers should be based in Burma rather than in Yunnan, where they would be vulnerable to enemy air attack. By November 1941, Chiang still had reservations about the combat worthiness of the group: he would have been happy for the US Army to take control of the AVG as well as the CAF, if it meant that the United States became involved in the war with Japan.

The British, by contrast, saw the volunteer group in a more modest and realistic light. From February to November 1941, Brigadier General Lance Dennys worked with Chiang's most trusted officers on military cooperation. Once British officials found out about the AVG, they saw its military potential. The AVG had a hundred planes and eventually three hundred personnel, which doubled the assets available to the British to defend their Far East territories. So whereas the US government never appreciated the volunteers as potential combatants, the British did; they wanted to make the group combat worthy as quickly as possible. To that end, they made the key decisions that governed where, how, and when to deploy the American Volunteer Group.

Their plan was straightforward: the IAF, as the British consistently termed the AVG, would fly alongside the RAF to defend Yunnan and Burma *if and only if* Japan declared war on the British Empire. The British and Chinese succeeded in keeping their mutual security arrangements secret from the Americans until the summer of 1941. Once the War Department (and Currie) found out about Sino-British cooperation, they were determined to muscle in and do what they could to make the Chinese feel that their principal ally in peace and war was the United States, not Britain.

How did Claire Chennault fit into this world of competing foreign policies and interests? From November 1940 to March 1941, Chennault and his colleagues in the Chinese delegation were on the receiving end of initiatives generated by the Plus Four: Henry Morgenthau, Cordell Hull, Frank Knox, and Henry Stimson. Morgenthau thought up the project to bomb Tokyo, which gave way to a scheme devised by George Marshall for the Chinese to use their newly acquired P-40 fighters to lure the Japanese toward the Burma Road and away from Singapore. During this period, Chennault was on the sidelines, present at the creation but hardly the father of the Flying Tigers.

It is a myth that Chennault ever persuaded the president or anyone else in the administration to endorse his idea of "a small but well-equipped air force" in China to smash the Japanese.[1] Before Pearl Harbor, the only plan that existed for the deployment of the AVG was that approved by British and Chinese officials for the defense of their joint territories once the Japanese had declared war on the British Empire.

Sino-British relations were not without their stresses and strains. In 1939–1941, China resented being pushed to the back of the line for American arms and aircraft, which went automatically to the British. The British were skeptical about the ability of Chiang's military to hold up their side of the bargain in any joint guerrilla or air operations against Japan when the time came. They also were worried about the failure of the Chinese to keep plans secret from the enemy. Nonetheless, the archival record reveals sincere efforts of two allies who were both at war to help one another within their limited means. This sentiment came through in discussions about the IAF/AVG, in communications between Chiang and Churchill, as well as in reports from British officials in the Far East about "unobtrusive" talks with Chinese officials. Therefore this book has made the case that without the British, the Flying Tigers would never have gotten off the ground.

In January 1941, the British provided the Tomahawks, even if they did so reluctantly. From February 1941 onward, the British recognized that the IAF/AVG would double the air assets available for the defense of Burma and Yunnan once the Japanese declared war on the British Empire. By June they had decided that the group should be based in Burma, and by mid-August they were prepared to let the group undergo full operational training. From that point onward, British officials did what they could to provide munitions and to bring the group up to combat standard. In the autumn of 1941, the IAF/AVG had become the backbone of air defense for Burma and Yunnan. Under no circumstances, however, were Chennault and his volunteers to launch attacks on the enemy before a state of war existed. In line with this

Sino-British agreement, on December 20, 1941—nearly two weeks after Pearl Harbor—the Flying Tigers took to the air against the Japanese. Apart from an initial detour to Yunnan, their orders were to defend Rangoon against the Japanese; they retreated once and for all to defend Yunnan after the enemy had occupied most of Burma in March 1941.

The volunteers knew little or nothing about the politics or politicians who shaped their strange existence in Burma. They also knew very little about Claire Chennault, who according to the archival record appears to have expressed little interest or confidence in them before Pearl Harbor. He spent the first six weeks or so of their life in Burma elsewhere, meeting officials of every stripe across the Far East. He was not overly eager to start instructing the youngsters in tactics or whipping them into shape: he never made provision for transition training, and when asked to provide it in the autumn of 1941, he told the army that he had no means to do so. There was no such thing as a kindergarten conducted by the "old man." The volunteers ran their own playgroup, taught themselves to fly the Tomahawk and to spar (and sometimes collide) with each other midair.

Before Pearl Harbor, Chennault despaired of his young charges. Perhaps there was nothing unusual about this, as the US military tended to be hard on subordinates, especially new recruits. Furthermore, no one in the US government believed that the volunteers would ever amount to anything. The saving grace was the fearlessness of the pilots and the peculiar character of their supervisor. Chennault was a maverick who proved to have a talent for inspiring men to fight. Under his command, a bunch of rookies were transformed into the legendary Flying Tigers.

The historiography of the Flying Tigers remains puzzling. Why, for over seventy years, have historians so rarely called into question a narrative spun by wartime propagandists and postwar apologists of the Nationalist cause?

Soon after the Pacific war broke out, as the historian Jonathan Utley has pointed out, propagandists transformed the AVG / Flying Tigers into a mascot of Sino-American friendship: in developing an account of how the group came about, publicists and historians used the Tigers as proof of Roosevelt's prescience and his desire to help China resist Japan *even* before

Pearl Harbor.[2] Interest in the Tigers was greatest in the immediate postwar period, as the United States digested the loss of China in December 1949. In *Way of a Fighter*, Chennault portrayed himself as the man who had tried to save China through airpower, first using the AVG and then the air strategy in the China-Burma-India theater: he savaged anyone who opposed him before the war and during the war, as well as all those who he felt had contributed to the collapse of the Nationalist regime.

In the 1950s, US military historians Charles Romanus and Riley Sunderland for the army, as well as James Cate and Wesley Craven for the air force, wrote official histories of the US Army in World War II. In discussing the origins of the Flying Tigers, they downplayed the role of President Roosevelt and his cabinet colleagues while mentioning almost in passing the contribution of Lauch Currie and the directors of Intercontinent. Instead they portrayed George Marshall, Hap Arnold, and Claire Chennault as the competent military planners who created the AVG. Ironically, Marshall, more than any other military leader, did the most to thwart the AVG specifically and military supplies to China generally.

In 1963, Arthur Nichols Young assessed the record of American aid for the Nationalists in *China and the Helping Hand*. Young quoted extensively from *Way of a Fighter* and characterized Chennault as "the dramatic figure on whom centers the story of China's military aviation from 1937."[3] By including a lengthy extract from Chennault's memoir in a book published by Harvard University, Young greatly enhanced the academic reputation of Chennault as an authority on US-China relations before, during, and after the war. Through the 1970s, popular historians accepted that *Way of a Fighter* was a true account of the decisive influence that Chennault had over the formation of the Flying Tigers.

That so little has been known about the British side of the story is due in large measure to their defeat in the Far East. US government officials as well as the US press rapidly became contemptuous of the British military for losing Burma, Singapore, and Hong Kong. Americans seemed to forget that the British already had spent two years fighting the Germans and could not afford a war on two fronts. In June 1942, James McHugh reflected the anti-British bias when he wrote to Frank Knox about the British failure in

Burma. He contended that Britain had never intended to hold Burma and pointed to the experience of Chennault in dealing with the British to get the AVG organized and trained: "He was continually blocked and baffled at every turn . . . and when he overcame these objections, he was pinned to a promise that his force would defend Burma first in the event of war."[4] Not only does the archival record contradict McHugh's charges, but so did Claire Chennault. In *Way of a Fighter* he stated explicitly that without the British, the AVG would not have gotten into fighting condition. No historians, however, explored this angle: they continued to omit the British from the story, treat them as stuffy fools, or, like James McHugh, accuse them of obstructing the Flying Tigers.

British historians have never done anything to correct this dismal perception of their government's role in the AVG. Dozens of files about the International Air Force have gathered dust in the National Archives, all of which were declassified in 1972 under the thirty-year rule. As far as I can see, only one British historian, Peter Lowe, has referred to a few files in describing Britain's financial and air assistance to China in 1940 and 1941.[5] American historians have not cited a single one of the records to do with the IAF in writing about the Flying Tigers.

This is not entirely surprising. For decades historians have accepted as articles of faith the gospel according to Chennault, reinforced by Arthur Young and a host of popular chroniclers of the AVG. Under such circumstances there has never been any reason to find out the contributions that others made to the group's formation.

This lack of curiosity applied especially to the role of Intercontinent and CAMCO in the AVG — one that has been documented but never explored in any depth. The official US Army historians Romanus and Sunderland consulted a range of company records in Bill Pawley's office at Intercontinent's New York headquarters while preparing *Stilwell's Mission in China* in the early 1950s. Footnotes revealed that they consulted Bill Pawley's AVG files, including one labeled "Leighton."[6] Historians, however, never had a chance to look again at these documents, because all of Pawley's files went missing in the 1960s. I discovered from his niece Anita Pawley that Bill decided to donate his AVG archive to the Air Force Academy in Taiwan: the Republic of China's embassy in Washington sent a truck to collect his filing cabinets from his home in Miami, but they went missing thereafter.[7] This means that my collection of Bruce Leighton's papers are probably all that is left of Intercontinent records not only about the Flying Tigers but the firm's business in China from 1937 to 1940.

I am confident that other new sources will come to light about the Flying Tigers, because they already have. In November 2016, Dr. Cynthia Chennault allowed me to look at the collection of AVG flight reports that her father had kept and which had been miraculously preserved all these years. It seems that I was the first historian to ever look at these folders. Here were reports handwritten in pencil and ink by the volunteer pilots. Although typewritten copies exist in other archives, some appeared to be unique accounts of their combat in December 1941 to July 1942.

It is beyond the scope of this book to go back over these documents and compare them to all the other flight reports in Claire Chennault's papers at Stanford University or elsewhere. I hope that others will take a fresh look at all the evidence and reconsider the significance of the Flying Tigers in the history of air warfare. Controversy still surrounds estimates of their "kills," but Claire Chennault's personal collection may eventually tell us exactly what the Flying Tigers did before they "passed into history."[8]

Acknowledgments

So many people have helped me over the past ten years with research for this book that their names could fill a telephone directory. I apologize if I have not mentioned all of them. Special thanks for their generosity in sharing documents or photographs go to Lennart Andersson, Ed Amaczyk, and Marilyn Brown of the Tonawanda-Kenmore Historical Society, and Alan Armstrong, Anthony Carrozza, Dr. Cynthia Chennault, Nicholas Dennys, Lila Garnett, Ge Shuya, Andrew Leighton, David Leighton, Sarah Leighton, Hsiao-ting Lin, William C. McDonald III, Tracy Minter, Professor Richard Overy, Anthony Slessor, and David Yao. Several have helped me along the way or shown special interest in the project: my agent Ronald Goldfarb, and Gerrie Sturman, Dan Ford, Diana Fortescue, Peter Harmsen, Robert Keatley, Emma Oxford, Anita Pawley, James Srodes, and Jay Taylor. Others have listened patiently to updates about the story: Elizabeth Llewellyn, Alison Rea, and last but not least my husband David Buchan.

Notes

Abbreviations Used in the Notes

AAC [United States] Army Air Corps
AAF [United States] Army Air Forces
ABC America Britain Canada
AFB air force base
AIR Air Ministry (Great Britain)
AIRWHIT Air Ministry Whitehall (Great Britain)
ANY Arthur Nichols Young Papers
AVG American Volunteer Group
AVIA Ministry of Aviation (Great Britain)
BGLA Bruce Gardner Leighton Archive
BRINY British Purchasing Mission New York
CAB Cabinet Office (Great Britain)
CAF Chinese Air Force
CAMCO Central Aircraft Manufacturing Company
CC carbon copy
CCAC Cynthia L. Chennault and Anna C. Chennault, "Five Year Diary of Claire Lee Chennault"
CDF Central Decimal File (US State Department)
CHS chapters
CKS Chiang Kai-shek
CO Colonial Office (Great Britain)
CUL Cornell University Library
EML Ethel Major Leighton (BGLA)
EP export pursuit (aircraft)
FDRL Franklin Delano Roosevelt Library

FO Foreign Office (Great Britain)

FRUS *Foreign Relations of the United States*

HBM His Britannic Majesty

HISU Hoover Institution, Stanford University

HM Henry Morgenthau Jr.

HMS his majesty's ship

IAF International Air Force

JB Joint Board

MAP Ministry of Aircraft Production (Great Britain)

NA North American [Aviation]

NAI National Archives Identifier (NARA)

NARA National Archives and Records Administration (US)

NMNA National Museum of Naval Aviation

NYT *New York Times*

PREM prime minister (Great Britain)

PSF President's Secretary's File (in FDRL)

RAF Royal Air Force (Great Britain)

RG record group (NARA)

SDASMA San Diego Air and Space Museum Archive

TMC Tracey Minter Collection (Letters of Mamie Porritt)

TNA The National Archives (Great Britain)

TVS T. V. Soong

USAAC United States Army Air Corps

USAFHS United States Air Force Historical Study

USMC United States Marine Corps

USNR United States Navy Reserve

USSR Union of Soviet Socialist Republics

WO War Office (Great Britain)

WPD War Plans Department (US)

WSC Winston Spencer Churchill

Introduction

1. *New York Times* (hereafter *NYT*), "Labels Americans 'Flying Tigers,'" January 27, 1942, 10.

2. The number of enemy aircraft brought down by the Flying Tigers is a source of enormous controversy, about which I cannot comment. I have cited the figure provided by the AVG veteran Erik Shilling in a May 15, 1996, message to the newsgroup rec.aviation.military, which is available at yarchive.net/mil/avg_record.

html. Dan Ford offers a far more conservative estimate of 115: Dan Ford, *Flying Tigers: Claire Chennault and His American Volunteers, 1941–1942* (Washington, DC: Smithsonian/HarperCollins, 2007), x.

3. William D. Pawley, *Americans Valiant and Glorious* (privately printed, 1945).

4. Kung Hsiang-hsi (1881–1967) (孔祥熙; pinyin, Kǒng Xiángxī), Nationalist finance minister 1933–1944.

5. Pawley, *Americans Valiant and Glorious*, 6.

6. Chiang Kai-shek or Chiang Chieh-Shih (1887–1975) (蔣介石; pinyin, Jiang Jieshi) was the political as well as military head of the Nationalist government of China from 1928 through World War II.

7. *Time*, "Tigers over Burma," February 9, 1942.

8. Russell Whelan, *The Flying Tigers: The Story of the American Volunteer Group in China* (New York: Viking, 1942), 24.

9. Robert B. Hotz, *With General Chennault: The Story of the Flying Tigers* (New York: Coward-McCann, 1943).

10. Claire Lee Chennault, *Way of a Fighter: The Memoirs of Claire Lee Chennault, Major General, U.S. Army (ret.)*, edited by Robert Hotz (New York: G. P. Putnam's Sons, 1949).

11. Annalee Jacoby, "Fighting Man, Fighting Words," *New York Times Book Review*, January 30, 1949, 1.

12. Ford, *Flying Tigers*, 2: Ford treats *Way of a Fighter* with notable skepticism in that he acknowledges Robert Hotz as its ghostwriter.

13. Soong (Song) Mei-ling (1898–2003) (宋美齡; pinyin, Sòng Měilíng).

14. T. V. Soong, Soong Tse-ven (1891–1971) (宋子文; pinyin, Sòng Zǐwén), finance minister 1928–1933; personal representative of Chiang to the US government 1940–1942.

15. Chennault, *Way of a Fighter*, 96–97.

16. Bruce Gardner Leighton Archive (hereafter BGLA; these papers are in the author's possession), folder CAMCO, AVG, "Leighton to Col. C. T. Chien," September 5, 1944, 2–3.

1. Chiang's Rotten Air Force

1. The [UK] National Archives (hereafter TNA), FO 371/23463, F3687/118/10, "Secret Report on the Chinese Air Force," HBM Air Attaché, April 17, 1939, 6 (hereafter TNA, "Secret Report").

2. Ibid.

3. TNA, FO 371/20968, F2527/31/10, "Annual Report in Aviation in China 1936," May 3, 1937, 90.

4. TNA, FO 371/20967, F477/31/10, "Chinese Air Force," January 25, 1937, "Confidential, Minute of Interview Wing Commander H. S. Kerby, Air Attaché with Mr. W. H. Donald," November 17, 1936, 263.

5. John Magruder, "The Chinese as a Fighting Man," *Foreign Affairs*, April 1931, 469.

6. Ibid., 470.

7. TNA, FO 371/20968, F1837/31/10, "Chinese Air Force — Preparedness for War," January 27, 1937.

8. *Information Bulletin, Office of the Chief of Naval Operations* 18, no. 1, "Notes on the Present Conflict in China, March 1939" (Washington, DC, 1939), 43.

9. Aleksandr Ya. Kalyagin, *Along Alien Roads* (New York: East Asian Institute, Columbia University, 1983), 11.

10. Ray Wagner, *Prelude to Pearl Harbor* (San Diego, CA: San Diego Aerospace Museum, 1991), 27–28.

11. FDR Presidential Library & Museum (fdrlibrary.marist.edu), Diaries of Henry Morgenthau, Jr. (hereafter FDRL Morgenthau), vol. 146, October 14–20, 1938, "To Secretary Morgenthau from J. Lossing Buck: Interview with Minister Kung," October 7 and 13, 1938, 361.

12. "Soviet Military Aid to China, 1937–1939," by 1.JmA (Jagdmoroner Abteilung) member Skoreny (http://1jma.dk/articles/1jmachina.htm), who cites Y. Chudodeev, "Defending Chinese Skies," in *On the Eve*, ed. N. Yakovlev, O. Stepanova, E. Salynskaja (Moscow, 1991), 118–27, and "On the Chinese Soil," *Nauka* (Moscow, 1977).

13. Cornell University Library, James M. McHugh Papers (hereafter CUL McHugh), passim. In 1934–1938 McHugh had the rank of captain and in 1939–1941 of major. He was promoted to colonel early in 1942. For a brief profile of McHugh see Robert E. Mattingly, *Herringbone Cloak — GI Dagger: Marines of the OSS*, Occasional Paper (Washington, DC: History and Museums Division, Headquarters, US Marine Corps, 1989), 55–58.

14. CUL McHugh, box 2, folder 13, "The Chinese Air Force," June 7, 1938; BGLA, folder Misc. Chinese Correspondence, Leighton to George Sellett, March 20, 1938, 3.

15. CUL McHugh, box 2, folder 13, "Confidential the Chinese Air Force," June 7, 1938.

16. BGLA, folder Misc. Chinese Correspondence, "Leighton to Pawley," April 3, 1938, 1, 7.

17. Ibid., 3.

18. TNA, FO 371/22140, F10951/298/10, "Soviet Assistance to Chinese Air Force," October 18, 1938, 175.

19. William H. Donald was a crusty old Australian journalist who had come

to China in the early part of the century and become an adviser to one Chinese warlord after another. In 1936 he went to live with the Chiangs. See Earl Albert Selle, *Donald of China* (New York: Harper, 1948), 305–6.

20. TNA, FO 371/ 22139, F3951/298/10, "Secret from B. A. Hankow," February 4, 1938, 270, and F877/298/10, "Russian Aircraft for China," January 20, 1938, 164.

21. TNA, "Secret Report," 8, 31.

22. Ibid., 31.

23. Mao Pang-chu (1904–1987) (毛邦初; was also known as Peter or P. T. Mow, Mao Bangchu, and Mow Pang Tsu).

24. Chien Ta-chun (1892–1982) (钱大钧; pinyin Qian Dajun), one of Chiang's most trusted officers. He was head of the CoAA and in the mid-1930s also served as mayor of Shanghai and Chiang's aide-de-camp.

25. TNA, "Secret Report," 9–10. For a biography of T. C. Chien see *Who's Who in China*, 5th ed. (Shanghai: China Weekly Review, 1936), 49.

26. TNA, "Secret Report," 8.

27. Ibid., 36.

28. Ibid., 12.

29. Chennault retired from the US Army Air Corps with the rank of captain, but the Chiangs gave him the honorific title of colonel so that he would have a superior rank to most Chinese officers. See Martha Byrd, *Chennault: Giving Wings to the Tiger* (Tuscaloosa: University of Alabama Press, 1987), 68.

30. TNA, "Secret Report," 28.

31. Ibid., 30.

32. "Five Year Diary of Claire Lee Chennault," courtesy of Cynthia L. Chennault and Anna C. Chennault, Washington, DC (hereafter CCAC): "Roster of Ams. Dec. 1938": W. C. McDonald, H. R. Mull, W. W. Pannis, R. S. Angle, B. R. Carney, R. M. Reynolds, J. L. Bledsoe, G. L. Cherymisin, E. S. Scott, F. L. Higgs, C. B. Adair, D. E. Long, R. M. Lancaster.

33. TNA, "Secret Report," 29.

34. Ibid., 38.

35. Ibid, 30. In 1935–1941, different authorities referred to Chinese currency as *fapi, yuan*, or Chinese or Mexican dollars (as the Chinese historically used a silver standard). A Chinese dollar in February 1939 was worth about sixteen cents (US), so MacDonald's bonus was relatively generous if converted to Chinese dollars. For background on Chinese currencies see Arthur N. Young, *China's Wartime Finance and Inflation, 1937–1945* (Cambridge, MA: Harvard University Press, 1965), 5–6, and table 59, p. 360.

36. Ibid., appendix C, "General Chiang kai shek's questionnaire and Colonel Chennault's answers."

37. Ibid.

38. National Archives and Records Administration (NARA), RG 59, Central Decimal File 893.248/106, "In strict confidence to the Secretary of State [from Willys Peck]," December 13, 1938.

39. TNA, FO 371/23462, F197/118/10, "Export credits for aircraft for Chinese government," January 6, 1939, 32–34, and *NYT*, "Britain Will Help China Get Imports," December 12, 1938, 42.

40. TNA, CO 129/580/4 (1939), "Sir A. Clark Kerr (Shanghai), Important, Secret," December 21, 1938.

41. TNA, "Secret Report," 41.

42. Ibid.

43. Hoover Institution, Stanford University (hereafter HISU), Arthur Nichols Young Papers (hereafter ANY), box 36, folder Mil/Av, "John Jouett to Arthur Young," September 18, 1933.

2. Burma Roads

1. Norman D. Hanwell, "China Driven to New Supply Routes," *Far Eastern Survey* 7, no. 22 (November 9, 1938): 259.

2. *NYT*, "US Envoy Praises China-Burma Road," January 10, 1939, 13.

3. *NYT*, "China's Back Door," January 11, 1939, 15.

4. Hanwell, "China Driven," 259.

5. CUL McHugh, box 2, folder 9, "Memorandum for the Ambassador, Subject: the Burma Road," December 31, 1938, 6.

6. Franco David Macri, *Clash of Empires in South China* (Lawrence: University Press of Kansas, 2012), 107–9.

7. FDRL Morgenthau, vol. 151, "November 19, 1938, 9 a.m. at the Secretary's home," 308.

8. Ibid., 309.

9. Ibid., 301–6.

10. FDRL Morgenthau, vol. 151, "November 19, 1938," 310; FDRL Morgenthau, vol. 152, "Memorandum on Yunnan-Burma Road" from K. P. Chen for the President, November 18, 1938, 336.

11. FDRL Morgenthau, vol. 152, "Chen Memorandum," 336; *NYT*, "US Envoy Praises China-Burma Road," January 10, 1939, 13.

12. Michael Schaller, *The U.S. Crusade in China, 1938–1945* (New York: Columbia University Press, 1979), 29. Schaller cites K. C. Li to H. H. Kung, December 23, 1938, in the papers of Arthur Young, but I could not find this document.

13. BGLA, "Bruce Leighton to Carl Dolan Intercontinent New York," November 27, 1938, 2, 3.

14. TNA, FO 371/ 22157, F13499/3284/10, "Projected aeroplane factory on Chinese side of Burma-China frontier," December 20, 1938, 170; note by A. H. Seymour, Defence Department Rangoon, November 14, 1938, 177.

15. BGLA, "Bruce Leighton to Carl Dolan Intercontinent New York," November 27, 1938, 2–3.

16. TNA, FO 371/20968, F6021/31/10, "Plan for establishment in Hong Kong of aeroplane assembly depot for China," September 2, 1937; FO 371/20969, F8440/31/10, "Assembly of aeroplanes for China in Hong Kong," October 25, 1937, 6–7, minute by Fitzmaurice; FO 371/22157, F3284/3284/10, "Proposed erection in Hong Kong of factory for manufacture of commercial and military aeroplanes," Geoffrey Northcote to W. G. A. Ormsby, Gore Colonial Secretary, February 5, 1938, and William D. Pawley to His Excellency, the Officer Administering the Government, October 22, 1937; FO 371/22157, F4832/3284/10, "Proposed erection in Hong Kong of factory for manufacture of commercial and military aeroplanes," May 6, 1938.

17. TNA, FO 371/22157, F13800/3284/10, "minute by M. J. R. Talbot [Milo John Robert Talbot, Baron of Malahide (1912–1973)], December 23, 1938," 178–79.

18. TNA, FO 371/22157, F4832/3284/10, Note of a meeting held on the 28th April [1938], 109; N. B. Ronald to the Undersecretary of State Colonial Office, June 24, 1938, 114; telegram from the Secretary of State for the Colonies to the Governor of Hong Kong, July 5, 1938, 116.

19. TNA, FO 371/23462, F1215/118/10, "Mr. Pawley's schemes for assembling aircraft for Chinese Government," February 7, 1939, 68: telegram from Governor of Hong Kong to Secretary of State for the Colonies, January 29, 1939, 70.

20. TNA, FO 371/22157, F13800/3284/10, minute by G. G. Fitzmaurice, December 31, 1938, 181–82.

21. TNA, FO 371/23462, F408/118/10, "telegram from Japan R. Craigie," January 13, 1939, 51.

22. TNA, FO 371/23462, F408/118/10, minute by N. B. Ronald, January 20, 1939, 50.

23. TNA, FO 371/23462, F1861/118/10, "Construction of aircraft factories on the Sino-Burmese border," February 27, 1939, 72, minute by N. B. Ronald, February 28, 1939, 74.

24. TNA, FO 371/23462, F408/118/10, "Desire of Chinese Government to assemble aircraft at Rangoon and fly them to China," January 13, 1939, minute by M. J. R. Talbot, 49.

25. TNA, FO 371/23463, F5552/118/10, "Report on aviation plant on Sino-Burmese frontier," June 9, 1939, 157–61.

26. Tracey Minter Collection, Letters of Mamie Porritt (secretary for Intercontinent, 1938–1942) (hereafter TMC Porritt), "Dearest Jims," July 10, 1939.

27. TNA, FO 371/23463, F9709/118/10, "Proposed aeroplane service between Hong Kong and Loiwing in connexion with factory at Loiwing," August 30, 1939; "The Intercontinent Corporation to the Harbor Master Hong Kong," July 28, 1939, 191–95.

28. TNA, Air 2/4133, "Minute by B. E. Embry," August 3, 1939.

29. TNA, CO 529/129/580/4, "Minute by Andrews," August 22, 1939, 21.

30. TNA, FO 371/23463, F9709/118/10, "Foreign Office to Colonial Office," September 7, 1939, 197.

3. Plane Aid

1. FDRL, President's Secretary's File (hereafter PSF) box 32, folder Germany—Wilson, Hugh R., March–November 1938, "Hugh Wilson to the President," July 11, 1938, 2. For German aircraft output in 1938 see Richard J. Overy, *The Air War, 1939–1945* (Washington DC: Potomac Books, 2005), 21.

2. Mark Watson, *Chief of Staff: Prewar Plans and Preparations* (Washington, DC: Center of Military History United States Army, 1950), 132 and fn13. German aircraft production in 1938 was 5,235. See Overy, *Air War*, 21.

3. Harold L. Ickes, *The Secret Diary of Harold L. Ickes*, vol. 2 (New York: Simon & Schuster, 1954), 469.

4. I. B. Holley, *Buying Aircraft: Matériel Procurement for the Army Air Forces* (Washington, DC: Office of the Chief of Military History, Department of the Army, 1964), 174.

5. FDRL, PSF box 30, folder France, Wm. C. Bullitt 1938, "Sec State Washington Rush—September 28 3pm," 4.

6. Watson, *Chief of Staff*, 132; Robert Dallek, *Franklin D. Roosevelt and American Foreign Policy, 1932–1945* (New York: Oxford University Press, 1979 and 1995), 186–87.

7. See William Emerson, "Franklin Roosevelt as Commander-in-Chief in World War II," *Military Affairs* 22, no. 4 (Winter 1958–1959): 187.

8. Holley, *Buying Aircraft*, 199.

9. Emerson, "Franklin Roosevelt," 185.

10. FDRL Morgenthau, vol. 146, "Budget and Armament Plans," October 20, 1938, 279.

11. R. Modley et al., *Aerospace Facts and Figures, 1962* (Washington, DC: American Aviation Publications, 1962), 6–7.

12. Ickes, *Secret Diary*, vol. 2, December 24, 1938, 531–32.

13. Office of Statistical Control, *Army Air Forces Statistical Digest World War II* (Washington, DC, 1945), 127.

14. Watson, *Chief of Staff*, 300.

15. Quoted ibid., 133.

16. FDRL Morgenthau, vol. 172 (French Mission [Planes] — Part I), "December 21, 1938, group meeting," 12.

17. William O. Watson, "Hawk 81, Latest Curtiss Flyer," *Curtiss Flyleaf* 23, no. 24 (Fall 1940): 6.

18. FDRL Morgenthau, vol. 216, "French purchases in the United States October 9, 1939," 206F; TNA, AVIA 38/732, "Basis of information for draft cable reply MAP-887," August 15, 1940. On October 5, 1939, the French ordered 530 Hawk 75s but within weeks cut the amount to 265 because of lack of engines. See Lionel Persyn, *Les Curtiss H-75 de l'Armée de l'Air* (Outreau, France: Éditions Lela Presse, 2008), 17.

19. TMC Porritt, "Dear Jim Prims," June 26, 1939, and "Dearest Jims," July 10, 1939.

4. Bruce Leighton's Guerrilla Air Corps

1. BGLA, folder EML, "Leighton to his wife," June 24, 1939, 1; CUL McHugh, box 4, folder 4, handwritten update to "10/4/39 Aircraft Industry Report," 10; see NARA, RG 59, CDF 893.248/168, "Memorandum Joseph Green," September 14, 1939, 6, which reveals that the contract was modified to thirty-four Curtiss-Wright 21 Interceptors and fifty-six P-36s plus spare parts at a value of US$6 million.

2. CUL McHugh, "American Aircraft Industry, April 10, 1939," 18; HISU, ANY, Young Consolidated, "Agreement between the Chinese Government and Consolidated Trading Company Ltd. 25th March 1939," 1.

3. CUL McHugh, box 1, folder 4, "Dear Timp[erley]," July 9, 1939. Harold Timperley had been the China correspondent of the *Manchester Guardian*.

4. CUL McHugh, box 3, folder 3, typed notes, October 3, 1939.

5. Ibid.

6. CUL McHugh, box 2, folder 14, "From Am. Consul Rangoon Feb 14, 1940," handwritten note; FDRL, collection of miscellaneous manuscripts too small to be named as collections, folder Joint Board #355 — Aircraft Requirements of the Chinese Government, "R. A. Boone to the Office of the Chief of Naval Operations [Harold Stark] concerning report of interview with Lieutenant-Commander Bruce G. Leighton USNR," January 17, 1940 (hereafter FDRL Misc. J.B. 355).

7. BGLA, "Leighton to Chien," September 5 1944, 3.

8. Sun Yat-sen, *International Development of China* (Shanghai: Commercial Press, 1922), 10.

9. BGLA, folder CAMCO, AVG, "Bruce Leighton to W. D. Pawley," February 10, 1943, 2.

10. *Foreign Relations of the United States* (hereafter FRUS) 1937, vol. 4, "The Commander in Chief of the United States Asiatic Fleet (Yarnell), to the Chief of Naval Operations (Leahy), [Shanghai]," September 22, 1937, 352; *NYT*, "To 'Accept Risks,'" September 25, 1937, 1.

11. FRUS, 1937, vol. 4, "Memorandum by President Roosevelt to the Secretary of State," Aboard Presidential Special, October 2, 1937, 362, and "Memorandum by the Secretary of State to President Roosevelt," Washington, October 4, 1937, 363.

12. *Life*, July 3, 1939, "An American Admiral and His 36 Warships Stand Guard on Asia's War," 9. *Life* featured Yarnell on the cover and emphasized that he had more power than US diplomats to keep the Japanese in their place.

13. *NYT*, "Japanese Policy Scored: Admiral Yarnell Would End Our Economic Cooperation," January 17, 1940, 10, and "Defense of Pacific Urged by Yarnell," October 25, 1940, 9.

14. *NYT*, "Sergeant York Ready to Join War on Japan," November 12, 1937, 3.

15. BGLA, folder CAMCO, AVG, Handwritten letter from Captain R. P. Molten; "Alice H. Leonard to B. G. Leighton," April 19, 1944; "Bruce Leighton to W. D. Pawley," February 10, 1943, 2.

16. *NYT*, "R. P. Molten Dies, Navy Officer, 53," May 30, 1940, 16.

17. BGLA, folder CAMCO, AVG, "Leighton to Pawley," February 10, 1943; "Memorandum for the Chief of Naval Operations by W. S. Anderson and attached memo by Bruce G. Leighton," January 16, 1940.

18. NARA, RG 127, box 8, "R-2 Reports by Headquarters, Fourth Marines, Shanghai China, August–October 1937," by Captain R. A. Boone, Regimental Intelligence Officer.

19. BGLA, "Anderson memo and attached Leighton memo," January 16, 1940.

20. FDRL Misc. J.B. 355.

21. FDRL, "Boone Report," January 17, 1940.

22. BGLA, folder CAMCO, AVG, "Bruce Leighton to Bill Pawley," February 19, 1943, 1.

23. The meeting occurred in the week of January 22–26. See BGLA, folder CAMCO, AVG, "E. J. King to Bruce G. Leighton," [Monday] January 29, 1940 [letterhead Department of the Navy General Board, Washington].

24. BGLA, folder CAMCO, AVG, "Leighton to Pawley," October 3, 1943, 1.

25. Ibid.

26. Ibid., 3.

27. BGLA, folder CAMCO, AVG, "Leighton to Pawley," May 14, 1942.

28. Ibid., 1.

29. BGLA, folder CAMCO, AVG, "Bruce Leighton to Captain Oscar Badger," May 6, 1940, 2.

30. BGLA, folder CAMCO, AVG, "Leighton to Pawley," May 14, 1942, 1; "Leighton to Pawley," February 10, 1943.

31. FDRL Morgenthau, vol. 255, April 17–19, 1940, "Conference HM Jr, Mr. Purvis, Mr. Young and Mrs Klotz," April 18, 1940, 141. Initially there were 215 H-81As for the French air force and 385 for the RAF. TNA, AVIA 38/732, "BRINY 2359 P-40 Aircraft," January 7, 1941. The original French order was 600 P-40s in April 1940, but the Anglo-French Purchasing Board increased it to 630, allowing 415 P-40s for the British.

32. Ray Wagner, "P-40," *American Combat Planes of the Twentieth Century*, http://www.americancombatplanes.com/p40_1.

33. TMC Porritt, "Dearest Jim Prim," May 25, 1940.

34. TNA, FO 371/25194, W8101/8101/49, "Production of aeroplanes for the Allies at Loiwing factory," May 31, 1940, and "Governor of Burma to Secretary of State for Burma," June 21, 1940, 219.

35. TNA, FO 371/25194, W8101/8101/49, "W. D. Croft to Nigel Ronald," October 7, 1940, 243.

36. Gangadhar Devrav Khanolkar, *Walchand Hirachand: Man, His Time and Achievements* (Bombay: Walchand & Co., 1969), 331; TNA, FO 371/25194, W10349/8101/49, "Secretary of State to Governor of Burma," October 1, 1940, 240.

37. TNA, CAB 67/8/19 W.P. (G), (40) 219, "The Manufacture of Aircraft in India, Memorandum by the Secretary of State for India," August 21, 1940, 1.

5. Business, the Chinese Way

1. Ancestry.com, California, Passenger and Crew Lists, 1882–1959 (database online). NARA, RG 85, Passenger Lists of Vessels Arriving at San Francisco, NAI no. 4498993.

2. *Miami Herald*, "Speed Record Is Broken," January 10, 1935, 12-A-1, with photo featuring W. D. Pawley and Colonel C. F. Wang; *NYT*, "Army Air Armada Opens Miami Meet," January 11, 1935, 11.

3. NARA, RG 59, CDF 893.248/175, "File note by Joseph Green," May 4, 1940, and "K. C. Li to Joseph Green," April 29, 1940.

4. Joseph Green, "Supervising the American Traffic in Arms," *Foreign Affairs* 15, no. 4 (July 1937): 732, and Elton Atwater, *American Regulation of Arms Exports*

(Washington, DC: Carnegie Endowment for International Peace, 1941), 208–10.

5. NARA, RG 59, CDF 248/175, "May 4, 1940," note by Joseph Green on his meeting with Chinese officers.

6. FDRL Morgenthau, vol. 260, "Memorandum for the Secretary," May 4, 1940, 5.

7. FDRL Morgenthau, vol. 317, "Report of the President Liaison Committee on Foreign Purchasing other than British," October 1, 1940, 288.

8. *Code of Federal Regulations of the United States 1940 Supplement Titles 1–20* (Washington, DC, 1941), "Proclamation 2417," 55, and "Regulations of October 15, 1940," 345.

9. Atwater, *Arms Exports*, 257.

10. FDRL Morgenthau, vol. 276, "To Secretary Morgenthau from Mr. Cochran," June 27, 1940, 190; for Young, Ancestry.com, NARA, RG 85, Passenger Lists of Vessels Arriving at San Francisco, NAI no. 44989.

11. Wu Jingping and Tai-chun Kuo, eds., *Select Telegrams between Chiang Kai-shek and T. V. Soong (1940–1943)* (Shanghai: Fudan University Press, 2008) (hereafter *Select Telegrams*), "Telegram from Chiang on US governmental loan negotiation," July 12, 1940, 264.

12. FDRL Morgenthau, vol. 273, "Conversation Henry Morgenthau and Arthur Purvis," June 17, 1940, 124–25.

13. For background on Jean Monnet as French purchasing agent see John McVickar Haight Jr., "France's First War Mission to the United States," *Airpower History* 11 (January 1964): 12; FDRL Morgenthau, vol. 337, "Copy of letter Winston Churchill to Jean Monnet," July 18, 1940, 264.

14. CUL McHugh, box 2, folder 12, "Airforce Administration," March 7, 1938, 2; TNA, FO 371/22139, F8132/298/10, "Strength of Soviet Air Group in Chinese Air Force," July 28, 1938, 270.

15. *Select Telegrams*, "Telegram from Chiang on military procurement and on loans (July 7, 1940)," 262.

16. HISU, ANY, box 105, Mil/Av 39–41, "Memorandum regarding Airplane Purchase," July 8, 1940, "Memorandum from Colonel Huang," August 1, 1940, and "Memorandum on conversation with Major B. M. Jacobson," August 27, 1940.

17. *NYT*, "Planes for Sweden Held," April 26, 1940, 10; FDRL Morgenthau, vol. 282, "Aide memoire for Mr. Morgenthau from Arthur Purvis," July 15, 1940, 561, and vol. 289, August 5–6, 1940, "Re: Ship movements control," August 6, 1940, 284, 290.

18. HISU, ANY, box 105, Mil/Av 39–41, "Huang Memorandum," August 1, 1940.

19. FDRL Morgenthau, vol. 282, "Aide memoire for Mr. Morgenthau from

Arthur Purvis," 561; vol. 289, "Re: Ship movements control," August 6, 1940, 284–86.

20. TNA, Air 8/539, "BRINY 4313 5/4/[41]," April 5, 1941, 85.

21. HISU, ANY, box 105, Mil/Av 39–41, "Jacobson Memorandum," 40/08/27.

22. HISU, ANY, box 105, Mil/Av 39–41, "Memorandum of September 6," September 7, 1940.

23. NARA, RG 59, CDF 893.248/179, "Confidential," July 27, 1940, note by Joseph Green of conversation with Arthur Young.

24. HISU, ANY, box 105, Mil/Av 39–41, "Memorandum of September 6," September 7, 1940, 2.

25. HISU, ANY, box 105, Mil/Av 39–41, "Estimated cost of Airplanes," October 2, 1940.

6. T. V. Soong's Mission to Washington

1. Ancestry.com, NARA, RG 85, Passenger Lists of Vessels Arriving at San Francisco, NAI no. 4498993.

2. FDRL Morgenthau, vol. 218, "Confidential from Nicholson," October 18, 1939, 2. Martin Richard Nicholson was one of the most trusted sources for Morgenthau on Chinese politics and finance. See his obituary, *NYT*, "Martin R. Nicholson, Official of Treasury," November 11, 1941.

3. Arthur Nichols Young, *China and the Helping Hand* (Cambridge, MA: Harvard University Press, 1963), 133–34; Schaller, *U.S. Crusade*, 33–34.

4. For discussion see Jonathan L'Hommedieu, "Roosevelt and the Dictators: The Origin of the US Non-recognition Policy of the Soviet Annexation of the Baltic States," in *The Baltic Question during the Cold War*, ed. John Hiden, Vahur Made, and David J. Smith (London: Routledge, 2008).

5. James McHugh, quoted by Brenda A. Ericson in *The Making of an Ally: Chiang Kai-shek and American Foreign Policy, 1936–1941* (Albuquerque, NM: University of New Mexico Press, 2004), 290.

6. FDRL Morgenthau, vol. 266, "Group Meeting," May 27, 1940, 341. Morgenthau evidently pronounced "Soong" as "Song."

7. FDRL Morgenthau, vol. 276, "To Secretary Morgenthau from Mr. Cochran," June 27, 1940, 190.

8. FDRL Morgenthau, vol. 255, "April 18, 1940 Present Mr. Purvis, Mr Young, Mrs Klotz," 183.

9. FDRL Morgenthau, vol. 277, "June 28, 1940, 10:30 am," 146-C.

10. FDRL Morgenthau, vol. 278, "Memorandum for the President," July 1, 1940, 82.

11. FDRL Morgenthau, vol. 281, "July 9, 1940," 129.

12. FDRL Morgenthau, vol. 282, "Memorandum for the Secretary," July 15, 1940, 533, and "The USSR as a Source of Strategic and Critical Materials," September 12, 1940, 544.

13. FDRL Morgenthau, vol. 282, "Aid to China, received from T. V. Soong," July 12, 1940, 293–95.

14. *Select Telegrams*, "Telegram from Chiang on interruption of Burma transportation," July 16, 1940, 265.

15. FRUS 1940, vol. 1, "Statement by the Acting Secretary of State," July 23, 1940, 401.

16. FDRL Morgenthau, vol. 307, "September 20, 1940 Present: the Russian Ambassador Mr. Oumansky, Mr. Jesse Jones, Dr. White," 149.

17. Morton Blum, *From the Morgenthau Diaries: Years of Urgency, 1938–1941* (Boston: Houghton Mifflin, 1964), 348–50.

18. FRUS 1940, vol. 4, "Memorandum of Conversation, by the Adviser on Political Relations (Hornbeck) [Washington]," August 15, 1940, 665.

19. FRUS 1940, vol. 4, "Hornbeck Memorandum," 666.

20. *Select Telegrams*, "Telegram from Chiang on reorganization of the Executive Yuan," August 15 and 23, 1940, 267–68.

21. FRUS 1940, vol. 4, "Hornbeck Memorandum," 667–68.

22. FDRL Morgenthau, vol. 146, "Morgenthau to the President [first draft]," October 17, 1938, 147.

23. FDRL Morgenthau, vol. 303, "Group Meeting," September 6, 1940, 250.

24. FDRL Morgenthau, vol. 307, "September 23, 1940," 294.

25. FRUS 1940, vol. 4, "Memorandum of conversation by the Assistant Secretary of State (Berle)," September 13, 1940, 668.

26. FDRL Morgenthau, vol. 307, "Conversation with Cordell Hull," September 20, 1940, 141.

27. Ibid.

28. FDRL Morgenthau, vol. 307, "September 20, 1940 Present: the Russian Ambassador Mr. Oumansky, Mr. Jesse Jones, Dr. White," 150.

29. Roger Moorhouse, *The Devil's Alliance: Hitler's Pact with Stalin, 1939–1941* (New York: Basic Books, 2014), 155–56.

30. *Select Telegrams*, "Telegram from Chiang on failure of Russian airplane delivery and demands for American airplanes," October 7, 1940, 274.

31. FDRL Morgenthau, vol. 307, "Conversation with Cordell Hull," September 20, 1940, 142.

32. Harold L. Ickes, *The Secret Diaries of Harold L. Ickes*, vol. 3, *The Lowering Clouds, 1939–1941* (New York: Simon & Schuster, 1954), September 15, 1940, 322.

33. FDRL Morgenthau, vol. 308, "Conversation with Leon Henderson," September 24, 1940, 43.

34. FRUS, Japan 1931–1941, vol. 2, "Press Release no. 48 Issued by the Federal Loan Agency on September 25, 1940," 222.

35. FDRL Morgenthau, vol. 334, "Re Chinese Loan, Sunday December 1, 1940, 8:30 pm," 55–56.

36. FDRL Morgenthau, vol. 308, "Conversation with Henderson," September 24, 1940, 43.

37. *Select Telegrams*, "Telegram from Chiang on Soong as delegate plenipotentiary for loan negotiations," September 26, 1940, 269.

38. *Select Telegrams*, "Telegram from Chiang on formation of the Axis and on US aids to China," September 28, 1940, 269–70.

39. HISU, ANY, box 105, Mil/Av 39–41, "Draft of telegram: substance sent in Chinese TVS to CKS," September 27, 1940.

40. *Select Telegrams*, "Telegram from Chiang on procurement of airplanes, fuel and ammunition," October 4, 1940, 274.

41. CCAC, entry for October 12, 1940.

42. CCAC. Chennault so valued his encounters with the Chiangs that he tended to record them in his diary. After February 12, 1940, when he met Madame Chiang in Hong Kong, he noted no further meetings or communication with the Chiangs until October 12, 1940.

43. NARA, RG 38, E-98, box 96, file A-1-Q Register no. 12592-E, folder Aeronautics in China 1939–40, "Personal Observation and Conversations," by Captain H. J. McQuillan [Francis J. McQuillan], USMC, October 8, 1940, 3.

44. HISU, ANY, box 105, Mil/Av 39–41, "Memorandum to Welles 10/18," October 17, 1940; *NYT*, "Swedish Planes Await U.S. Action," October 11, 1940, 2. The *New York Times* reported that seventy-five planes had been constructed.

45. FDRL Morgenthau, vol. 323, "Memorandum to the Secretary from James C. Buckley, Re: Swedish Export Situation," October 17, 1940, 89.

46. HISU, ANY, box 105, Mil/Av 39–41, "Memorandum to Welles 10/18," October 17, 1940.

47. *Select Telegrams*, "Telegram from Chiang to Soong and Hu Shi on Chiang's interview with US ambassador," October 18, 1940, 277.

48. Hsiao-ting Lin and Wu Jingping, *T. V. Soong: Important Wartime Correspondences (1940–1942)* (Shanghai: Fudan University Press, 2009). Telegrams to Pei and [Cyril] Rogers, October 17–20, 1940, 314–16.

49. FDRL Morgenthau, vol. 308, "Group Meeting September 25, 1940," 153.

7. A Few Planes for China

1. William Doyle, *Inside the Oval Office* (London: London House, 1999), 31–32. For the Japanese apology about this article see FRUS 1940, vol. 1, "The Counselor of the Japanese Embassy (Morishima) to the Chief of the Division of Far Eastern Affairs (Hamilton), Washington," October 5, 1940, 662.

2. Doyle, *Inside the Oval Office*, 32.

3. Ibid., 34.

4. TNA, FO 371/24709, F4621/G, "War Cabinet. Far Eastern Committee," October 3, 1940, 359; F4569/193/61, "Foreign Office, October 17, 1940," 330, and F4556/193/61, "To the Marquess of Lothian (Washington)," October 8, 1940, 345.

5. TNA, FO 370/24709, F4615/G, "The Marquess of Lothian (Washington)," October 7, 1940, 341–42.

6. FRUS 1940, vol. 4, "The Ambassador in China (Johnson) to the Secretary of State Chungking," October 17, 1940, 427.

7. TNA, FO 371/24709, F4621/G, "Far Eastern Committee 7th Meeting Draft minutes," November 17, 1941, 364.

8. *Select Telegrams*, telegrams from Chiang to Soong, October 4, 1940– November 14, 1940, 272–82.

9. *Select Telegrams*, "Telegram from Chiang on the urgency of American airplane procurement," October 7, 1940, 275.

10. FRUS 1940, vol. 4, "The Ambassador in China (Johnson) to the Secretary of State Chungking," October 20, 1940, 673.

11. FDRL Morgenthau, vol. 324, "Stimson and Morgenthau telephone call," October 23, 1940, 197.

12. Ibid., 198.

13. FDRL Morgenthau, vol. 325, "Conversation Morgenthau, Philip Young and Arthur Purvis," October 25, 1940, 50, and "To the Secretary from Mr. Young," October 26, 1940, and "Planes ordered by Thailand," 61. These were NA-69 twin-seater fighters designated as A-27 and used for training by AAC pursuit squadrons in the Philippines.

14. FDRL Morgenthau, Presidential Diary, vol. 3, "November 28 1940," p. 0713.

15. FDRL Morgenthau, vol. 325, "To the Secretary from Philip Young, October 25, 1940," 60, and "Planes ordered by Thailand," 61.

16. FRUS 1940, vol. 4, "The Secretary of State to the Ambassador in China (Johnson) Washington," October 24, 1940, 681.

17. FDRL Morgenthau, vol. 328, "Telephone Conversation Morgenthau and Stimson," November 1, 1940, 9.

18. Ibid., 10.

19. FDRL Morgenthau, vol. 330, "Group Meeting," November 7, 1940, 40–41.

20. Watson, *Chief of Staff*, 420–22; William H. Bartsch, *December 8, 1941: MacArthur's Pearl Harbor* (College Station: Texas A&M University Press, 2003), xlv–xlvi.

21. FDRL Morgenthau, vol. 324, "Stimson and Morgenthau," October 23, 1940, 197; *NYT*, "President Takes 110 Planes," October 23, 1940, 13.

22. NARA, RG 59, CDF, 893.248/183, "Joseph Green to the Secretary of State," October 31, 1940, 238–40.

23. NARA, RG 59, CDF 893.248/185, "Joseph Green to the Secretary," November 5, 1940.

24. NARA, RG 59, CDF 893.248/184, "Hornbeck to Green," November 6, 1940.

25. FDRL Morgenthau, vol. 330, "Group Meeting," November 7, 1940, 40–41.

26. They were not powerful dive-bombers: the army designated the ten NA-69s as A-27s. Pursuit squadrons based in the Philippines used these as well as the Republic EP-1s for training before graduating to flying P-40s. See Glen Williford, *Racing the Sunrise: The Reinforcement of America's Pacific Outposts, 1941–1942* (Annapolis, MD: Naval Institute Press, 2010), 12.

27. NARA, RG 59, CDF 893.248/186, "Dr. Soong and Joseph Green," November 7, 1940.

28. FDRL Morgenthau, vol. 330, "Group Meeting," November 7, 1940, 41.

29. Ancestry.com, NARA, RG 85, M1410: 366 Passenger Lists of Vessels Arriving at San Francisco, Ship Manifest "American Clipper Passenger List 40419," November 14, 1940. The flight typically took six days from Hong Kong to San Francisco.

30. HISU, ANY, box 105, Mil/Av 39–41, "Data re types of planes for use by China," November 25, 1940; NARA, RG 59, box 5864, CDF 893.248/188, "Joseph Green to the Under Secretary," November 25, 1940.

31. NARA, RG 59, box 5864, CDF 893.248/189 PS/FF, "Joseph Green memorandum," November 22, 1940.

32. NARA, RG 59, box 5864, CDF 893.248/193, "Joseph Green to Under Secretary Welles," November 23, 1940.

33. FRUS 1940, vol. 4, "Memorandum of conversation by the Secretary of State," November 26, 1940, 697.

34. FRUS 1940, vol. 4, "The President of the Chinese Executive Yuan (Chiang) to President Roosevelt," November 28, 1940, 699. The original is in NARA, RG 59, CDF 893.248/194, "Aid to China, Memorandum of Conversation, Secretary Hull and Dr. T. V. Soong," November 28, 1940. See also HISU, ANY, box 105, Mil/Av 39–41, "SECRET Data re types of planes for use by China," November 25, 1940, probably by Arthur Young and Claire Chennault.

35. FDRL Morgenthau, vol. 334, "Conversation Hull and Morgenthau December 2, 1940 9:40 a.m.," 153–55.

36. NARA, RG 59, CDF 893.248/194, "Unsigned confidential communication from Chiang Kai-Shek," November 28, 1940, 3.

37. Ibid., 4.

38. Ibid., 3.

39. HISU, ANY, box 105, Mil/Av 39–41, "Memorandum on the Aviation Situation in China [by Claire Chennault]," November 19, 1940, 2.

8. Roosevelt's Dilemma

1. FRUS 1940, vol. 4, "The Ambassador in Japan (Grew), to the Secretary of State," Tokyo, June 19, 1940, 26–27.

2. Ickes, *Secret Diaries*, vol. 3, September 15, 1940, 322; FDRL Morgenthau, vol. 308, "Conversation with Leon Henderson," September 24, 1940, 43.

3. FDRL Morgenthau, vol. 334, "Re Chinese Loan," December 1, 1940, 8:30 p.m., 39–40. There were several meetings on one day so the references are distinguished by time of day.

4. FDRL Morgenthau, vol. 333, "Re: Loan to China," November 29, 1940, 11:30 a.m., 31.

5. Ibid., 33; "China-Japan: Treaty concerning Basic Relations Signed at Nanking November 30, 1940," *American Journal of International Law* 35, no. 3, Supplement: Official Documents (July 1941): 125–28.

6. FDRL Morgenthau, vol. 333, "Re China Loan, November 30, 1940, 10:20 a.m.," 241.

7. FDRL Morgenthau, vol. 333, "Re Chinese Loan, November 30, 1940, 11:05 a.m.," 252–54.

8. FDRL Morgenthau, vol. 333, "Conversation Morgenthau and Hull, November 29, 1940, 1:02 p.m.," 94–95.

9. FDRL Morgenthau, vol. 333, "Re: Chinese Loan, November 30, 1940, 10:20 a.m.," 244; "Re: Chinese Loan, November 30, 1940, 11:05 a.m.," 251.

10. Ickes, *Secret Diaries*, 3: 384.

11. FDRL Morgenthau, vol. 333, "Re: Chinese Loan, November 29–30, 1940, 11:05 a.m.," 253.

12. Ickes, *Secret Diaries*, 3:384.

13. Ibid., 3:385.

14. Ibid., 3:387–88.

15. FRUS 1940, vol. 4, "Memorandum of conversation by the Secretary of State," November 26, 1940, 697.

16. FDRL Morgenthau, vol. 333, "Re: Chinese Loan, November 30, 1940, 11:20 a.m.," 269.

17. FDRL Morgenthau, vol. 334, "Re: Chinese Loan," December 1, 1940, 8:30 p.m.," 63.

18. FDRL Morgenthau, vol. 333, "Re: Chinese Loan, November 30, 1940, 11:05 a.m.," 253.

19. Ibid.

20. FDRL Morgenthau, vol. 333, "Re: Chinese Loan, November 30, 1940, 10:20 a.m.," 243.

21. FDRL Morgenthau, vol. 333, "Conversation with Sumner Welles," November 30, 1940, 267.

22. FDRL, PSF Safe File, "Navy 'Plan Dog,' Memorandum for the Secretary," November 12, 1940, by Admiral Harold R. Stark, 22; Blum, *From the Morgenthau Diaries*, 82–83.

23. Quoted by Mark Watson, *Chief of Staff*, 122.

24. For the evidence see Frederick W. Marks III, *Wind over Sand: The Diplomacy of Franklin Roosevelt* (Athens: University of Georgia Press, 1988), 88–93.

25. Ibid., fn226.

26. Quoted ibid., 92.

27. Ibid., 88.

28. Warren F. Kimball, ed., *Churchill and Roosevelt: The Complete Correspondence*, vol. 1, *Alliance Emerging, 1933–November 1942* (Princeton, NJ: Princeton University Press, 1984), 93.

29. FDRL Morgenthau, vol. 334, "Re: Chinese Loan, December 1, 1940, 8:30 p.m.," 63–64.

9. Bombing Japan

1. David Reynolds, "Lord Lothian and Anglo-American Relations, 1939–1940," *Transactions of the American Philosophical Society*, new series, vol. 73, no. 2 (1983): 48; *NYT*, "Envoy Flies Here," November 24, 1941, 1.

2. FDRL Morgenthau, vol. 342A, China: Bombers December 3–22, 1940: "Dictated December 3 1940," 1.

3. FDRL Morgenthau, vol. 342A, "December 7, 1940," 2.

4. FDRL Morgenthau, vol. 342A, "December 8, 1940," 2.

5. Ibid.

6. Ibid.

7. FDRL Morgenthau, vol. 342A, "December 10, 1940," 10.

8. *NYT*, "Bomber Is Forced to Return to Base," January 6, 1941, 8.

9. NARA, RG 59, CDF 893.248/208, "Memorandum by Joseph Green," December 5, 1940.

10. Ibid.

11. *Select Telegrams*, "Telegram from Chiang on Chiang's letter to Roosevelt," December 13, 1940, 293.

12. FDRL Morgenthau, Presidential Diary vol. 3, "December 17, 1940," pp. 0742–43.

13. NARA, RG 165, box 887, NM 84, entry 31, file: Office Chief of Staff, Notes on Conferences, decisions by Chief of Staff, Deputy Chiefs of Staff, and other Information, September 26, 1940–December 31, 1940: "Memorandum of Army and Navy Conference," December 16, 1940.

14. NARA, RG 165, "Memorandum of Army and Navy Conference," December 16, 1940.

15. FRUS 1940, vol. 4, "The President of the Chinese Executive Yuan (Chiang) to the Secretary of the Treasury (Morgenthau)," December 16, 1940, 712.

16. FDRL Morgenthau, vol. 342A, "December 18 1940," 12.

17. FDRL Morgenthau, Presidential Diary, vol. 3, "December 17, 1940," p. 0743.

18. FDRL Morgenthau, vol. 342A, "December 20 1940 4:00 pm, Present: T. V. Soong, Mrs Klotz, Mr. Young," 18.

19. Harold Gullan, "Expectations of Infamy: Roosevelt and Marshall Prepare for War, 1938–1941," *Presidential Studies Quarterly* 28, no. 3 (Summer 1998): 515.

20. Emerson, "Franklin Roosevelt," 184, and Waldo Heinrichs, *Threshold of War: Franklin D. Roosevelt and American Entry into World War II* (New York: Oxford University Press, 1988), 18.

21. FDRL Morgenthau, vol. 342A, "December 20 1940 4:00 pm," 18.

22. See chapter 13.

23. FDRL Morgenthau, vol. 342A, "Notes on a Conference at Home of the Secretary," December 21, 1940, 5:00 p.m., 24.

24. Ibid., 25.

25. Yale University Library, Manuscripts and Archives, Diary of Henry Stimson, Series 14, Diaries box 74, vol. 36, entry for December 22, 1940, 1.

26. FDRL Morgenthau, vol. 342A, "December 22, 1940," 27.

10. Tomahawks for China

1. Wagner, "P-40."

2. *NYT*, "New Army Plane to Be Exhibited," May 16, 1940, 40.

3. FDRL Morgenthau, vol. 263, "May 16 1940 2:30 p.m. Present: General Brett, Major Lyon, Mr. Young, Mrs Klotz," 53.

4. Francis H. Dean and Dan Hagedorn, *Curtiss Fighter Aircraft: A Photographic History, 1917–1948* (Atglen, PA: Schiffler Military History, 2007), 260.

5. "Curtiss Expansion Well Under Way," *Curtiss Flyleaf* 24, no. 1 (January–February 1941): 10.

6. Wagner, "P-40," 40; TNA, AVIA 38/732, "BRINY 2536," January 16, 1941.

7. FDRL Morgenthau, vol. 337, "Copy of letter Winston Churchill to Jean Monnet," July 18, 1940, 264.

8. TNA, AVIA 38/732, "BRINY 2704," January 24, 1941.

9. TNA, AVIA 38/732, "Secret P-40 Aircraft," January 7, 1941.

10. TNA, AVIA 38/732, "British 81A (Tomahawk) airplanes as per proposed schedule, Nov. 2, 1940."

11. TNA, AVIA 38/732, "BRINY 2704," January 24, 1941.

12. TNA, AVIA 38/732, "ZAX 644," January 10, 1941.

13. San Diego Air and Space Museum Archive (hereafter SDASMA), American Volunteer Group (Flying Tigers) Special Collection, box 3, Papers of Walter Pentecost (hereafter Pentecost), folder Ferry Pilot Forms, "Flight Log Book Chinese P-40s Test Pilot B. A. Glover H-81-A-2."

14. TNA, AVIA 38/732, "BRINY 2106," December 23, 1940.

15. TNA, AVIA 38/732, "Mr. C. R. Fairey from Lewis Orde," October 28, 1940; AVIA 38/843, "Urgent, Tomahawk Spares Situation," August 22, 1941.

16. TNA, AVIA 38/732, "Tomahawk Curtiss 81A Aircraft," January 29, 1941, and "Tomahawk Curtiss 81A Aircraft," December 10, 1940.

17. TNA, AVIA 38/732, "Briny 2359 to Ministry of Aircraft Production from Self," January 7, 1941.

18. *Pearl Harbor Investigations*, vol. 15, "Exhibit No. 55, 'Conference in the Office of the Chief of Staff at 10:00 A.M., Tuesday, February 25 1941,'" p. 1629.

19. Curtiss-Wright Corporation and US Army Air Corps, "The Other Side of the Question: The P-40 in the Limelight," *Curtiss Flyleaf* 24, no. 4 (September–October 1941): 6. Tricycle landing gear with a nose wheel instead of a tail wheel was introduced on US fighter planes later in the war.

20. HISU, box 105, Mil/Av 39–41, "Extract from Pilot's letter," February 1941.

21. TNA, AVIA 38/732, "British 81A (Tomahawk) airplanes as per proposed schedule," November 2, 1940.

22. Dean and Hagedorn, *Curtiss Fighter Aircraft*, 265.

23. Ibid., 265–68 and 383–84; Curtiss-Wright and USAAC, "Other Side of the Question," 8; TNA, AVIA 38/732, "British 81A (Tomahawk) airplanes as per proposed schedule," November 2, 1940.

24. Dean and Hagedorn, *Curtiss Fighter Aircraft*, 265, 268; Curtiss-Wright and USAAC, "Other Side of the Question," 8.

25. TNA, AVIA 38/732, "Secret, P-40 Aircraft," January 7, 1941.

26. TNA, AVIA 38/732, "To Self from Air Ministry X80," January 11, 1941.

27. Office of Statistical Control, *Army Air Forces Statistical Digest*, World War II, December 1945, 128.

28. FDRL Morgenthau, vol. 338, "December 11, 1940, conversation Henry Morgenthau and Cordell Hull," 249.

29. FDRL Morgenthau, vol. 337, "To the Secretary from Mr. Young, Re: Planes for Greece," December 9, 1940, 259.

30. TNA, AVIA 38/732, "Memorandum Re: Additional Capacity for Production of P-40 Type Aircraft—construction Possible Release to Greece," December 10, 1940.

31. FDRL Morgenthau, vol. 338, "British Purchasing Program, December 11, 1940, 3:30 p.m.," 256.

32. FDRL Morgenthau, vol. 337, "To the Secretary from Mr. Young Re: Planes for Greece," December 9, 1940, 259.

33. TNA, AVIA 38/732, "To Self from Air Ministry ZAX 644," January 10, 1941.

34. TNA, AVIA 38/732 "Secret P-40 Aircraft," January 7, 1941.

11. Robbing Churchill to Pay Chiang

1. NARA, RG 165, box 887, NM 84, entry 31: "Conference in the Office of the Chief of Staff, December 23, 1940, 8:30 a.m."; TNA, AVIA 38/732 "Memo from Mr. E. N. Gray to Mr. C. R. Fairey," December 12, 1940.

2. NARA, RG 165, "C/S conference," December 23, 1940.

3. Virtually all the Martin bombers were destroyed through CAF pilot error in 1937. See BGLA, folder China Misc. Correspondence, "Leighton to Pawley," September 20, 1937, 2. The Japanese destroyed one Martin and several Russian bombers on the ground the night of March 14, 1938. See TNA, Air 2/3558, British Air Ops1938, January 25, 1939, appendix D.

4. NARA, RG 165, "C/S conference," December 23, 1940.

5. Ibid.

6. FDRL Morgenthau, vol. 342, "Notes on Conference in office of the Secretary of State, Monday, December 23, 1940, 9:30 a.m.," 47.

7. FDRL Morgenthau, vol. 342, "Hull P-40 conference 23/12/40," 49.

8. TNA, AVIA 38/732, "BRINY 2106 Self to Ministry of Aircraft Production," December 23, 1940.

9. Ibid.

10. FDRL Morgenthau, vol. 342, "Re: British Purchasing Program, December 23, 1940, 4:30 p.m.," 79.

11. Ibid., 80.

12. Ibid.

13. FDRL Morgenthau, vol. 344, "Notes on Conference at Home of the Secretary, January 1, 1941, 6 p.m.," 12.

14. Ibid.

15. Ibid.

16. FDRL Morgenthau, vol. 344, "Re Eccles' Announcement of Federal Reserve Board's Report, January 2, 1941, 10:56 a.m.," 35.

17. *NYT*, "Airplanes for China," January 1, 1941, 22.

18. FDRL Morgenthau, vol. 344, "Eccles' Announcement of Federal Reserve Board's Report, January 2, 1941, 10:56 a.m.," 35.

19. Ibid.

20. *Select Telegrams*, "Telegram from Chiang on Mao Bangchu's press interview," January 5, 1941, 301.

21. Ancestry.com, NARA, RG 85, Passenger Lists of Vessels Arriving at Honolulu, Hawaii, Ship manifest SS *Lurline* sailing from Los Angeles, January 24, 1941; *NYT*, "Japanese Emperor Greets President," January 26, 1941, 21.

22. FDRL Morgenthau, vol. 344, "Aid to Britain, January 3, 1941, 10:50 a.m.," 258.

23. TNA, Air 19/500, "To Ministry of Aircraft Production from British Air Commission," January 3, 1941.

24. FDRL Morgenthau, vol. 344, "Re: Chinese Purchasing program," January 2, 1941, 50.

25. Ibid., 52.

26. Ibid., 57 and 59.

27. Ibid., 54.

28. Ibid., 59.

29. Ibid., 60.

30. Ibid.

31. Ibid., 76.

32. FDRL Morgenthau, vol. 346, "Translation of Chinese telegram from General Chiang kai-shek to Secretary Morgenthau," dated January 6, 1941, 50.

33. TNA, CAB 9/1, "Appreciation by the Commander-in-Chief Far East," December 10, 1940, 289.

12. The Private Military Contractor

1. BGLA, folder CAMCO, AVG, "Bruce Leighton to W. D. Pawley," May 14, 1942.

2. FRUS 1940, vol. 4, "The Secretary of the Navy (Knox) to the Secretary of State Washington," October 19, 1940, 671.

3. See also *United States Statutes at Large, 1939–1941, vol. 54,* 76th Cong., 3d Sess.—CHS 875,876—October 14, 1940, 1168–69.

4. FRUS 1940, vol. 4, "Secretary of State to Secretary of the Navy," October 23, 1940, 678.

5. BGLA, folder CAMCO, AVG, "Leighton to Pawley," May 14, 1942, 2.

6. Ibid.

7. Ibid.

8. Anthony R. Carrozza, *William D. Pawley* (Washington, DC: Potomac Books, 2012), 75 and 337 fn81.

9. FDRL Morgenthau, vol. 346, "Planes for China," January 10, 1941.

10. NARA, RG 59, CDF 841.248/813, "Note by Stanley Hornbeck," January 15, 1941.

11. FDRL Morgenthau, vol. 344, "Re: Chinese Purchasing program," January 2, 1941, 76.

12. TNA, AVIA 83/843, "D. W. Howard [BAC] to C. W. Miller," February 12, 1941.

13. BGLA, folder CAMCO, AVG, "Telegram Leighton to Pawley," January 16, 1941.

14. BGLA6, folder CAMCO, AVG, "Telegram Leighton to Pawley," January 18, 1941.

15. Ibid.

13. Diplomatic Skirmishes

1. Watson, *Chief of Staff,* 124. He cites Memo, C of S for A C of S WPD, January 17, 1941, sub: White House Conference of Thursday, 16 Jan 41, WPD, 4175–18.

2. Herbert Feis, *Road to Pearl Harbor: The Coming of the War between the United States and Japan* (New York: Atheneum, 1967), 153–54.

3. Dorothy Borg, *The United States and the Far Eastern Crisis, 1933–1938* (Cambridge, MA: Harvard University Press, 1965), 68–81.

4. BGLA, folder CAMCO, AVG, "Bruce Leighton to Captain M. H. Deyo," January 20, 1941 (dictated January 18), 1.

5. Ibid., 2.

6. Ibid., 3.

7. TNA, Air 19/500, "Foreign Office to Viscount Halifax (Washington) re: Briny No. 2665 [of January 22: aircraft for China]," January 29, 1941.

8. Ibid.

9. TNA, Air 19/500, "Briny 2663 Ministry of Aircraft Production from British Air Commission," January 22, 1941.

10. TNA, FO 371/27606, F332/G, "Release of United States Aircraft for China," January 22, 1941: minute by Ashley Clarke, January 24, 1941.

11. TNA, FO 371/27606, F332/G, "Minute by Anthony Eden," January 25, 1941.

12. TNA, CAB 66/14/35, "Supply of Aircraft to China from the United States," January 27, 1941.

13. TNA, FO 371/27606, F332/G, "FO to Halifax re: Briny No. 2665," January 29, 1941.

14. FDRL Morgenthau, vol. 353, "Group Meeting, January 30, 1941, 9:30 a.m.," 20–21.

15. Ibid.

16. Ibid.

17. HISU, ANY, box 105, Mil/Av 39–41, "Draft telegram to the Generalissimo sent — *CKS approved*," January 25, 1941.

18. *Select Telegrams*, "Telegram from Chiang on recruitment of American Volunteers," January 27, 1941, 307.

19. National Museum of Naval Aviation (NMNA), Emil Buehler Naval Aviation Library, RG 4.9, U.S. Navy American Volunteer Group Papers, "Memorandum for Secretary Procurement of Personnel for China by Mort L. Deyo," February 3, 1941.

20. Ibid.

21. HISU, ANY, box 105, folder Mil/Av 39–41, "Young to James McHugh," February 13, 1941.

22. *NYT*, "Knox Says Greece Refuses 30 Planes . . . Chinese Are Getting 100," February 6, 1941, 8; *Scotsman*, "US Planes for China, 100 Which Were to Have Come to Britain," February 6, 1941.

23. TNA, FO 371/27638, F757/G, "Viscount Halifax (Washington), to the Foreign Office," February 5, 1941.

24. TNA, FO 371/27638, F1051/45/10, "Release of U.S. aircraft to China, Viscount Halifax (Washington)," February 8, 1941, 34–35.

25. TNA, FO 371/27638, F1073/45/10, "Release of U.S. aircraft to China February 18 1941: minute by J. C. Sterndale Bennett," 36–37.

26. FRUS 1941, vol. 4, "Memorandum of Conversation, by the Assistant Chief of the Division of Far Eastern Affairs (Ballantine) (Washington)," January 22, 1941, 10–14.

27. David Mayers, *FDR's Ambassadors and the Diplomacy of Crisis* (Cambridge: Cambridge University Press, 2013), 16.

28. FRUS, Japan 1931–1941, vol. 2, "Memorandum by the Counselor of Embassy in Japan (Dooman) [Tokyo]," February 14, 1941, 138–39.

29. FRUS, Japan 1931–1941, vol. 2, "The Ambassador in Japan (Grew) to the Secretary of State," Tokyo, February 26, 1941, 137–38.

30. Marks, *Wind over Sand*, 94, and FRUS, Japan 1931–1941, vol. 2, "Memorandum by the Counselor of Embassy in Japan, ([Eugene] Dooman) Tokyo," February 14, 1941, 138–39.

31. Marks, *Wind over Sand*, 95.

32. Dallek, *Franklin D. Roosevelt*, 284.

14. Reinforcing the Philippines

1. Walter D. Edmonds, *They Fought with What They Had* (Boston: Little, Brown, 1951), 16.

2. US Air Force Historical Study (USAFHS) no. 111, *Army Air Action in the Philippines and Netherland East Indies, 1941–1942* (Maxwell AFB, AL, 1945), 6.

3. FDRL Morgenthau, vol. 324, "Group Meeting," October 23, 1940, 162; Williford, *Racing the Sunrise*.

4. USAFHS no. 111, 6–7.

5. Ibid., 6; Edmonds, *They Fought*, 14.

6. Edmonds, *They Fought*, 14.

7. Ibid.

8. Bartsch, *December 8, 1941*, 25.

9. Phillip Meilinger, *Hoyt S. Vandenberg: The Life of a General* (South Bend: Indiana University Press, 1989), 25.

10. Maochun Yu, *OSS in China: Prelude to Cold War* (Annapolis, MD: Naval Institute Press, 2013), 53.

11. Meilinger, *Vandenberg*, 25.

12. Bartsch, *December 8, 1941*, 29.

13. Ibid., 53.

14. FDRL Morgenthau, vol. 333, "Conversation Morgenthau and Sumner Welles," November 29, 1940, 27.

15. Meilinger, *Vandenberg*, 26.

16. Bartsch, *December 8, 1941*, 9–10.

17. Richard Overy, *The Battle of Britain* (London: Andre Deutsch digital edition, 2010), location 288.

18. Bartsch, *December 8, 1941*, 9.

19. Quoted in Watson, *Chief of Staff*, 423.

20. Ibid., 124–25.

21. Bartsch, *December 8, 1941*, xlix, citing *Washington Post*, "US Warns She'll Protect Philippines," October 24, 1940, 7.

22. Watson, *Chief of Staff*, 424.

23. Ibid.

24. Bartsch, *December 8, 1941*, 60.

25. Ibid., 17.

26. Ibid., 62.

27. Ibid., xvii.

28. Ibid., 42.

29. Ibid., 41.

30. Watson, *Chief of Staff*, 440.

31. USAFHS no. III, 13.

32. Edmonds, *They Fought*, 3–4.

33. See Richard Overy, *The Bombing War: Europe, 1939–1945* (London: Penguin, 2013), 89.

15. Favoring Currie

1. FDRL Morgenthau, vol. 334, "Re Chinese Loan, December 1, 1940, 8:30 p.m.," 39–40.

2. FDRL, PSF China 1941, "The importance of Singapore to the defense of the British Isles and the British Empire and to the interests of the United States," December 4, 1940, revised April 23, 1941 (Lauchlin Currie).

3. John Paton Davies Jr., *China Hand: An Autobiography* (Philadelphia: University of Pennsylvania Press, 2012), 31.

4. FDRL Morgenthau, vol. 348, "Conversation with Lauchlin Currie," January 16, 1941, 177–78.

5. FDRL, PSF Adm. Assts: Laughlin Currie—Subject File, June 1940–1945, "Memorandum for the President: Re: China Trip," January 18, 1941.

6. *NYT*, "Roosevelt Sending Aide to Chungking," January 24, 1941, 4.

7. FDRL Morgenthau, Presidential Diary, vol. 4, "April 21 1941," p. 0901.

8. Ancestry.com, NARA, RG 85, Passenger and Crew Manifests of Airplanes Arriving at Honolulu, Hawaii, "Passenger List NC 18606 American Clipper from San Francisco, California January 29 1941."

9. CUL McHugh, box 1, folder 7, "My dear McHugh from Frank Knox," January 25, 1941.

10. CUL McHugh, box 1, folder 7, "Dear Mac," January 26, 1941.

11. CUL McHugh, box 1, folder 6, "Your Excellency [Chiang Kai-shek]," November 15, 1940.

12. CUL McHugh, box 7, folder 1, "Dear Lauch," April 14, 1941, 2.

13. FDRL, PSF China, 1941—Currie Report, March 15, 1941, 27, 30.

14. Ibid., 27.

15. Ibid., 22.

16. Ibid., 22–23.

17. Ibid.

16. The Mercenary's Contract

1. FDRL, PSF Thomas G. Corcoran, "Dear Tommy," January 20, 1941.

2. FDRL Morgenthau, vol. 374, "Conversation H. M. Jr and Tom Corcoran," February 21, 1941, 165.

3. Ibid., 164.

4. FDRL Morgenthau, vol. 157, "Group Meeting," December 21, 1938, 175.

5. Ibid., 177–78.

6. FDRL Morgenthau, vol. 374, "Conversation H. M. Jr and Tom Corcoran," February 21, 1941, 163–65.

7. *Select Telegrams*, "Telegram from Chiang on dispatch of senior US air force officers," March 5, 1941, and "Telegram from Chiang on American volunteers," March 13, 1941, 312–13.

8. FDRL (http://fdrlibrary.marist.edu), Day Log, March 19, 1941; HISU, Lauchlin Bernard Currie Papers (hereafter HISU Currie), box 5, "John K. Fairbank, Memorandum on Air Program for China, 1942," (hereafter Fairbank memo), 18.

9. BGLA, folder CAMCO, AVG, "Strictly Confidential to Central Aircraft Manufacturing Company Federal Inc., U.S.A.," March 21, 1941.

10. Ibid.

11. CUL McHugh, box 1, folder 7, "My dear Major [McHugh] from Frank Knox," March 22, 1941.

12. NARA, RG 160, entry 120 (NM-25), box 1, location 390/27/31/6, "Memorandum for the Chief of Staff, subject Pilots for the Chinese Air Force," March 29, 1941.

13. CUL McHugh, box 2, folder 10, "From Major J. M. McHugh, Conversation with the Generalissimo, 11 January 1941: his requests for American Advisor Missions for Transport and Aviation."

14. HISU, ANY, box 105, Mil/Av 39–41, "Dear Arthur Chungking," January 14, 1941, received January 28, 1941, 1.

15. Ibid., 2.

16. HISU, ANY, box 36, Mil/Av, "Letter from Chiang Kai Shek to Colonel

John H. Jouett, Shanghai," July 25, 1932, 3: the American instructors were barred by their contracts from combat missions. NARA, RG 38, box 136, file A-1-u, Register no. 7348, "Central Aviation Academy, Hangchow, China," May 18, 1935; Archivio Storico del Ministero degli Affari Esteri (Italy), [file] Anno 1934, CINA R. Ambasciata Shanghai Arrivo, "Situazione in Cina—Missione aeronautica italiana," n. 492 R, Shanghai, February 2, 1934.

17. *Select Telegrams*, "Telegram from Chiang on recruitment of American volunteers," January 27, 1941, 307.

18. *Select Telegrams*, "Chiang to Soong about American Volunteers," March 13, 1941, 313; "Telegram from Chiang on recruitment of air force instructors and volunteers," April 12, 1941, 318.

19. TNA, Air 8/586, F3856/523/G, "From Chungking to Foreign Office Most Secret," May 6, 1941.

20. TNA, FO 371/27640, "Burma 2240 1941 from Governor of Burma to Secretary of State for Burma Rangoon," June 14, 1941.

21. *Select Telegrams*, "Telegram to Chiang on transportation of P-40 fighters," June 6, 1941, 340.

22. FDRL Morgenthau, Diaries, book 4, President Roosevelt, March 1, 1941, through December 31, 1941, "April 21, 1941," p. 0901.

23. FDRL Morgenthau, vol. 390, "Re: Chinese Loan," April 21, 1941, 137.

24. FDRL Morgenthau, vol. 390, "Group Meeting," April 21, 1941, 10:00 a.m., 73.

17. Recruiters and Recruited

1. NARA, RG 160, entry 120 (NM-25), box 1, location 390/27/31/6, "Memorandum for the Chief of Staff, subject Pilots for the Chinese Air Force," March 29, 1941.

2. Ibid.

3. Headquarters, AAF, Office of Flying Safety, *Pilot Training Manual for the P-40*, 1943, 5.

4. W. F. Craven and J. L. Cate, *The Army Air Forces in World War II* (Chicago: University of Chicago Press, 1955), 4:572, 615.

5. See chapter 10.

6. Charles R. Bond Jr. and Terry H. Anderson, *A Flying Tiger's Diary* (College Station, TX: Texas A&M University Press and the Texas Book Consortium, 1984), 38.

7. I estimate that fourteen AAC pilots had some experience of a P-40 before going to China—eight from Mitchell Field (New York), five from Selfridge Field

(Michigan), and one from Hamilton Field (California). See Carl Molesworth, *Curtiss P-40 Long-Nosed Tomahawks* (Oxford: Osprey, 2013), 42, and Ford, *Flying Tigers*, for references to pilots recruited from units based at these airfields.

8. HISU, ANY, box 105, Mil/Av 39–41, "Extract from Letter of April 7 1941, from Colonel C. L. Chennault to Mr. W. D. Pawley," 1; "Exhibit 'A' Employees Required," April 1, 1941.

9. HISU, ANY, "Extract from Letter of April 7 1941."

10. HISU, ANY, box 105, Mil/Av 39–41, "Exhibit 'A' Employees Required," April 1, 1941.

11. Ibid.

12. HISU, ANY, box 105, Mil/Av 39–41, "Extract from Letter of April 7 1941, from Colonel C. L. Chennault to Mr. W. D. Pawley," 10.

13. TNA, Air 5/586 "W. M. (41) 71st Meeting, International Air force for China (W. P. (41) 165)," July 17, 1941, and Extract from W. M. (41) 71st Conclusions, July 17, 1941.

14. Craven and Cate, *Army Air Forces*, 6:575–76.

15. HISU Currie, Fairbank memo, 18, and Library of Congress, microfilm, Papers of Claire Lee Chennault, "CAMCO contract April 15 1941."

16. HISU Currie, box 2, folder AVG Corr and Mem, May–Sept 1941, "Agreement between CAMCO and employee"; Fairbank memo, 19.

17. HISU Currie, Fairbank memo, 20.

18. Ibid., 20–22.

19. HISU Currie, box 2, folder AVG Corr and Mem, May–Sept 1941, "May 3 1941."

20. HISU Currie, Fairbank memo, 22.

21. Byrd, *Chennault*, 123–24.

22. Ford, *Flying Tigers*, 43–44.

23. Charles Baisden, *Flying Tiger to Air Commando* (Atglen, PA: Schiffler Military History, 1999), 12; Byrd, *Chennault*, 123–24; Ford, *Flying Tigers*, 47.

24. Carrozza, *William D. Pawley*, 111; *American Aviation*, "India Plans Factory," July 1, 1941, 41.

25. Estimates vary, but the current satellite map of Taungoo airport at Kaytumati shows a small airfield of about fifteen hundred meters long next to a runway that is about a mile long.

26. HISU Currie, box 2, folder AVG Corr and Mem, Dec. 1941, "Information from Lt. Estes Swindle," December 6, 1941, 8.

27. Baisden, *Flying Tiger*, 20.

28. SDASMA, Pentecost, 1941 Calendar, entry for July 29, 1941.

29. FDRL, Subject Files, box 91, folder Adm, Assts: Laughlin Currie, June

1940–1945, "Memorandum for the President: Protection of American pilots sailing to China," June 21, 1941. Roosevelt wrote "O.K." next to the CC to Frank Knox on June 26, 1941, at the bottom of the memo.

30. HISU Currie, box 2, folder AVG Corr and Mem, May–Sept 1941, "Confidential to Dr. Laughlin Currie from Richard Aldworth," July 1, 1941: Jennifer Holik-Urban, *To Soar with the Tigers: The Life and Diary of Flying Tiger, Robert Brouk* (Woodridge, IL: Generations, 2011), 10.

31. Holik-Urban, *To Soar*, 26.

32. Bond and Anderson, *Flying Tiger's Diary*.

33. *Washington Post*, "US Releases Pilots to Fight for China," June 1, 1941, 1.

34. HISU Currie, box 2, folder AVG Corr and Mem, May–Sept 1941, "H. R. Stark to Lauchlin Currie, the White House," August 27, 1941.

35. *Straits Times*, "U.S. Pilot Leader on Way to Chungking," July 19, 1941, 13, eresources.nlb.gov.sg/newspapers.

36. *China Weekly Review*, "People in the News," July 26, 1941, 256.

37. CCAC, July 28–29, 1941.

38. Olga Greenlaw, *The Lady and the Tigers*, ed. Dan Ford (Durham, NH: Warbird Books, 2012), 21.

39. Ford, *Flying Tigers*, 66–67.

40. *Daily Herald* (Biloxi and Gulfport, MS), January 18, 1943, cited on Wikipedia, "United States Court for China," wikipedia.org/wiki/United_States_Court_for_China#cite_note-25.

41. Baisden, *Flying Tiger*, 20.

42. Ibid.

43. HISU Currie, box 2, folder AVG Corr and Mem, Dec. 1941, "Information from Lt. Estes Swindle," December 6, 1941, 7; Holik-Urban, *To Soar*, 18–19.

44. Chennault, *Way of a Fighter*, 100–101.

45. Ibid., 106.

18. The International Air Force

1. TNA, FO 371/24708, War Cabinet C.O.S. (40) 592, "The Situation in the Far East in the event of Japanese Intervention against us," July 31, 1940, paragraph 62, p. 19.

2. John Grehan and Martin Mace, compilers, *Disaster in the Far East: The Defense of Malaya, Japanese Capture of Hong Kong, and the Fall of Singapore* (Barnsley, UK: Pen & Sword Military, 2015), "Dispatch" by Robert Brooke-Popham, 1948, 56.

3. Ibid., data derived from appendix J, p. 84.

4. Alan Axelrod, *Encyclopaedia of World War II*, vol. 1 (New York: Facts on File, 2007), 470–71.

5. TNA, WO 3555A, "F.E. (40) instructions for Brigadier Dennys." Relatively little is known about Lancelot Dennys (1890–1942), despite his considerable influence over Sino-British relations in this period. He died in a CNAC plane crash on March 14, 1942, en route from Kunming to Chungking.

6. *North China Herald*, "New British Military Attaché to China," January 8, 1941, 42.

7. TNA, FO 371/27615, F/3176/G, "Report on conversations between Major-General L. E. Dennys Military Attaché to the British Embassy in CHINA and General Ho Yao-Tsu, Chief of the Adjutant's Department of the Generalissimo's Personal Headquarters," January 30–February 3, 1941, 116–22.

8. TNA, FO 371/27615, F/3176, "Third Discussion Held on 3rd February, 1941," 119.

9. TNA, Air 8/539, "Following for the War Office and the Air Ministry from Dennys," February 12, 1941, 118.

10. TNA, Air 8/539, Dennys cable, February 11, 1941.

11. TNA, WO 3555A, "Sir A. Clark Kerr following for War office from Military attaché," February 5, 1941. 79a.

12. For background on Monnet in the interwar years see François Duchêne, *Jean Monnet, the First Statesman of Interdependence* (New York: W. W. Norton, 1994), 49–97.

13. Feis, *Road to Pearl Harbor*, 165–66.

14. TNA, Air 8/586, "To Air Ministry repeat C. in C. China from Slessor 11.2.40 [*sic*; 41] 1250 recirculated 12/2/41."

15. TNA, Air 8/586, "Slessor cable," February 11, 1941.

16. Ibid.

17. Grehan and Mace, *Disaster*, 83.

18. TNA, Air/8/586, "Slessor cable," February 11, 1941.

19. Ibid.

20. HISU, ANY, box 36, Mil/Av, "Additional information for Memorandum from Col. C. F. Huang," August 1, 1940; TNA, Air 8/539, "To Chief of Air Staff from Slessor," March 16, 1941, 107.

21. TNA, Air 8/586, "To Air Ministry (R), C. in C. Singapore, Most Secret. Personal for C.A.S. from Slessor," February 21, 1941.

22. Ibid.

23. Ibid. Lord Beaverbrook complained to Portal about the "scope of Slessor's activities in America, stating it was undesirable for him to discuss the disposal of aviation such as the Vultee Vanguards." See TNA, Air 8/539, "my dear C.A.S. from Beaverbrook," April 7, 1941.

24. TNA, Air 8/539, "My Dear Beaverbrook from C. S. Portal," March 6, 1941, 92–94.

25. TNA, Air 8/539, "My Dear C.A.S. from Beaverbrook," March 6, 1941, 91.

26. TNA, Air 8/539, "Slessor for C.A.S.," April 7, 1941, 84; "To British Air Commission, Washington from Ministry of Aircraft Production," April 26, 1941; Air 8/586, "To Ministry of Aircraft Production from British Air Commission," May 22, 1941.

27. TNA, Air 8/539, "Slessor for C.A.S.," April 7, 1941, 84.

28. See Richard L. Dunn, "Airplanes of the Chinese Air Force, 1942–1943: The Vultee P-66 and Other Aircraft" (2005), http://www.warbirdforum.com/dunnp663.htm.

29. For background on the Dennys mission see TNA, WO 3555A, "Assistance to China," vol. 1 passim: TNA, Air 8/539, "C. in C. Far East to the War Office 6/3/41."

30. TNA, WO 208/327, "G. O. C. Malaya to War Office Ref. Slessor's telegrams 12/2 and 20/2," February 26, 1941, 2.

31. Ibid.

32. Ibid.

33. TNA, WO 208/327, "Air Ministry to C. in C. Far East," March 4, 1941, 3; WO 106/3555A, "Foreign Office to Sir A. Clark Kerr (Shanghai)," March 24, 1941, 124A.

34. TNA, Air 8/586, "Foreign Office to Lord Halifax," March 15, 1941, and "Foreign Office to Lord Halifax," March 24, 1941.

35. TNA, FO 371/27638, F1073, "Release of US aircraft to China": "Viscount Halifax to Foreign Office," February 18, 1941.

36. Ibid.

37. TNA, FO 371/27638, F1073, "Release of US aircraft to China": minute B. E. T. Gage, February 22, 1941.

38. TNA, Air 8/539, "From Sir A. Blackburn (Chungking) to Foreign Office," March 10, 1941.

39. TNA, FO 371/27638, F1073, "To Sir A. Blackburn (Chungking) from Foreign Office," March 21, 1941.

40. TNA, FO 371/27615, F3077/60/10, "Mr Eden to Sir A. Clark-Kerr (Shanghai)," April 16, 1941.

41. TNA, FO 371/27615, F3017/G, "Anglo-Chinese Cooperation in event of war with Japan," April 16, 1941, 98.

42. TNA, FO 371/27615, F3017/G, "Minute by John Brenan," April 16, 1941, 98–99, and TNA, FO 371/27616, F4038/60/10, "From Foreign Office to Tokyo," May 14, 1941.

43. TNA, FO 371/27616, F4276, "From Chungking to Foreign Office," May 20, 1941.

44. Ibid.

45. TNA, FO 371/27615, F2965/G, "Anglo-Chinese, Military Cooperation in China, 15 April 1941: minute Ashley Clarke April 20 1941."

46. TNA, CAB 121/639, "From the Foreign Office to Chungking," May 10, 1941, 66.

47. TNA, CAB 121/639, "From C in C Far East to the War Office," April 4, 1941, 77.

48. TNA, Air 8/586, "F.O. to Lord Halifax Washington," March 13, 1941.

49. TNA, Air 8/539, "From Foreign Office to Chungking," May 10, 1941, 66.

19. Staying on in Burma

1. TNA, Air 8/586, "To A.A. Washington from Air Ministry X.221-29/4[/41]."

2. TNA, Air 8/586, "To Air Whit from A.A. Washington No. 249 5/5/[1941]."

3. TNA, WO 208/327, "Telegram from Secretary of State to Government of Burma," May 13, 1941, 10.

4. TNA, Air 8/586, "To A.A. Washington from: Air Ministry, Your 249 5/5[/41]."

5. TNA, Air 8/586, "To Air Whit from A.A. Washington No. 257 9/5[/41] your X.933 6/5."

6. TNA, Air 8/586, F/3856/523/G, "From Chungking to Foreign Office Most Secret," May 8, 1941.

7. TNA, FO 371/27639, F3923/523/G, "Telegram Foreign Office to Lord Halifax," May 20, 1941, 28.

8. NARA, RG 38, box 116, Strat. Plans War Plans Div., "Memorandum for British Military Mission Aid to China," June 25, 1941.

9. NARA, RG 38, box 116, Strat. Plans War Plans Div., "From Director of Naval Intelligence to Chief of Naval Operations Aid to China," [July 8, 1941].

10. NARA, RG 38, box 116, Strat. Plans War Plans Div., "Memorandum for the Director, Comment on Proposed Aid to China," A. H. McCollum, July 8, 1941.

11. TNA, WO/208/327, "Foreign Office to Chungking [re:] telegram no. 256," June 6, 1941, 14.

12. TNA, WO/208/327, "B.A.D. Washington addressed Admiralty 17.8.41" [about release of ammunition for IAF Tomahawks].

13. TNA, FO 371/27639, F4661/G, "From C-in-C Far East to the War Office," May 27, 1941, 100.

14. TNA, Air 8/586, "From Washington to Foreign Office, Viscount Halifax No. 2357," May 26, 1941.

15. TNA, FO 371/27639, F5248/230/G, "Minutes of a Meeting held in Mr. Butler's Room at the Foreign Office," June 6, 1941, at 11:30 a.m., 152.

16. TNA, WO/208/357, "Ashley Clarke, Foreign Office to Colonel Scott War Office," June 6, 1941, 15, and "To C-in-C Far East from Air Ministry Whitehall," June 8, 1941, 17.

17. TNA, WO/208/357, "C in C Far East to Air Ministry," June 17, 1941, 18.

18. TNA, Air 8/586, "To British Ambassador Chungking repeated Air Ministry, War Office Please Forward. From: C-in-C Far East," June 20, 1941.

19. TNA, Air 8/586, "From Chungking," June 24, 1941.

20. TNA, Air 8/586, "To the War Office repeated Ambassador at Chungking from C. in C. Far East," June 25, 1941.

21. TNA, WO/208/327, "From Washington to Foreign Office," June 24, 1941, 20.

22. TNA, Air 8/539, "C.-in-C. Far East to War Office, 359/3 cipher 25/6 25/6/41."

23. SDASMA, Pentecost, folder Personal Daily Calendar, entries for May 23, 1941, and following.

24. HISU Currie, box 2, folder AVG Corr and Mem, May–Sept 1941, "American Consulate Rangoon, Burma July 14 1941 Subject American airmen for planes for China . . . July 14 1941 by Austin Brady"; TNA, AVIA 83/843, "D. W. Howard [BAC] to C. W. Miller 12th February 1941" suggests that the last thirty-two Tomahawks left Buffalo within a few weeks of the first sixty-eight.

25. SDASMA, Pentecost, Daily Calendar, July 18, 1941.

26. SDASMA, Pentecost, Daily Calendar, November 28, 1941.

27. TNA, WO/208/327, "To Air Ministry, from Warburton Chungking," July 22, 1941. The bombers in question were thirty-three Lockheed Hudsons with a range of two thousand miles and thirty-three Douglas DB-7s of eleven hundred miles.

28. TNA, WO/208/327, "Secretary of State to Governor of Burma," July 19, 1941, 27; TNA, Air 5/586, "W.M. (41) 71st Meeting, International Air Force for China (W.P. (41) 165)," July 17, 1941, and "Extract from W.M. (41) 71st Conclusions," July 17, 1941.

29. TNA, Air 5/586, "W.M. (41) 71st Meeting, International Air Force for China (W.P. (41) 165)," July 17, 1941, and "Extract from W.M. (41) 71st Conclusions," July 17, 1941.

30. TNA, Air 5/586, "W.M. (41) 71st Meeting, International Air Force for China (W.P. (41) 165)," July 17, 1941.

31. HISU Currie, box 3, folder Chiang kai-shek Mme, "C. L. Chennault Memo for H. E. Madame Chiang Kai-shek subject: Report upon conference with British Officials in Burma and Singapore," August 5, 1941, 1.

32. HISU, "C.L.C. memo for Madame Chiang," [August 5], 1941, 2.

33. TNA, WO 208/327, "Governor of Burma to Secretary of Ste for Burma," July 26, 1941, 28.

34. Ibid.

35. TNA, WO/208/327, "From C.-in-C., Far East to the War Office," July 27, 1941, 29.

36. TNA, WO/208/327, "C in C Far East to the War Office 1/8[/41]," 31, and "Extract from C. in C. Far East No. 263/4," August 12, 1941, 34.

37. TNA, WO/208/327, "C in C Far East to the War Office," August 1, 1941, 31.

38. TNA, WO/208/327, "Extract from C.-in-C. Far East 263/4,12/8" [refers to War Cabinet's decision in response to Air Ministry on July 30, 1941], 34.

39. HISU, "C.L.C. memo for Madame Chiang," [August 5,] 1941, 2.

20. Squabbling over Bullets

1. Chennault, *Way of a Fighter*, 107.

2. HISU Currie, Fairbank memo, 13.

3. Quoted by Richard M. Leighton and Robert W. Coakley, *Global Logistics and Strategy, 1940–1943* (Washington, DC: Center of Military History, United States Army, 1955), 94–95.

4. TNA, WO/208/327, "Extract from: GLEAM 103 Washington-Admiralty 1229R/5 August," 32.

5. TNA, WO/208/327, "Military Attaché Chungking to C-in-C Far East," August 8, 1941, 36.

6. TNA, WO/208/327, "C in C Far East, 261/4 of 11/8[/41]," 33.

7. CUL McHugh, box 1, folder 8, "Dear Lauch," August 3 and 6, 1941, 5.

8. TNA, WO/208/327, "C in C Far East, 261/4 of 11/8[/41]," 33.

9. Ford, *Flying Tigers*, 57. SDASMA, Pentecost, "Royal Dutch Mail 1941 Calendar," entry for August 16, 1941.

10. HISU Currie, Fairbank memo, 14.

11. TNA, WO/208/327, "B.A.D. Washington to Admiralty," August 17, 1941, 39.

12. HISU Currie, Fairbank memo, 14.

13. TNA, WO/208/327, "To: AHQ Far East for C in C Far East from Air Min. Whitehall," August 22, 1941, 40.

14. TNA, Air 8/586, "Prime Minister Copy 21st August 1941": "Do you approve? If so, I agree (Intld.) W.S.C."

21. AVG Summer Camp

1. Philip D. Caine, *Eagles of the RAF: The World War II Eagle Squadrons* (Washington, DC: National Defense University Press, 1991), 78–86.

2. SDASMA, Pentecost, "1941 Calendar," entry for August 16, 1941.

3. SDASMA, Pentecost, folder Ferrying Log: September 4, Erik Shilling [AAC], 20 hours.

4. SDASMA, Pentecost, folder Ferrying Log: September 5, Bright [navy] 3 hours, Wright [navy] 4 hours, Howard [navy] 4 hours; September 6 Geselbracht [navy] 2 hours, Mangleburg [AAC] 145 hours. Mangleburg was exceptional for his experience on a P-40 but unfortunately was one of the first volunteers to die in December 1941 on a reconnaissance. See Ford, *Flying Tigers*, 124–25.

5. CCAC, August 22, 1941.

6. CCAC, entries for August 5–September 19, 1941.

7. Ford, *Flying Tigers*, 73.

8. CCAC, Thursday, June 3, 1937.

9. CCAC, September 19, 1941.

10. CCAC, September 22, 1941.

11. Holik-Urban, *To Soar*, 27. Chennault never recorded the demonstration flights staged by the volunteers for visitors.

12. HISU Currie, box 2, folder AVG Corr and Mem, May–Sept 1941, "to Lauchlin Currie from Robert Lovett," August 7, 1941.

13. HISU Currie, box 2, folder AVG Corr and Mem, November 1941, "Dear Dick [Aldworth] from Claire L. Chennault," November 5, 1941.

14. HISU Currie, box 2, folder AVG Corr and Mem, November 1941, "To Central Aircraft Mfg. Co. New York from Claire Chennault," November 7, 1941.

15. Ibid.

16. FDRL, J.B. 355, "From the Joint Planning Committee to the Joint Board July 9 1941: item 15."

17. HISU Currie, Fairbank memo, 22.

18. Bond and Anderson, *Flying Tiger's Diary*, 41.

19. Ibid., 46.

20. Ibid., 50–51.

21. Bartsch, *December 8, 1941*, 66 and 128.

22. Quoted ibid., 128.

23. Ibid., 66.

24. Ibid., 118–19.

25. Quoted ibid., 66–67. He quotes a letter of Ted Fisch to his wife, July 6 and 9, 1941.

26. HISU Currie, Fairbank memo, 28.

22. *The Short-Term Air Program for China*

1. FDRL, PSF China 1941, "A Tentative Aircraft Program for China," May 9, 1941.

2. FDRL, PSF China 1941, "Memorandum for the President, Aircraft program for China," May 9, 1941; see also CUL McHugh, box 1, folder 7, "Dear Lauch from McHugh," April 14, 1941, 1.

3. FDRL, PSF China 1941, "The President to Lauchlin Currie," May 15, 1941.

4. TNA, Air 8/539, "To British Air Commission, Washington from Ministry of Aircraft Production 26.4.41"; HISU Currie, Fairbank memo, 31–32. General Burns was in charge of coordinating the requests of foreign purchasing missions. See Leighton and Coakley, *Global Logistics and Strategy*, 78.

5. TNA, FO 371/27639, F/3923/523/G, "No. 2694 Secret," May 20, 1941.

6. HISU Currie, Fairbank memo, 34.

7. See chapter 16.

8. FDRL Morgenthau, vol. 406, "Dear Mr Secretary, Lauchlin Currie," May 21, 1941, 360, and "Dear Mr Currie from H Morgenthau Jr," June 10, 1941, 359.

9. TNA, Air 8/539, "To Britman from: AIRWHIT. Webber WX.396," August 20, 1941.

10. FDRL, J.B. 355, "Memorandum for Mr. Lovett; status of Chinese requests for aid," June 11, 1941.

11. "Bombers for Allies Could Be Delivered under Own Power," *Science News-Letter* 37, no. 21 (May 25, 1940): 326.

12. TNA, Air 8/539, "From AIRWHIT to BRITMAN," August 20, 1941.

13. TNA, Air 8/539, "From Foreign Office to Washington," May 26, 1941.

14. TNA, Air 8/539, "Dear C.A.S. from A. T. Harris," September 2, 1941.

15. HISU Currie, Fairbank memo, 36; TNA, Air 8/586, "Royal Air Force Delegation (British Air Commission) Secret," September 2, 1941.

16. TNA, RG 38, box 147a, entry 355, ABC-1, ABC-2, "United States–British Staff Conversations Air Policy U.S. Serial 011512–15, B.U.S. (J) (41) 39," March 29, 1941, 2.

17. FDRL, J.B. 355, "Aircraft Requirements of the Chinese Government—Short Term Aircraft Program for China," letter from Lauchlin Currie to Secretary of the Navy, May 28, 1941.

18. TNA, Air 8/539, "To Airwhit from Britman, Caesar 448 Washington," August 22, 1941; "To Airwhit from Britman, Caesar 457 Washington," August 23, 1941; "To Airwhit from Britman, Caesar 504 Washington," August 28, 1941; "Dear C.A.S. from A. T. Harris," September 2, 1941.

19. FDRL, J.B. 355, "The Joint Planning committee to the Joint Board: Aircraft Requirements of the Chinese Government," item 11.

20. TNA, Air 8/539, "To Airwhit from Britman, Caesar 448 Washington," August 22, 1941.

21. Ancestry.com, NARA, RG 85, Crew lists of Vessels Arriving at Boston, MA, 1917–1943, Publication no. T938, roll 451, Passenger list HMS *Rodney*, June 12, 1941.

22. TNA, Air 8/539, "To Airwhit from Britman, Caesar 448 Washington," August 22, 1941.

23. Currie Gets in a Jam

1. HISU Currie, box 5, folder Harry Hopkins, "Memorandum for Mr. Hopkins," August 18, 1941.

2. TNA, Air 8/5/539, "To Airwhit from Britman, Caesar 448 Washington," August 21, 1941, and "Dear C.A.S. from A. T. Harris," September 2, 1941, 2.

3. TNA, Air 8/539, "To Airwhit from Britman, Caesar 448 Washington," August 21, 1941.

4. Ibid.

5. Ibid.

6. TNA, Air 8/539, "To Airwhit from Britman, Caesar 457 Washington," August 23, 1941; "To Airwhit from Britman, Caesar 448 Washington," August 21, 1941.

7. HISU Currie, Fairbank memo, 60. At the War Department, General Burns was in charge of coordinating the requests of foreign purchasing missions. See Fairbank memo, 78.

8. TNA, Air 8/539, "To Airwhit from Britman, Washington Caesar 504," August 27, 1941, 2.

9. Ibid.

10. Ibid.

11. Ibid.

12. HISU Currie, Fairbank memo, 61; Currie, box 5, "Memo for Mr. Hopkin[s]," August 18, 1941; FDRL, PSF Adm. Assts: Laughlin Currie—Subject File, June 1940–1945, "Memorandum for the President: bombers for China," August 26, 1941.

13. TNA, Air 8/539, "To Airwhit from Britman, Washington Caesar 506," August 28, 1941; HISU Currie, box 5, folder Harry Hopkins, "To AMEMBASSY London for Sir Archibald Sinclair," September 2, 1941.

14. TNA, Air 8/539, "To Airwhit from Britman, Washington Caesar 506," August 27, 1941.

15. TNA, Air 8/539, "To Britman, Washington from AIRWHIT, Webber WX.226," August 21, 1941.

16. HISU Currie, box 5, folder Harry Hopkins, "To AMEMBASSY for Sir Archibald Sinclair from Hopkins London," September 2, 1941.

17. TNA, FO 371/27642, F9029, "Air Ministry to H. Ashley Clarke Foreign Office," September 5, 1941; Air 8/539, "To Ministry of Aircraft Production from British Air Commission, Washington Briny 8833," September 12, 1941.

18. HISU Currie, Fairbank memo, 61–62.

19. Roger James Sandilands, *The Life and Political Economy of Lauchlin Currie: New Dealer, Presidential Adviser, and Development Economist* (Durham, NC: Duke University Press, 1990), 113.

20. NARA, RG 225, J.B. 355, "To the President from Robert B. Patterson acting secretary of War and Frank Knox Secretary of the Navy," July 18, 1941. Roosevelt wrote by hand on this cover letter a message about military mission versus the attaché method on July 23, 1941.

21. CUL McHugh, box 1, folder 8, "Dear Mac from Lauch," August 29, 1941.

22. NARA, RG 225, J.B. 355, handwritten note, "My dear Scobey from Turner."

23. See Overy, *Bombing War*, 279–80 and 339–40.

24. FDRL, PSF Adm. Assts: Laughlin Currie—Subject File, June 1940–1945, "T. V. Soong to Colonel William Donovan," August 16, 1941.

25. TNA, FO 371/27642, F9394, "From Chungking to Foreign office," September 16, 1941.

26. *Select Telegrams*, "Telegram to Chiang on miscellaneous affairs," September 18, 1941, 383–84.

27. FDRL, Soong to Donovan, August 16, 1942, 3.

28. TNA, FO 371/27645, F12972/145/10, "Aircraft for China," November 25, 1941.

29. HISU, Fairbank, 29.

24. Magruder's Mission

1. *NYT*, "US Army Mission Will Assist China," August 27, 1941, 1.

2. TNA, FO 371/27642, F8572/145/10, "United States Military Mission to China: Sir R. I. Campbell to Foreign Office," August 28, 1941.

3. HISU Currie, box 2, folder AVG Corr and Mem, May–Sept 1941, "Memorandum for the President Re: Pilots for China from Lauchlin Currie," September 18, 1941.

4. HISU Currie, Fairbank memo, 65.

5. HISU Currie, box 2, folder AVG Corr and Mem, May–Sept 1941, "Memorandum for the President Re: Pilots for China from Lauchlin Currie," September 18, 1941.

6. HISU Currie, box 2, folder AVG Corr and Mem, October [19]41, "To H. E. T. V. Soong from C. L. Chennault," September 29, 1941.

7. HISU Currie, Fairbank memo, 66.

8. TNA, FO 371/27642, F8572/145/10, "United States Military Mission to China," August 30, 1941.

9. TNA, FO 371/27642, F9095/145/10, "Most Secret from B.A.D. Washington to Admiralty," September 9, 1941.

10. TNA, FO 371/27642, F9095/145/10, "Most Secret to Britman Washington from Admiralty," September 8, 1941.

11. TNA, FO 371/27642, F9217/145/10, "Assistance in connexion with United states aircraft sent to China," September 12, 1941.

12. TNA, FO 371/27642, F9351/145/10, "Most Secret from B.A.D. Washington to Admiralty," September 12, 1941.

13. TNA, CAB 121/689, "C. in C. Far East to War Office," October 7, 1941.

14. Ibid.

15. TNA, Prem 3/90/1, "Most Secret from Washington," November 1, 1941 [a British report about two cables from Magruder covering air aid and a purported Japanese attack on Kunming].

16. NARA, RG 59, CDF 893.248/258, "From Chungking to AMISSCA," November 8, 1941" [Magruder's report to Stimson and Marshall].

17. NARA, RG 59, LM183, reel 30, Confidential US State Department Central Files: China, Internal Affairs, 1940–1944, "From Chungking (Magruder) to AMISSCA," November 8, 1941.

18. NARA, RG 59, CDF 893.248/252, "To Max Hamilton Far East desk from Stanley Hornbeck," October 30, 1941, and "Cordell Hull to AMEMBASSY," November 10, 1941.

19. NARA, RG 59, CDF 893.248/252A, "For Chennault, from Currie," November 12, 1941.

25. Countdown to War

1. TNA, FO 371/27642, F8762/145/10, "International Air Force: From C. in C. Far East to Governor Burma," August 26, 1941.

2. Grehan and Mace, *Disaster in the Far East*, 127–28.

3. TNA, Air 8/586, "To Air Ministry from A.H.Q. F.E.," October 11, 1941.

4. TNA, Prem 3/90/1, "Most Secret from Washington," November 1, 1941.

5. HISU Currie, box 5, folder Soong, T. V., "Memorandum for the President," October 30, 1941.

6. TNA, CAB 121/689, vol. 1, "From Chungking to Foreign Office," November 1, 1941.

7. TNA, Prem 3/90/1, "Most Secret from Washington," November 1, 1941.

8. TNA, Prem 3/90/1, "Most Secret," January 11, 1941.

9. Leighton and Coakley, *Global Logistics and Strategy*, 105.

10. TNA, Air 8/586, "From War Office to C-in-C Far East," November 5, 1941.

11. Ibid.

12. CCAC, November 8, 1941; HISU Currie, box 2, folder AVG Corr and Mem, November [19]41, "Message from Col. Chennault," received November 12, 1941.

13. HISU Currie, box 2, folder AVG Corr and Mem, November [19]41, "Cable received from Joseph Alsop," November 20, 1941.

14. TNA, Air 8/586, "Most Secret Immediate to the War Office from C in C Far East," November 10, 1941; HISU Currie, box 2, folder AVG Corr and Mem, November [19]41, "Message from Col. Chennault," received November 12, 1941.

15. TNA, Prem 3/90/1, "From Chungking to Foreign Office, Chiang Kai-Shek's message to Prime Minister," November 2, 1941.

16. TNA, Prem 3/90/1, handwritten draft of telegram from Churchill to Roosevelt, 66.

17. TNA, Prem 3/90/1, "Telegram dated November 7 1941 Personal and Strictly Confidential from the President to the Former Naval Person," 49–50.

18. TNA, Prem 3/90/1, "War Cabinet. Chiefs of Staff Committee Minutes of meeting 6th November 1941," 42.

19. TNA, Prem 3/90/1, "General Ismay for C.O.S. Committee WSC, 9.XI," 39.

20. TNA, Prem 3/90/1, "General Ismay for C.O.S. Committee WSC, 11.XI," 33.

21. TNA, Prem 3/90/1, "To Sir A. Clark Kerr (Chungking): Following for Chiang Kai-Shek from Prime Minister," November 11, 1941.

22. FRUS 1941, vol. 5, "President Roosevelt to the President of the Chinese Executive Yuan (Chiang Kai-shek)," November 14, 1941, 758–59.

23. TNA, Prem 3/90/1, "From Chungking to Foreign Office," November 15, 1941, 12.

24. Quoted by Bartsch, *December 8, 1941*, 140.

25. Quoted ibid., 141.

26. Quoted ibid.

27. Quoted ibid., 130.

28. Quoted ibid., 100 and 132.

29. Edmonds, *They Fought*, 69–70.

30. TNA, Air 8/586, "To C in C Far East from War office," November 13, 1941.

31. TNA, Prem 3/90/1, "From C in C Far East to War office," November 15, 1941, para. 2.

32. TNA, Prem 3/90/1, "From C in C Far East to War office," November 15, 1941, para. 5.

33. TNA, Prem 3/90/1, "Secret L. C. Hollis, Office of the Minister of Defence to the Prime Minister 18th November": handwritten note by Churchill dated November 19, 1941.

34. TNA, Air 8/586, "To C in C Far East from Air Ministry," November 17, 1941.

35. SDASMA, Pentecost, Daily Calendar, entry November 18 and 19, 1941; BGLA, folder, Extra Letters, "W. D. Pawley to Mr. Bruce G. Leighton," November 18, 1941, 2.

36. TNA, Air 8/586, "To Whitehall from Singapore," November 11, 1941.

37. BGLA, folder, Extra Letters, "W. D. Pawley to Mr. Bruce G. Leighton," November 18, 1941, 2.

38. Ibid.

39. "Adair, Claude Bryant 'Skip,'" Flying Tigers Association American Volunteer Group, http://flyingtigersavg.com/index.php/avg-biographies/100-adair-claude-bryant.

40. TNA, Air 8/586, "To Air Ministry Whitehall from Singapore," November 22, 1941.

41. William G. Grieve, *The American Military Mission to China, 1941–1942: Lend-Lease Logistics, Politics and the Tangles of Wartime Cooperation* (Jefferson, NC: McFarland, 2014), 171.

42. Ibid., 192.

43. Document reproduced in Chuck Baisden, *Flying Tiger*, 19.

44. Bond and Anderson, *Flying Tiger's Diary*, 46.

45. Ibid., 45.

46. CUL McHugh, box 1, folder 4, "Dear Paul [Meyer]," August 5, 1939.

47. CUL McHugh, box 1, folder 8, "Dear Lauch, from McHugh," October 5, 1941.

48. TNA, Air 8/586, "To the War Office from the C.-in-C. Far East," December 16, 1941. See also TNA, Air 23/4657, "Air attaché Chungking to RAF Rangoon," November 7, 1941. Chiang believed that the air warning system in Yunnan was adequate.

49. TNA, FO 371/27645, "From Governor of Burma to the Secretary of State for Burma," December 17, 1941.

50. CCAC, album 23, an untitled eight-page list of enemy aircraft destroyed listed by pilot, squadron, and date (hereafter "kill log"). I have tried to avoid

duplication of "kills" shared or assigned to several pilots in calculating the figure of 283 total enemy planes brought down.

51. CCAC, album 23, "kill log."

Epilogue

1. Chennault, *Way of a Fighter*, 96.

2. Jonathan Utley, *Going to War with Japan, 1937–1941* (New York: Fordham University Press, 2005), 136.

3. Arthur Nichols Young, *China and the Helping Hand* (Cambridge MA: Harvard University Press, 1963), 22–24.

4. CUL McHugh, box 1, folder 5, "Frank Knox from McHugh," June 11, 1942.

5. Peter Lowe, *Great Britain and the Origins of the Pacific War: A Study of British Policy in East Asia, 1937–1941* (London: Oxford University Press, 1977), 295.

6. Charles Romanus and Riley Sunderland, *China-Burma-India Theater: Stilwell's Mission to China*, United States Army in World War II (Washington, DC: Center of Military History, United States Army, 1953), 11–12 and fn18.

7. Author interview with William D. Pawley's niece Anita Pawley, June 5, 2007; author inquiries to Air Force Academy library and Taiwan military attaché in 2008.

8. Chennault, *Way of a Fighter*, 140.

191–92; Chen and, 35–36; and China Lobby, 117–18; and Chinese plan to bomb Japan, 61, 62–64, 66–67, 68, 75, 109, 189, 192; Corcoran and, 111, 117–18; Currie and, 106–7, 118, 157–58; on Hull, 39, 54; and Japanese aggression, 38, 41, 42; and Lend-Lease, 65; and loans to China, 42, 55, 56–57, 58, 105; and planes for China, 10–11, 47–48, 50, 52, 65, 77–81, 91–92, 157–58, 189; and planes for Greece, 73; and president's liaison committee, 30, 96, 100, 166; and proposed Soviet-US-China alliance, 40; and sale of planes to allies, 19–20, 30, 32; Soong and, 35–40, 105, 112, 118; views on aid to China, 36–37

Navy Department: and Leighton's lobbying for air aid for China, xiii, 23–27; release of pilots for AVG service, 114; support for China, 23, 107–8, 109
Neutrality Act of 1935, 29–30

Office of Naval Intelligence (ONI): 3, 9, 24–26, 107, 113–14, 137

P-40 fighter planes: for AAC, 20, 69, 72, 73, 102; for Britain, 70–71, 72, 74, 79; design and production of, 19–20, 69, 71; as difficult to fly, 119–20, 153, 154; export models of, 69–70; nomenclature for, 71, 72, 102; performance of, 69, 102; in Philippines, 102; problems with, 71–72, 120; promised to Greece, 73–74, 76, 79, 93; Roosevelt's plane aid and, 188; sales to Allies, 19–20, 69–70; and

shipping problems, 71, 72–73; type of runway needed for, 73; as untested in battle, 74. *See also* planes for AVG
P-40s, for China: Burma Road defense as rationale for, 78, 79–80, 81, 82, 96; and Burma Road "distraction," Chinese concerns about, 51; decision to use, 75–76; as diversion, 80, 82, 96, 189–90, 192; and redirection of British planes, 75–81, 84, 90–91; secrecy surrounding, 88–89, 90–91, 93–94; training of pilots for, 81
Panay (US naval ship), 54
Patterson, A. L. "Pat," 6, 12, 21, 32, 50
Pawley, William D.: and AVG, origins of, xi, xi–xii, xiii, 83, 84; and AVG plane commissions, xiv, 32–33, 85, 91, 125; and AVG, recruitment for, 92–93, 130–31; on AVG unrest, 183; and British interest in AVG, 129–30, 183; CAMCO factory, 3, 12–13, 14, 15, 20; Chennault and, 125–26, 152, 183–84; and Chinese visit in 1935, 29; and Indian Air Force, 28, 122; as Intercontinent president, ix, x; Leighton on, 89; and plane sales to China, 6, 12, 14, 22, 27–28; records of, 195–96; Young's views on, 32
Pearl Harbor attack, 185
Pentecost, Walter, 123, 141, 148, 150
Philippines: as base for bombing Japan, 96, 99, 101, 102–3, 181; Europe first strategy and, 60; living conditions on, 154–55; in Stark's strategy, 87
Philippines, defense of: air assets on, 96–99, 101–3, 181, 182; Battle of Britain as model for, 99–101, 103; and diversion of planes from China, 48–49, 97, 103–4; and faith